ESCAPE!

ESCAPE!

*Memoir of a World War II Marine
Who Broke Out of a Japanese
POW Camp and Linked Up with
Chinese Communist Guerrillas*

BY JAMES D. MCBRAYER, JR.

McFarland & Company, Inc., Publishers
Jefferson, North Carolina, and London

To my wife, Helen Jean Paterson ("Skip") McBrayer

Unless noted otherwise in the Acknowledgments,
all names are pseudonyms

British Library Cataloguing-in-Publication data are available

Library of Congress Cataloguing-in-Publication Data

McBrayer, James D., 1916–
    Escape! : memoir of a World War II marine who broke out of
a Japanese POW camp and linked up with Chinese communist
guerrillas / by James D. McBrayer, Jr.
        p. cm.
    Includes bibliographical references and index.
    ISBN 0-7864-0058-7 (lib. bdg. : 50# alk. paper) ∞
    1. Sino-Japanese Conflicts, 1937–1945 — Prisoners and prisons,
Japanese.   2. Sino-Japanese Conflicts, 1937–1945 — Personal
narratives, American.   3. McBrayer, James D., 1916–   . I. Title.
DS777.5315.M42   1995
940.54′7252′092 — dc20   94-24528
[B]   CIP

Manufactured in the United States of America

McFarland & Company, Inc., Publishers
Box 611, Jefferson, North Carolina 28640

Acknowledgments

I wish to thank my wife Skip, whose assistance in editing and fine-tuning the manuscript was invaluable.

My sincere appreciation to the Marine Corps Historical Foundation for its encouragement and financial support of my endeavor to write this story of my experiences in China.

My thanks to Tom Bartlett, the managing editor of the *Leatherneck*, for his helpful suggestions and editing of my manuscript.

My thanks also to Richard A. Long, oral historian, Marine Historical Center, for his invaluable assistance in providing me with historical data, for encouraging me to write my story, and for meticulous editing.

Melanie Beauston has my grateful thanks for deciphering my penmanship after I had a stroke in April 1993 and for typing and retyping the many revisions of my manuscript.

My humble thanks to both our sons for their unflagging support of this project. Jim skillfully interpreted my descriptions and translated them into meaningful sketches. John A., a graduate of Parris Island, a lawyer, and a good Marine, provided legal advice.

Unless otherwise stated, permission has been granted to use the real names of all Americans mentioned in this book or their names have appeared in other publications.

Table of Contents

Preface

THIS BOOK is an account of my experiences in a Japanese prisoner of war camp in China (1941–45), my escape from the Japanese in 1945, and my adventures with the Chinese Communist guerrillas. It was compiled from extensive notes I wrote immediately upon my return to the United States in 1945. A few gaps in my notes and memory were filled in by casual conversations and letters from my four fellow escapees.

I was not and am not a student of the Chinese language, but I learned some Chinese words and phrases before my imprisonment. Other Chinese words and phrases used in this story are my interpretation of the Wade-Giles system of translation of Chinese. I do not attempt to place accent, aspiration, or diacritical marks on words; hence the pronunciation of words is left to the reader.

Words in the Wade-Giles system of translation are not to be confused with the words of the modern Hangu Pinyin system of translation introduced by the People's Republic of China in 1958, nor with the Chinese postal system of naming towns and geographical areas. The names of towns used in this book are based on the Wade-Giles system and hence may not appear on modern maps. All coordinates of towns, unless otherwise stated in the story, have been taken from the map illustrating our route of escape.

Reconstructed conversations among the five escapees or with the Chinese are included to enliven the story, as are the occasional instances in the narrative in which in some nonsubstantive way I "depart from history," as Mark Twain wrote. Though these passages of dialogue and action may seem more stylistically typical of a novel than of a memoir, they in no way fictionalize the basic factual account.

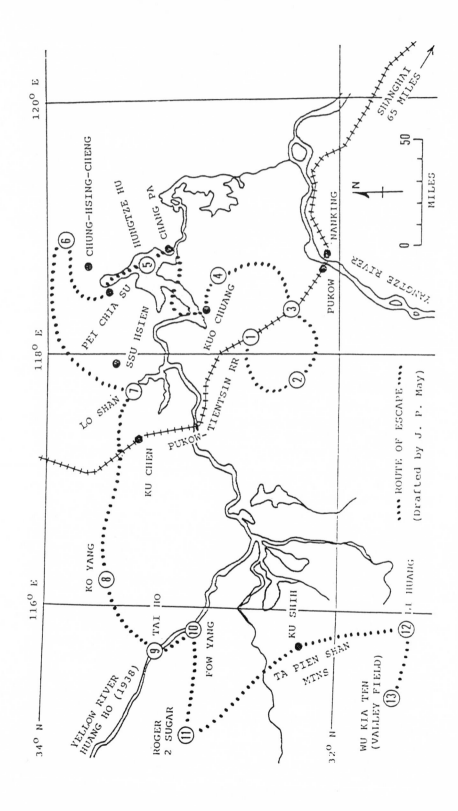

COORDINATES OF TOWNS ON MAP

CITY	LATITUDE	LONGITUDE
CHANG PA	33°07′N	118°45′E
CHUNG-HSING-CHENG	33°42′N	118°40′E
FOW YANG	32°53′N	115°48′E
KU SHIH	32°11′N	115°40′E
KO YANG	33°31′N	116°12′E
KU CHEN	33°19′N	117°18′E
KUO CHUANG	32°54′N	118°18′E
LI HUANG	31°30′N	115°54′N
LO SHAN	33°20′N	117°40′E
NANKING	32°06′N	118°46′E
PEI CHIA SU	33°32′N	118°28′E
PUKOW	32°08′N	118°42′E
ROGER 2 SUGAR	33°02′N	115°21′E
SSU HSIEN	33°29′N	117°53′E
TAI HO	33°08′N	115°38′E
WU KIA TEN	31°25′N	115°35′E

CHRONOLOGY OF THE ESCAPE

10 May 1945	Escape from a Japanese prisoner of war train
16 May	Five escapees reunited by Chinese Communist guerrillas
19 May	Forced crossing of Pukow-Tientsin (P-T) Railroad west to east en route to Communist New Fourth Army (NFA) headquarters
23–31 May	Activities in NFA area included dodging Japanese and their puppet troops; visiting guerrilla arsenals, schools, and hospitals
1–3 June	Crossing Hungtze Hu in a junk from Chang Pa to Pei Chia Su
4–11 June	Escapees movements in 4th Guerrilla Division area similar to those in NFA area
12–13 June	Lo Shan; crossover from Communist troops to Nationalist troops
13–15 June	Crossing of P-T Railroad from east to west en route to Ko Yang
15–17 June	Tai Ho
17–18 June	Fow Yang
19–21 June	Roger 2 Sugar, an OSS intelligence post
26 June	Li Huang
27 June	Wu Kia Tien (Valley Field); flight to Kunming
27 June–5 July	Kunming, China

Opposite: **This map was taken from one prepared under the direction of the chief of engineers, Army Map Service, U.S. Army, Washington, D.C. Compiled in 1945 from China, 1:50,000, Central Land Survey, 1926.38, and road maps and intelligence reports, 1943.45. Location names in text and on map are in Wade-Giles System and are different from modern Pin-Yin translation. First Edition (AMSI), 1945, pp. 337.38, 467.69.**

CHAPTER ONE

Leap into the Unknown

A DARKENED TRAIN of old boxcars rattled through the dreary night, lumbering its way toward Peking. The red glow of the firebox flared briefly as the fireman fed the flames a shovelful of coal. No other light shone from the train, and no signal lights gave direction along the track. The endless gloom of the Chinese countryside swallowed evidence of the train's passage. Silence was broken only by the clacking of the wheels on the rough track and the wheezing of the ancient steam engine.

Prisoners of war, tightly packed and wired inside the boxcars, pondered their fate and tried to sleep. Japanese guards in the middle of each car muttered as they counted bodies. The thump of a rifle butt slammed against the floor told of their all too obvious presence.

Inside the next to the last boxcar, four U.S. Marine officers were preparing to escape. The four of us whispered arrangements on final tactics. Then, attempting to rest, we awaited the appropriate moment to execute our plans. For three and a half years, we had planned, hoped, and dreamed of escaping from the Japanese. Would the night of 10 May 1945 bear fruit after our years of labor and determination?

With the aid of God, a bit of luck, a hacksaw blade, and a pair of pliers, we jumped off a Japanese prisoner of war train for freedom and the unknown. We did not know what was in store for us. We only knew that here was a chance to free ourselves from a hellish existence.

We simply hoped for the best—hoped that none of us would hit a utility pole, jump off a bridge, or land in the middle of Japanese forces. Instinctively, we knew that such a gamble was better than going to the prison camps we were headed for in Japan. Certainly, we had a greater chance for a better life by acting rather than remaining passive.

The four of us had been on duty at two widely separated points on

5

the Asiatic-Pacific front. Richard Marvin Huizenga and I, both U.S. Marine lieutenants, were captured by the Japs in North China on 8 December 1941. Marine lieutenants John A. McAlister and John F. Kinney were captured at Wake Island on 23 December 1941. Our commonly used names were, in sequence, "Hi," "Mac," "Johnny Mac," and "Kinney."

For the past years of imprisonment, Hi and I had one thought uppermost in our minds and that was to escape from the Japanese prisoner of war camp. With the exception of food, it was the prevailing topic of our conversations. We had been held first in a prisoner of war camp at Woosung for almost a year, then moved to a camp at Kiangwan in December 1942. Both camps lay a few miles outside of Shanghai. Neither was conducive to escape attempts because both were located in flat, densely populated areas swarming with Japanese troops. Additionally, two heavily guarded, electrified, barbed-wire fences surrounding each camp discouraged efforts to escape.

Throughout our imprisonment, to be prepared for any opportunity to escape, both Hi and I stole tools and other items that might be useful in an attempt. Camp regulations contained only one statement about punishment for escape: "Escape will be punished by death or exile." We always wondered to what place we would be exiled.

It was our hope that once free, we could contact Chinese guerrillas or sympathizers who would guide us to either regular Chinese Communist (Kungchantang) or Nationalist (Kuomintang) forces. Huizenga and I, having been stationed in North China for almost two years, spoke some Mandarin Chinese, which we believed would be useful.

In view of the many dialects in China, however, we had a Chinese fellow prisoner named Li, formerly stationed on the gun boat USS *Wake*, prepare two pointee-talkees in Chinese characters for us. Each consisted of a sheet of paper on which simple questions and answers were counterpoised in English words and Chinese characters. (See Document 1 in the Appendix.) The sheets included an offer of a large reward from the U.S. government for safely guiding the bearer to friendly troops. They also included requests for *leng kai shwei* (cold boiled water), *re cha* (hot tea), or *wo yao fan* (rice).

Later, when Kinney and McAlister approached us about escaping and decided to make the attempt with us, copies of the pointee-talkees were made for them. They would need them more than Hi and I since neither of them spoke Chinese.

Although we had been collecting items for our escape, some items we needed, such as medical supplies, were severely limited. We managed to get hold of some iodine for water purification and ground charcoal and bismuth for dysentery. Canteens were made from disinfectant cans discarded by the Japanese. By spending a little of the U.S. currency we had

A guard tower at Japanese camp for POWs at Kiangwan, China, 1942–45.

managed to save, we obtained some "pain alleviating medicine" through
black market operations conducted by several guards.

As for infectious disease prevention, we believed that we had suffered
most of the common types and had developed subclinical immunity for the
remainder. I, for instance, had suffered beriberi, pellagra, scurvy,
dysentery (both bacilli and parasitic), etc. Most of us had acquired immunity to the many common diseases in China. (See Document 2 of Appendix.)

We originally planned to travel for several days evading everyone including the Chinese because we knew there were many individuals and
organizations who would gladly turn in Americans to the Japanese for
rewards. Both Hi and I had learned of the probable disposition of Japanese
troops from our duty in China while attached to the U. S. Embassy in
Peking, 1940–41.

I was also well aware of the contents of Edgar Snow's *Red Star Over
China*. Reports about the Chinese Communist Eighth Route Army and
Wang Ching Wei's Chinese puppet troops supporting the Japanese had
come to my attention. (Upon his death, Wang was succeeded as head of

the puppet government by Chen Kun-po in May 1942. The Chinese puppet government which supported the Japanese still was referred to as "Wang's government," however.) My hunting experiences in North China had provided me with information about Chinese guerrillas and bandits, as well as the habits and customs of the Chinese peasantry. I also knew of the Communist New Fourth Army in Anwhei and Kiangsu provinces. Both the Communists and Nationalists were considered to be friendly toward Americans.

In addition to Japanese troops, the troops of Wang's puppet government in Nanking were scattered throughout Japanese-occupied China. Also, there were swarms of bandits around the landscape eager for a little money and material goods. Our problem would be to recognize friend or foe before making our presence known. The general idea was to stay away from railway lines, as the Japanese and their puppets maintained a strong guard along their lines of communication.

Our plans became firm in April 1945 as we surmised that the Japanese were planning on moving the prisoners of war at Kiangwan by railroad through Nanking and Peking and thence by ship to Japan. A few days before we were to leave the Shanghai camp area, an advance detail of prisoners was sent to the rail yard to prepare the train for our departure. From the prisoners who were in this advance detail, we learned of some specific plans for the move.

About 50 prisoners were to be placed in each "40 and 8" boxcar (40 men or 8 horses, so named in WWI): 25 men in each end, along with their personal effects and straw mattresses. The space between the two sliding doors of each car was to be wired off from the prisoners with barbed wire, thus making a secure space for the six Japanese guards assigned to each car. One small, high window located on either side near opposite ends of each car was secured with barbed wire in addition to the existing iron bars.

In one corner of each end of the car, a five-gallon tin can was placed for use as a head, or latrine, by the 25 men in that end of the car. As the boxcars had been used for transporting horses, the advance detail removed most of the horse manure, and straw was placed over what could not be shoveled out the door. The straw was to provide some warmth and comfort. Each prisoner was to carry his straw tick (mattress) and personal effects, if any, to the train. The straw tick became our foil for taking our escape gear onto the train.

Hi and I, over the years, had collected (stolen from the Japanese) two sets of tools—an auger, pieces of a wood saw, a hacksaw blade, pliers, and two small pry bars. We each carried a set of tools in our tick. Fortunately, when our turn came to board the train, the Japanese guards made only perfunctory searches and both of us were able to get our tools aboard our boxcar.

Sketch of a boxcar like the one from which the author and four other POWs escaped on 10 May 1945.

Most Chinese boxcars had steel sides, but all had wooden floors and small windows with iron bars near each end of the car. Accordingly, we had two plans. The primary plan was to cut a hole in the floor as near to the end of the car as possible, crawl through the hole, and escape via the under-carriage supports. Once we got through the hole and reached the under-carriage, we would catch hold of the brakeman's ladder on the side of the car, swing to the side, and jump clear of the tracks.

The second plan was to saw through or pry loose the iron bars across the window. Once out the window, we would grab the brakeman's ladder, swing to the side, and jump off the tracks. How we would accomplish either of the two plans without attracting the attention of the guards remained to be seen. We believed we could execute the first plan with less chance of detection.

A bit of explanation may be in order. Our original plan was for Hi and Johnny Mac to go together and Kinney and me to go together via the brakeman's ladder, where the first to emerge would wait for the second. This pairing was thought necessary. As mentioned earlier, Hi and I spoke some Chinese. Johnny Mac and Kinney did not.

At about four o'clock in the morning of 9 May 1945, one group of prisoners (of which Hi and I were members) left in advance of the main body to finish preparing the boxcars. We marched for a few hours to the Kiangwan railway station guarded by many soldiers who were somewhat nervous because of the darkness and the impending move. All of us were aware that U.S. bombers and P-51 fighter-bombers had been operating frequently in the area, and we found evidence of train strafing on the boxcars we were to ride.

Although only the high command of the prison camp knew our destination, the prisoners and the guards had long surmised that Japan was the destination. The guards were as unhappy as many prisoners were about the trip to Japan. Neither group savored the idea of a long train trip under air attack or possible guerrilla attack, the probability of even shorter rations in Japan, and particularly the trip by ship to Japan once the train reached the Korean straits. Some Taiwanese guards said, "Too many submarines." The only happy group seemed to be those of us planning our escape.

When we arrived at the Kiangwan station, only part of the train was on the siding. Many Jap officers were running around trying to get the rest of the train placed where they wanted it. This period of inactivity gave us a chance to take in the typical Chinese scenes, always bustling and lively. We had not seen so many people in a very long time. We, as officers, had been held in rather close confinement while working in the prisoner of war camp, but enlisted men and civilians were sent on work details outside the camp area to Shanghai and the countryside. So even such a common, prosaic scene as a Chinese railway station was interesting.

Finally, all appeared to be in order, and each group was assigned to a boxcar to complete the work started by the advance detail. With bated breath and silent prayers, Hi and I waited to see what the luck of the draw would be for our group of officers. Wonder of wonders, the car in which we were to ride had only two iron bars across the little window. (Later examination showed that both the bolts holding the bars and the bars themselves were very rusty.) The only additional obstacle to our use of the window was the barbed wire nailed across it. We could scarcely believe such a miracle. It gave us a better alternative than cutting a hole in the floor. Having to pry only two bars loose and snip the barbed wire was a much better solution.

Further events improved the possibility of going out through the window. Because of the likelihood of air raids, the Japanese ordered cotton blankets placed over each window as blackout protection for the train. We moved our five-gallon tin can that was to be used as a toilet into the corner of the boxcar near the window and dutifully covered the window with the furnished blanket. After making an attempt to further clean the car of all manure, we scattered straw around the area, covering the worst spots.

By the time we had finished these chores, the rest of the prisoners had arrived with their belongings, which had no value but were too valuable to throw away. The guards had trucked everything from the camp which they thought would be of use in Japan. When the Japs moved, they took everything except the main structural parts of the buildings. All easily removable items, including water pipes, scrap metal, doors, etc., were moved.

There was one very valuable item to us in our boxcar—a wooden door lying on the floor. Utilizing the wooden door, a cotton blanket, and the boxcar corner, we created a small toilet room around our five-gallon can toilet near the window. By enclosing our toilet, we blocked the view of the window from the six guards in the center of the car. Our luck was holding. The enclosure also directed any nauseous odors out the window. We thought the sweat and smell of our many unbathed bodies in the boxcar was bad enough.

One water can was placed in each end of the car along with a crate of hardtack. The rations were to be three hard tack biscuits per man per day washed down with a bit of water. This would be supplemented with food anyone had been able to save for the journey.

The POWs in the Kiangwan camp received several Red Cross food parcels over a period of about two years, the first boxes arriving in December 1942 and the last in January 1945. Each parcel usually consisted of a pound of Klim (powdered milk), a couple of cans of corned beef or Spam, a half pound of cheese, a small tin of jelly, crackers, a can of instant coffee, a couple of chocolate bars, and several packages of cigarettes wedged between the cans. None of the escape planners smoked, so we traded cigarettes for food and saved a cache for our escape.

Our straw ticks were placed on top of the straw on the stinking wooden floor. There was some argument about the placement of the ticks, as our group wanted to be near the toilet and our escape window and others wanted to be near the window for a possible breath of fresh air. Kinney, being a low ranking second lieutenant, won the honor of being placed immediately adjacent to the toilet, which was fortunate for us. We were the lowest ranking officers in our end of the car and hence had little choice. We naturally were given spaces near the toilet.

By the time all the ticks were on the floor, one couldn't move without stepping on another person. Imagine live sardines in a flat can vying for space and you have the picture.

After long hours of waiting, we were finally wired inside our cars, and the train chugged slowly toward the west and Nanking. Although we could see little of the countryside through the doors kept open by the guards, the glimpses were interesting. There is always something enchanting about travel, perhaps more so for a POW long confined. New scenes, new faces and situations . . . all were intriguing, especially when the final destination was unknown either to those who had planned nothing more than to move along with the forces of fate or to those who planned on dealing themselves another poker hand.

Where would we try to make the attempt? And at what time of the night? Could we remove the barriers from the window undetected? Would any of us be severely injured or killed? Thoughts of loved ones and possibilities of reprisals against the remaining prisoners filled our minds. The general and prevailing opinion of many POWs was that an escape attempt was not worth the risk.

As we settled down on our straw ticks to get as comfortable as possible for the scheduled long trip to Nanking, we began to converse in whispers about our next actions. Knowing that the rail lines ran from Nanking through Anwhei Province to the city of Tsinan in Shantung Province and then on to Tientsin, I whispered my ideas about where we should jump the train.

I was of the opinion that our best chance of reaching friendly forces would be in Shantung Province. The Chinese Communist Eighth Route Army had been operating in Shantung for many years and controlled much of the countryside. There was good reason to believe the Chinese Communist New Fourth Army was operating in Kiangsu and Anwhei provinces, but its positions were not as widespread nor as stable as those of the Eighth Route Army in Shantung.

I said I believed we should wait until the second night when we would be closer to Tsinan, and that we should plan to leave about midnight. Hi agreed and said he thought the best possibility of finding friendly troops might be west of the Pukow-Tientsin rail line in Shantung, but he wondered how we could determine where we would be at about midnight tomorrow.

"Are there any landmarks to determine our position?" Johnny Mac asked, and he added, "Those landmarks would have to be pretty big."

Hi said, "Just north of Tsinan, we'll cross the old Yellow River bed, a very distinct landmark at night or in daylight. But our problem is that we'll have to have one of us in the toilet all the time to look for the landmark. Impossible. Others have to crap." He finished with, "The guards will get suspicious."

Kinney, watching the guards, said, "The guards are keeping one of the sliding doors open a bit. Perhaps we can see the landmark through the cracks."

Johnny Mac squelched that. "I wouldn't like to depend on whether the guards' door is open or not."

Remembering the maps I had seen, I mentioned that we'd probably pass over the Whai River tonight and the old bed of the Yellow River our second night out, and I added that the train would slow for those large bridges.

Hi joined in with, "We're going to have to make up our minds whether it will be the first night out of Pukow or the second night."

He didn't need to remind us that it would take some time to get the bars and the barbed wire off the window. We knew we couldn't do it until just before we jumped, because the guards might notice the open window from their outside inspections when our train was placed on sidings to let more important trains pass. The Japanese troops on the outside might also notice the open window.

Captain Lewis Bishop of the "Flying Tigers," known to us as "Bish," who had been listening to our whispered conversation, told us he was interested in escaping. Bishop had resigned his commission in the U.S. Navy in 1940 and joined the famous "Flying Tigers" in Kunming, China. While flying a P-40 against the Japanese, he had been shot down over Indo-China and captured by the Japanese in April 1942. He was brought to our Kiangwan prison camp in May 1943. Like the rest of us, he had suffered the many diseases of the Orient and had acquired immunity to others.

We discouraged Bish from going with us because our plans were set. We believed that the addition of a fifth member would complicate and endanger our escape. Further, Bish didn't have a pointee-talkee or any escape gear, nor did he speak Chinese. When we explained this to Bish he said he'd think about it. He said he wished he'd known earlier we were planning to escape.

One of the other prisoners cut in at this point. "You guys are crazy as hell to try to escape. You'll be caught and executed or spend the rest of this war in some stinking Japanese prison and die of typhus or something worse."

Another prisoner chimed in. "Don't you guys have any feeling for the rest of us? You know very well that the Japs will cut our rations, beat the hell out of us, and give us worse treatment than they have in the past."

There was a wide gap between those going and those staying. It appeared that the discussion was getting out of hand as a few more prisoners voiced similar opinions. Consequently we decided to call a halt to the discussion before the guards became nervous.

It was an old issue among the prisoners, many of whom believed that no one should try to escape as it would be to the detriment of the group. Others believed that their best chance of living through the war was to remain a prisoner of war. Still others thought, as did we, that it was the duty of an individual to try to escape.

It may seem peculiar, but during my long years of Marine Corps training, I did not and still do not recall any directive issued prior to World War II that once captured, an individual should make every effort to escape. We marines believed, however, that it was the duty of each marine not to give aid or comfort to his captors. We believed it best to give them as much difficulty as possible without endangering our lives and to make every effort to escape.

My model was General Charles de Gaulle, who escaped from the Germans several times during World War I. He was always caught because of his great height. We realized reluctantly that as tall, white Caucasians dressed in ragged Japanese uniforms, we would be as conspicuous among the Chinese peasants as the proverbial whore in church.

The train rolled slowly westward. We could see the familiar skyline of Shanghai through the sliding doors kept open by the guards. This brought to mind the familiar sights of Bubbling Well Road, the Bund, and the "Mandarin" nightclub owned by Jimmy James, an old and faithful friend of the marines. I had watched his band play farewell tunes for the Fourth Marines as they marched to the Bund in late November 1941 to board ships (President *Harrison* and President *Madison*) bound for the Philippines.

Passing into the countryside, we caught glimpses of Chinese and Japanese erecting barbed wire entanglements and concrete pill boxes. Apparently, the Japanese intended to defend Shanghai, but against whom at this point of the war was questionable.

At last the train moved through the age-old countryside scenes of China: velvet green carpets of rice; raggedly clad honey bucket coolies carrying buckets of night soil (human feces) to fertilize fields; patient water buffalo slowly dragging rudimentary plows through thick muck in unplanted fields; and peasants pushing squeaking wheelbarrows on narrow paths atop the dikes separating the fields.

Frequently our train pulled onto sidings to permit higher priority trains to pass. Long trains loaded with timber, coal, and supplies moved toward Shanghai. Each train was covered with a thick frosting of Chinese puppet or Japanese soldiers. On rare occasions, a passenger train packed to the bursting point steamed furiously by us to meet its flexible Oriental schedule. We passed the time by trying to sleep, wiggling around to find a comfortable position.

Our first meal of hardtack for supper took lots of time. One broke off a small piece and let it absorb saliva or soaked it in water. The stuff was too hard to chew and our teeth were not in the best of shape. As usual while eating, many delighted in reciting recipes of delicious food or telling stories about their favorite meals. A navy ensign from Wake Island was among the best when talking about chocolate milk shakes and banana splits. He could verbalize the taste of whipped cream.

Darkness slowly drowned the landscape, and the Japanese guards lighted kerosene lanterns in their space between the sliding doors. The light from the lanterns was not very bright but enabled us to make out the outlines of bodies and detect movement. The guards used their flashlights to make occasional checks.

Finally the guards closed the sliding doors and started a charcoal fire in a brazier to cook their food. It smelled good and diluted some of the local body odor. A guard partially opened one of the doors for some fresh air, and a Chinese voice, sounding like a bullfrog, thundered through the crack, "Meigworen, Meigworen, shr ding hau." ("American, American, very good.") The guard slammed the door shut and grabbed his rifle as did the others. Our group regarded the words as a good omen, despite the increased alertness of the guards.

Early the next morning, 10 May, the gray walls of Nanking rose through the mists of the Yangtze River. The musty smell of its silt-laden water overrode the stench of the guards' fishy breakfast. Rolling slowly through the wall gates and into the rail yard, we fully expected to see a great deal of bomb damage, but we did not. However, we did see two locomotives that had been severely damaged by strafing.

Some sidings appeared to have been recently repaired. The rail yard was in a frightful state of activity. "Donkey" engines (small steam locomotives) were repositioning boxcars. Charcoal-powered trucks filled the air with smoke. Complete trains arrived and departed. Air raid shelters of bamboo, concrete, and dirt were being erected for locomotives. Hundreds of Japanese soldiers and milling Chinese workmen completed the ant hill scene.

We untangled, uncoiled, and stood for the inevitable "banco," count-off muster. The guards took their time as they pulled nails from the wall in order to lift the barbed wire barricade which separated us from them. The interpreter who ordered us to disembark from the boxcar told us to leave our gear in place because we would return to the same car on the other side of the Yangtze River.

Hi and I, perhaps the eternal pessimists, were not too trustful. To be on the safe side, we divided one set of tools and carried them with us, hidden in our clothing, in the event the Japanese plans to reload went awry and we were not returned to our old boxcar. The guards marched us about a mile to a grassy park where we were to remain for several hours. Large groups of Chinese came to ogle us but soon hurried away. The guards brought us measly servings of rice that was actually fresh cooked. The latter beat hell out of the single hardtack biscuit for breakfast.

Our small group of plotters took advantage of the space to find a fairly safe spot, a bit apart, to continue our discussion about future actions.

Hi asked if we had noticed the alarm wire tagged with tin cans along the side of our boxcar. I said I hadn't noticed but had seen that there was not a brakeman's ladder near our window at the end of the car. Of course, that would alter our plans to hang onto the ladder and go in pairs.

We decided that since we all had a pointee-talkee, we would just have to jump out the window and hope we found help soon.

"If the train is going slow," suggested Johnny Mac, "perhaps each pair will land close enough together to find each other."

Kinney said: "I wouldn't count on it. I think we'll just have to jump and hope for the best."

Hi added: "I agree, but we have the problem maybe we won't return to the same car. If it's a different boxcar, we may have a brakeman's ladder and can carry out the original plan of going in pairs. If a new boxcar doesn't have a brakeman's ladder or if it's the old boxcar, let's forget about going in pairs. How 'bout drawing straws to see who goes first?"

"OK. But we need to decide when we'll go," Kinney said.

I mentioned that I originally believed we should wait until we got closer to Tsinan. "But suppose others beat us to it? Then the goddamn Jap bastards would be running around all night and day screaming their damn heads off. What say? Let's go tonight." The conversation went back and forth.

Johnny Mac said, "Well, it's the dark of the moon and I agree."

"Hell, that's what I've thought all along!" Kinney added emphaticallly.

Hi asked if anybody had told Colonel Ashurst. None of us had, but I volunteered to tell him and said, "We owe him that as he is our senior marine. He has done a goddamn good job for us these past three years."

Hi said, "OK, so we leave tonight about midnight."

I picked up four pieces of straw and each of the other three drew one. Comparing the straws, Hi had the shortest. It looked like Hi would go first, Johnny Mac second, and Kinney third. "Looks like I'm last," I said, "If you guys screw up and I don't get a chance to jump, I'll shoot you the next time I see you."

We talked again about our original plan in case we were put in another car with a brakeman's ladder. The first man would hang on to the ladder until the second one emerged, and we would do our best to go off in pairs. If we got our old car or another without a ladder, each would simply have to go through the window, roll up in a ball, and pray to hit soft ground.

Kinney said: "My corn tells me that we're in a high pressure area so we should be able to see the stars tonight. The Pleiades [the Seven Sisters] will be a good guide to the west."

Hi asked, "What does your corn tell you about the rest of this week?"

"We'll probably have rain day after tomorrow," replied Kinney, "and you'll see your Chinese girlfriend again."

"I'll have you know that my friend was a Russian princess," Hi replied.

"Yeah!" I kidded. "She held court in the International Cabaret every night with most of North China in attendance."

Kinney said, "Let us get on with the business at hand."

"Yes, by all means," agreed Hi. "Now, shall we decide that if one or more are injured severely, none of the others will stop to assist?"

"If the train is making any speed at all, we'll be widely scattered along the track," I added. "We won't be close enough to know if anyone is injured. And since our objective is to move to the west as fast as possible, we won't have time to search the area."

Kinney said, "If we do see someone's hurt, the only thing we can do to assist is to tell any friendly person we contact where the injured person is located."

Johnny Mac, thinking the worst, said: "If one of us jumps off a bridge, or hits a utility pole or building, there won't be much use telling anyone. That will be it. C'est la guerre!"

The order came from the guards to line up and move out. Before we left the area, I managed to tell Colonel W. W. Ashurst that we were leaving that night. His only comment was: "This is the best chance you'll have. Good luck!"

We were marched to the piers along the Yangtze and herded onto ferries headed for the city of Pukow on the north bank of the river. There were no bridges across the Yangtze. The empty trains were ferried across separately from the prisoners and Japanese troops. I supposed it was considered too dangerous for the Japanese to ride across in boxcars.

Here at the river docks was the first good evidence of American air bombing. Many docks were damaged, as were the pavements and buildings facing the river. There was little activity except for the ferries and one small river boat tied to a pier. Apparently enemy shipping in this section of the river had been severely restricted by allied air activity. There were remarks among the prisoners that a swim in the dark, swirling waters of the Yangtze would not be too pleasant.

As we neared the north bank and the city of Pukow, we could see further evidence of bomb damage and scars of strafing on buildings and docks. The Pukow railroad station rose somewhat majestically among the battered surroundings, however. The main thought of the prisoners was that we get out of Pukow before any allied aircraft returned for further attacks. Our group also hoped, despite the predictions of Kinney's corn, that the weather would soon turn for the worse. Bad weather would not only provide air protection but would also give us better cover for our escape and time to get away from the tracks.

While awaiting the arrival of the train ferries, we sat around the railroad sidings and further discussed what we would do in preparation for our escape. The guards were anxious to get out of the area, so they were running around and not paying much attention to us.

The ferries with the trains arrived much faster than we thought they would, and we were soon on board the boxcars and headed north toward

Tsinan and Peking. Fortunately, we were back in our old boxcar with our cozy toilet and blackout blanket which covered our escape window. The only unfortunate change was that our old car was now in the middle of the train instead of near the end.

Being in the middle of the train meant that the Japanese to the rear would be more likely to see us. Also, it appeared that an extra contingent of Jap troops had been assigned to the train. Extra troops meant larger search parties if our escape was discovered early.

There was little we could do about these circumstances, so we resumed our old positions around the entrance to the toilet corner, Kinney with his feet sticking into the area. By this time, Bish became convinced that he also would go if the chance came. He produced a map of China, but it was of too small a scale to be of use. We told him that the best thing to do, if he did come, was to head west and use the words "Meigworen, feiji, pungeo" (American, airplane, friend) as the best passwords.

There was still some muttering among certain prisoners that "those bastards are going ahead with their plans." One man, thinking he might stop us, offered to change places with Kinney, whose feet were practically touching the five-gallon toilet. When Kinney said that he preferred to remain where he was, the other prisoner raised a bit of rhubarb and threatened to hold onto him if he tried to escape. Fortunately, this individual's actions and voice were overpowered by other prisoners saying, "For God's sake, shut up and go to sleep." More importantly, the guards did not take too much heed of the ruckus.

As midnight approached, four of the six guards were asleep and the other two did not appear too vigilant. We prisoners were sleeping in such close quarters that we believed it would be difficult for the guards to distinguish between bodies. To make sure the guards wouldn't notice our absence from our bunking space, however, we placed personal items under our blankets, thus creating a fair-looking dummy. With the others watching the guards, I went into the toilet room, slipped under the blackout blanket, and with my hacksaw blade sawed slowly and tediously through the two iron bars which were practically rusted through. Returning to my bunk space, we waited with bated breath to see if the guards had been disturbed. They had not.

We watched the guards again while Hi slipped behind the blackout curtain and cut the barbed wire from around the window with his trusty pliers. Some of the wire flapped back against the side of the boxcar, making a rather loud racket. We froze as the guards turned their flashlights in our direction. Hi came out of the toilet and sprawled into his bunk space. That seemed to satisfy the guards and they returned to their rest positions.

"Mac! Wake up! It's time to go." Somehow I had dozed for a few minutes between the time Hi came out of the toilet and the time he and

Johnny Mac left. Kinney had given me a swift kick and an impassioned whisper, "Hi and Johnny Mac are gone!" Kinney was on his way out the window. I grabbed my bundle of food, medicine, and water, placed my dummy, and slid across to the toilet. I glanced at the guards. They were looking at the other end of the car. I quickly ducked under the blackout blanket, vaulted through the window, pushed off from the side of the car, and rolled into a ball before hitting the ground.

I hit with a jolting thud and rolled alongside the tracks for some distance. The train was making about 15 knots. I finally stopped rolling in a ditch full of water. I must have been knocked unconscious for a time, as my first memory was seeing the train disappearing in the distance. That was one of the most welcome sights of my life! Fortunately, there was no alarm. We were clean so far.

Lying on my left side in a narrow ditch in about a foot of water, I cautiously raised my head to take stock of the surrounding terrain. From what I could see through the darkness, to the east of me and just across the tracks was a small building—a blockhouse or station. Slightly further to the east, there appeared to be a small village. I was cursing my landing spot, when I noticed some utility poles a few feet up the track and was grateful for my wet landing.

I heard someone singing on the other (east) side of the tracks. His outline against the pale night sky indicated an individual with a rifle— possibly a Japanese soldier? After a turn or two beside the tracks he entered the small building. Again I was thankful. If our escape window had been on the east side of the northbound train, I would have had him to contend with. I cautiously looked about and discovered that there was a steep bank about eight feet high just above me, and to the west a line of shrubs offered cover. It appeared that I would be much better off to crawl north before starting west.

By this time, the physical effects of my landing were taking their toll. There was a sharp, shooting pain in my back, and my left shoulder felt as though someone had hit it with a sledge hammer. My head throbbed like it did the morning after a Marine Corps birthday party. Fortunately, as far as I could tell, I hadn't broken any major bones. My left hand hurt badly, however; its little finger appeared to be broken and bent sideways. Taking stock of my belongings, I discovered that my canteen of water had been crushed in the fall.

Although the water in the ditch was shallow, all my gear and food were soaking wet. My iodine bottle was broken, but my other medicine was in a waterproof tin. I decided to keep the wet food in the hope that some of it would be edible. I buried the useless canteen in mud in the bottom of the ditch.

Regardless of the pain in my back and the discomfort of my rapidly swelling left hand, I knew I had to get out of the immediate area as fast as possible. For one brief moment I wondered: Where are the others?

Just as I started to crawl north, the Japanese soldier, probably a sentry, came out of the blockhouse across the tracks and lit a cigarette. Shortly thereafter, he began singing again; at least the Orientals call it singing. Having a sentry in the vicinity was not good, but a singing, smoking sentry was better than a regulation *Bushido* (GI issue) Jap.

As I moved through the water in the ditch with its muddy bottom, I made a good bit of noise, but apparently the sentry was thinking of a lovely geisha girl back home. He did not appear to notice anything as I inched cautiously along the ditch. When he stopped singing, I stopped. When he sang, I crawled. We played this little game for quite some time—it seemed more like centuries to me—when finally, on my left flank and to the west, I reached a low bank with many bushes on it. I elbowed up the bank, stood up cautiously, and looked west. It was open country. I felt like giving a whoop of Texas joy.

I ran west into the welcome, enfolding darkness.

CHAPTER TWO

Friendly Locals

T HE ENVELOPING DARK was both friend and foe. It hid me from enemies but caused me to stumble and fall many times as I ran west. My only thought was to get as far from the tracks as possible. I ran. I fell. I continued to run and fall. Out of breath and exhausted, I sprawled into a soft, muddy field. I lay like a fish out of water, gasping for air, when the thought struck me: "Where do I go from here?"

At night rural China was dark—totally black. When the sun faded, village smoke solidified descending night blackness. There wasn't a light to be seen. Peasants couldn't afford oil for lamps. The only evidence of nearby inhabitants was in the stench of night soil and the barking of wonks (large, ugly dogs). Fear of being recaptured was very nearly balanced by fear of falling into one of the many open pits of night soil, which were liberally scattered across Chinese farming areas. One could usually circumvent them by the intensity of the odor.

The hostile works, although a source of rabies, also served useful purposes. They usually stayed within village walls and barked their heads off. All villages had wonks to warn of approaching strangers or bandits. By listening to the barking, I could avoid the villages.

The first thing I had to do was to wring out my waterlogged clothes. They were heavy and added to the chill of the cool night air. Mud and water in my Japanese army shoes did not make for either speed or ease of movement. After I had done everything possible for comfort, I leaned against the dike surrounding the field to rest and oriented myself by the North Star. I located a cluster of stars to the west for guidance, the Pleiades.

Before moving out, I again took stock of my few possessions: my pointee-talkee and five U.S. twenty-dollar bills wrapped in oil cloth. All were dry.

In a double glass case, a small snapshot of my fiancée, Jean Paterson of

Towson, Maryland, was intact. We had been engaged since my graduation from the U.S. Naval Academy on 1 June 1939. In those days of strict discipline, if a graduate from the U.S. Naval Academy married within two years after graduation, it was good-bye to the service.

After a year at the Marine Corps Basic School in Philadelphia, I was sent to China in June 1940. It was now May 1945—a hell of a long time since I had last seen my girl. I hoped she was still waiting for me.

With a swift look at the Pleiades to guide me, I took off. The paths were narrow on two-foot-high dikes surrounding the fields. It was difficult to run on top of the dikes. I couldn't make much speed as I tripped and stumbled along in the dark. It was impossible to watch both the path and the stars. The whole world was full of barking wonks. Were they disturbed by escapees or pursuing troops? Would their barking disclose my presence and position?

Speed was essential. I had to put a good distance between me and the railroad before dawn. Darkness created visual deceptions. Some fields appeared to be only inches below the narrow path, but missing my footing, I would crash down two or three feet into the soggy mud of a rice field. Worse, I would hit the hard ground of a field of wheat or kaoliang (a type of maize), jarring my injured back. At the edge of a dike, thinking I saw water reflecting starlight, I would gingerly set one foot down to test the bottom and find good solid ground. Or, wading a small stream and thinking it shallow, suddenly I would plunge into water lapping around my waist.

In the dark it was impossible to see isolated huts or even villages, but wonks kept me oriented. At times, when surrounded by a horizon of barking animals, I was not sure which way to go. Was I being pursued? I couldn't wait around to see.

On through the darkness I went, stumbling, falling, and cursing, yet breathing thoughts of thankfulness for being there. Dawn caught me near the banks of a wide river. A few boats and fishermen forbade a close approach. There was little chance of a daylight crossing. I selected a couple of small hills and certain trees to serve as possible guidance features for a night crossing. Withdrawing from the river, I chose a field of winter wheat for a hiding place during the day.

The field was fairly large for a Chinese plot, about six mou (one acre). It encompassed a small hill and was some distance from the largest path in the area. This position allowed me to observe the immediate surroundings, but the steepness of the hill discouraged casual visitors. The wheat was about waist high and provided concealment. Additionally, it was heading and might offer a little food and moisture. I stretched out, bent some stalks over my body, and relaxed to catch the warming rays of the sun.

For the first time I took stock of my wet food. A few sugar cubes wrapped in oil cloth remained edible. I ate two for an early breakfast. The half pound of cheese could be eaten by peeling a thin layer off with my teeth and spitting out the wet, moldy outside. A bit of cheese is good for breakfast. My problem was water. One dare not drink the water in China unless it is purified or boiled. Cholera, typhoid fever, and amoebic dysentery were endemic in China. I did not need the dehydration and diarrhea of cholera or dysentery, and certainly not typhoid fever. I had no way to boil water and no iodine for purification. My iodine had vanished with my jump from the train. I pulled the tops off green wheat stalks and chewed them for moisture. Not much success. The green kernels were not any better. I wondered how long a person could go without water. Today was 11 May, and tomorrow would make two days. Could I hold out? Yes! With discretion—less speed and perhaps a good soaking in the river. That decided, what next?

To stay awake was impossible. As hard as I tried to keep alert, sleep came quickly. Exhaustion and the warmth of the sun were soporific. About noon the heat and my dry, burning throat awakened me. I chewed more wheat stalks, but my thirst persisted. As the day lengthened, the hot sun lingered above the horizon long beyond my wishes. I debated drinking river water and risking cholera. It wasn't a toss-up. No river water. But I couldn't go on much longer.

From the north came the lonesome wail of a train whistle. Had I walked in a semicircle? A cautious look north revealed a small village. A glance to the south brought a shock. A patrol of soldiers was moving east to west about a quarter mile from me. Their silhouettes were characteristic of Japanese troops. Rifles, kepi caps, and helmet humps on their backs identified them. There was nothing I could do but crouch where I was and wait. A Chinese farmer took a short cut through the field and passed within a few feet of me. I hugged the ground. More farmers passed as the day wore on, but not one saw me.

I was thankful when dusk pulled obscurity around me and I was able to assume a comfortable position to crap. Urination is not too difficult lying down, but "number two" requires another position. I was grateful that dysentery had not struck.

Thus ended a very long day, yet my "day" had only begun.

Preparation for the night hike consisted of munching three lumps of sugar and a bit of cheese. The sugar made the saliva flow and lessened my thirst for a moment. Dry clothes felt good against the sudden evening chill. Moving carefully to the edge of the river, I glanced in both directions. No boats. Searching for a stick to assist in crossing, I flushed some ducks, and their quacking startled me. Chinese usually herded ducks and chickens or kept them penned. Their presence meant there were Chinese living nearby. I froze for a few minutes and listened, but there was no further ruckus.

I found a stout, long stick, took off my clothes, and wrapped them around one end of the stick, hoping to hold my clothes up out of the water. No luck. Almost immediately, I was forced to swim and was back to square one. Wet clothes and more damage to my food supply. The water was not too cold, however, and felt good after the dry, hot day in the field. I hoped some would soak through my skin and relieve my thirst.

The west bank of the river afforded a little more cover. It was fairly high. Brush and weeds provided some concealment. Again, I wrung out my clothes, checked my gear, and crawled to the top of the bank. There were no huts or villages to the immediate west and even the wonks were quiet. That was good. The train tracks were north of me, and the Jap patrol was to the south. I had to go west.

With a few minutes of brisk walking, I was warm but my thirst was greater than before. I settled down to a less hasty pace. The area consisted primarily of wheat or kaoliang fields. Dikes were not as prevalent. Walking was easier. I walked slowly so as not to sweat. I had to conserve my body's fluid.

It was more difficult to remain oriented that second night because clouds covered much of the sky. During periods of cloudiness, I rested. Rain would have been most welcome. I visualized cupping my hands to catch enough water to dampen my dry throat.

The wonks again began their exchange of howls and provided some guidance. My biggest problem while plodding along was to maintain a westward course. Clouds were not welcome as I needed the stars for guidance, specifically the North Star and the Pleiades.

I was glad when dawn arrived, although it meant spending another day hiding in the hot sun. I was very tired and needed the rest. It also meant I had to reach a decision about approaching a local Chinese to ask for water and help. Of the many Chinese nearby, how was I to select one who would help me? One who would not betray me to the enemy?

As previously indicated, in this area there were Japanese and their Chinese puppet troops, bandits, and the Kungchantang (Communists). There was also the possibility of Kuomintang (Nationalist troops). It was my firm belief that the New Fourth Army (Kungchantang) had some well established bases in this area. In 1940, Chiang Kaishek's forces had driven the Nationalist Fourth Army north of the Yangtze River into Kiangsu and Anwhei provinces. There they had joined the Communists, renamed themselves the New Fourth Army, and established control over much of the area.

The Japanese were located in larger cities and villages and along the railroads and major thoroughfares. There were still pockets of bandits, Japanese, and puppet troops throughout the region. But it was the New Fourth, its guerrillas, or the Nationalists I wanted to find.

Early clouds obscured the sun and gave me more time to find a place to hide. After yesterday's experiences, I thought a more secure hiding place was in order. Among the many small hills I could see, there appeared to be one dotted with graves. It had grave markers and was surrounded by a wattle fence of kaoliang stalks and low bushes. A graveyard signified silence, and being offset with fencing, it appeared to be a good hiding place. The slight elevation also provided some observation of the area. I moved in among the bushes and graves and settled down for the day.

Time passed slowly. I ate a few heads of green wheat and a bit of cheese and two sugar lumps rounded out the meal. The sun burned away the clouds and left me sweltering in the heat. Flies came by the thousands. I was sorely reminded of the hordes of flies in our prison camps. There, when eating, one had to fan his mouth as well as the food constantly to keep from gulping down flies. Thousands of them were always emerging from the open latrines. Here in my hideaway, big ones and small ones buzzed around. Big horseflies bit and drew blood. Somewhere along the way fleas had found me. Fleas bit and bit hard. I scratched and scratched, only to attract more of those pests. Although I was exhausted, sleep escaped me.

About a hundred yards from me, there was a continuous parade of Chinese along a path. After some deliberation, I decided to move to the side of the hill opposite the path, away from the graves. The wheat there was high enough to conceal me and gave me another choice of something to chew for moisture. The flies followed, and the fleas bit harder. Toward dusk, I conceded victory to the heat, thirst, flies, and fleas and decided water and help were imperative. I crawled back among the graves and watched for someone on the path to ask for assistance.

At sunset the path appeared deserted except for an elderly man in ragged clothing with a thin, white, scraggly chin beard, who was carrying a bundle of sticks. I thought, if he's not friendly, I can get away from him even if violence is necessary.

I rose from my hiding place, walked toward him, and said, "Wu-an, syansheng." (Good evening, Mister.) "Wo shwo Junggwo wa yidyar. Wo shr Meigworen." (I speak a little Chinese. I am an American.)

The old man stopped, dropped his bundle, and stared at me in astonishment. He looked wildly around to see if other apparitions were nearby. I thought for a moment he was going to flee.

I said, "Wo shr eaguh pungeo." (I am a friend.)

He continued to stare and finally said, "Ni shr Meigworen?" (You are an American?)

"Wo shr Meigworen. Ching ni gei wo yisye cha—re kai shui." (Please give me some tea or hot water.)

I showed him my pointee-talkee, but he couldn't read the characters. He asked if I was Japanese.

I said no, I was not Japanese. I was an American and Japan was our enemy.

He continued to stare as though he couldn't believe what he was seeing. Slowly it began to dawn on him that I was not someone who would hurt him. His facial muscles relaxed, and he began to examine me quizzically. Slowly his eyes moved from my face to my feet, and back to my face. Then he asked an important question:

"Chrbow fan la?" (Have you eaten?)

"No, I have not eaten. I would like some rice and tea."

"Come with me."

"Are there any Japanese in this area?"

"No."

"Wang Ching Wei soldiers?" (Chinese puppet troops?)

"No."

"Kuomintang?" (Nationalists?)

"Yesyu." (Maybe.)

"Kungchantang?" (Communists?)

"Maybe."

"Where?"

He pointed west.

"How many li?" (About three li equals a mile.)

"One hundred, maybe two hundred."

My limited Chinese vocabulary had been strained. The old man's accent or dialect was different from my Mandarin. I was satisfied, however, that I had made a pretty good contact under the circumstances. He picked up his bundle of sticks and motioned me to follow. For better or worse, the die was cast. At least I appeared to have one friend out of the 500 million Chinese.

Once he stopped and said, "Russian?"

Again, my denial was immediate, and I added the words "American airplane."

He understood the word *feiji* (airplane) and seemed much more pleased with the situation. He led the way quite cheerfully. Although still cautious, I followed in his footsteps.

We soon arrived at a small village. My friend took a stick to the wonks growling at me, and they seemed to calm down. I was dirty, wet, and smelly. In the growing darkness none of the villagers took notice of me, but as we entered the old man's hut we were immediately surrounded by curious members of the household.

Each member of the family was trying to examine me carefully and talk to me at the same time. The old man gave some explanation of my presence which I didn't understand. The *furen*, his wife, gave orders and suddenly there was quiet. She bowed to a young man, probably her son, and must have encouraged him to ask me questions. He asked if I had eaten. At my response, the young man turned to his wife, who was holding a baby and restraining a young lad, and gave what appeared to be an order. She disappeared and brought back a bowl of white tea (hot water). I drank and asked for more. After four bowls of white tea and a bowl of cabbage soup, I felt as though I might live again.

CHAPTER THREE

Chinese Hospitality

T HE OLD MAN and I sat on the edge of the *whei k'ang*, a large, mud-brick bed covered with a thick layer of straw. The young man's wife disappeared again but soon returned with a bowl of millet gruel and another bowl of hot cabbage soup. I needed no encouragement. It was one of the best meals I have ever eaten. I was ashamed of myself for eating so much so fast. The family was eating rather slowly and watching every bite I took.

They continued to talk rapidly. From what little I could gather, it appeared I was accepted as an American. They were eager to be friendly, but they were not quite sure about the whole thing.

After we finished eating, the old man, whose name was Mr. Wang, left the hut and returned with two men. The older of the two was presented as "number one" in the village and the younger one as Mr. Tang. I assumed "number one" meant "head man."

I introduced myself: "Mi, shauwei, Meigwo haijyun lujandwei." (Mac, second lieutenant, American Marine Corps.)

He replied, "Wo shr Chen syansheng." (I am Mr. Chen.)

I pulled out my American money and the pointee-talkee.

Mr. Chen peered at the money, felt it, and seemed to understand that it confirmed my claim of being an American. None of them understood the English lettering, but they were impressed with the seals and pictures on the bills. Mr. Chen examined my pointee-talkee, searching for more information. He was still skeptical of my origin. I showed him the picture of my fiancée.

He asked, "Furen?" (Wife?)

Not knowing the word for fiancée, I lied, "Yes, my wife." Chinese are always interested in family pictures and family affairs.

"How many children?" he asked.

28

"None."

"Ding bu hau." (Very bad.) Chinese do not understand marriage without children.

He seemed to accept that I was an American since I was married to a "round eye." Because he appeared to need a little more convincing, I tried to tell him I had been a prisoner of the Japanese and had escaped, but my limited Chinese did not convey the message. Somewhat in desperation, I assumed the role of an aircraft pilot and began pantomiming. I pretended to strafe trains and bomb buildings. My act was a huge success. Every time a locomotive blew up, the thatched roof rocked with laughter and applause. It was a story that ran before me all the way to the headquarters of the New Fourth Army.

I gave a lump of my precious sugar to the young boy, and that gained me more acceptance. In the atmosphere of good fellowship, I asked for a bottle of water. Misunderstanding, Mr. Wang produced a bottle of some sort of alcoholic beverage. Considering my physical condition, I didn't think it wise to drink any alcohol, but my host insisted. I took a sip. Wow! It was very strong. One sip was more than enough. I thanked him — once I could talk. He took a sip and carefully returned the bottle to its hiding place. Again I pantomimed flying aircraft and shooting trains, urged on by my host. All appeared to be enjoying the proceedings.

Finally, we got down to business. My new friends were shocked and astounded when I asked to be taken to the Kungchantang. They insisted that the *Egwore'n* (Russians, meaning the Communists) would cut my throat, as well as theirs, and toss our bodies to the dogs. I then asked to be taken to the Kuomintang or to Chungking and added they would be liberally rewarded. The reply: "No can do. Too many Japanese, bandits, and puppets." After much discussion among the family members, I was told I could stay with them. Mr. Chen said he would find someone to guide me to an area of Communist operations. I was assured that no Japs had ever come near their village and I would be safe. I was not pleased with that decision but was too exhausted to think of an alternate plan that night. It was the old lady who brought the discussion to a close. She decided that foreigner or no foreigner, it was bedtime. Mr. Chen left and we were sent to bed.

My sleeping place was in a wattle shed at one end of a dirt threshing floor. My partner in the shed was the young male visitor, Mr. Tang. Apparently, he was there either to protect me or keep me from escaping. It wasn't a comfortable situation, but I reasoned I'd have to make the best of it. Mr. Tang settled himself on the dirt floor and went to sleep. My bed was a wooden door supported at either end by stacks of mud-bricks. I scattered kaoliang stalks on it to make it a little softer, laid down, and plummeted into unconsciousness.

Chinese rise early to take advantage of all daylight. On this morning (13 May 1945, my third morning after leaving the train), I was tired and wanted to sleep, but an urgent call of nature brought me to my senses. I had the trots. My infestation of fleas had increased, and other bugs had bitten me during the night. My legs and belly were covered with small red welts. Bedbugs? My resident fleas? This was not a good development, as fleas carry typhus, another endemic disease in China. What next?

Diarrhea is bad enough when one is near proper facilities, but here there was no paper. Neither were there corncobs, which one finds on a farm in the States. Soap was missing as well. In a sense, one becomes self-infecting and the disease goes in a circle. I swallowed some of my bismuth and charcoal and hoped for the best.

I knew I should refrain from eating because of my diarrhea. Needless to say, my hunger overcame any inhibitions. Tang brought some white tea and a bowl of millet gruel. It was good to have some food. When I left the train, my weight was down to about 110 pounds from my normal 180. My physical condition was not the best for traveling.

Mr. Wang came out to the threshing floor and indicated that I should leave at once because there were Japanese 30 li to the south. Tang was told to take me to a safer place.

I asked for Chinese clothes and shoes. I would be much less conspicuous in ordinary coolie clothes than in my prison garb, a ragged Japanese army uniform. Further, Chinese cloth shoes were a lot more comfortable than my stiff, leather, Japanese clodhoppers. I could walk faster in cloth shoes.

Wang handed me old clothes and shoes that were a reasonable fit. I discarded my Japanese uniform, the last remnants of Kiangwan. Wang gave Tang and me some *myanbau* (steamed bread) to carry with us.

Off again into the unknown...

Tang did not want to walk beside me because he wanted to be able to disassociate himself from me quickly. He walked about 50 yards ahead, looking right and left. He waited patiently when I had to stop for frequent calls of nature, but was not pleased to do so. He apparently thought that the Japs or puppet troops would catch up with us.

We stopped at one very small, isolated village where Tang obtained white tea to accompany our meager meal of steamed bread. Both food and drink were welcome. My stomach still felt like my throat had been cut, and the other end was an open valve. Toward dusk we came to another small village, and Tang led me directly to a wattle wall hut with a thatched roof. A young couple, three small children, and a large wonk responded to Tang's call.

Here we spent the night. The hut, much smaller than Mr. Wang's house, was a typical peasant's hut. It had a dirt floor and a whei k'ang, or brick bed with the usual fire box under it. A smoke tunnel running through the bed heated the dwelling in cold weather. At the other end, a low fence closed off a space for an ox. Since the weather was warm, the ox was tied outside. I was grateful for that.

I had stayed in many peasant huts before when hunting in North China and was acquainted with the layout. Dirt floors in huts were normal. Wonks wandered in and out, and chickens pecked about. Children often urinated and defecated on the floor. Despite hygienic considerations, the split pants of Chinese youngsters are very practical. Adults cleared their throats and spat on the floor. After a meal, to clean his teeth, a person swished water around in his mouth and spit it on the floor. When it was time to "tidy up," the woman of the house swept with a twig broom. Clouds of dust rose and settled on everything. Although vaguely repulsed, I was more interested in food and drink than the sanitary conditions.

I will call my host Kao (meaning "local farmer"), for want of a better name. Kao and his wife gave me hot water to drink and set about their evening chores. Tang left, saying he would return the next day. Soon there was a fire of kaoliang stalks and a boiling pot of millet gruel. I sat on the k'ang with the rest of the family and ate. The big wonk, with his ears erect, sat sniffing my leg but seemed somewhat benign.

The children were fascinated having a *da' bi-ze ren* (big nose man) in the house. If there are any cuter children in the world than Chinese youngsters, I don't know where you find them.

I reached for my bowl of gruel with my left hand and felt a warm splash on my wrist. I looked up to the rafters to see chickens roosting directly over me. But why should a little thing like that deter a hungry person?

After eating, I went out to the threshing ground, a flat and level area behind the hut, to find a place to sleep. My diarrhea was still active. My main concern with sleeping outside was that big wonk sniffing around me, but perhaps he would serve a useful purpose and alert me to any dangers.

Kao found some kaoliang stalks to soften the ground. He made me a pallet and offered a piece of cloth as a cover. The night air was chilly. I said good night and very quickly sprawled on the pallet because I wanted to beat the wonk to the bed. I was asleep before I hit the deck. The wonk was at my side through the night and kept me warm.

Early the next morning (14 May 1945), I was awakened by Tang, who told me another man would take me to the Kungchantang. Tang had passed the buck. My new guide was about 20 years of age with a pockmarked face. He was nervous and continually glanced around. He kept saying, "Kwai, kwai!" (Hurry, hurry!) I was ready to go, but food and drink came first. A bowl of gruel and hot water served as breakfast. Just before we left, I offered Tang some American money but he would not take it. He said: "America and China are friends. That is enough."

Tang must have been very sure of the loyalty of the people we had passed in our travels because retaliation by the Japs for harboring Americans would have been swift and severe. Not only would Tang have suffered, but all the villagers in the area would also have been punished.

I thanked Tang and the Kao family, turned to my guide, and said, "Kwai, kwai." Off we went at a dog trot to the west. My new guide also stayed ahead of me about 50 yards. After a short distance I slowed, and he accepted my somewhat slackened pace. I wanted to have some reserve in case of an emergency.

Again, frequent calls of nature slowed progress. We turned south for several miles and came to a small village about mid-morning. We stopped for water, and the guide bought some steamed bread. Slowly sipping the hot water and enjoying every morsel of the bread, I thought of my buddies from the train and wondered what had happened to them. I knew that we had been scattered along the track because of the speed of the train and the intervals between our departures. If they were in the area, however, the Chinese grapevine would have passed the word.

My reverie was broken as my guide walked up and picked a big, fat louse off my neck. He dangled the louse in front of my face as though tempting me with a choice morsel. He shattered the air with laughter and attracted a sizeable crowd, much to my consternation. Although I didn't like an audience, I was delighted when my guide pulled a louse from his own clothing and indicated we were *pungeos* (friends). He had more than an ample supply of lice and probably many other varmints. I had little interest in his menagerie, but believed his newly expressed friendliness would be an asset.

Although my guide was friendly now, thoughtful he was not. He kept trying to increase our speed, but I had to stop many times. He would race ahead and yell, "Kwai, kwai!" Some time after noon, we came in sight of a river and a large village on the opposite bank. We could see a wide road leading into the village. It was not the usual common country cart path. It appeared to have had lots of traffic. Motor vehicles? I questioned my guide about the village.

"Are there any soldiers in that village?"

"Yes."

I stopped, aghast, but he continued to walk. I ran after him, grabbed his jacket, and held him.

"What country soldiers?" I asked.

"Soldiers with guns."

"Japanese?"

"What people them?"

That reply set me back on my heels. Here was a nut trying to guide me to friendly troops, but he did not know there were a million bastardly

Japs occupying his country. I certainly didn't want to approach the village until I learned more about these "soldiers." I tried again to question the guide.

"Japanese make war on China."

"War, don't understand."

"Soldiers belong Mao Tse-tung?"

"Maybe."

"Soldiers belong to Chiang Kaishek?"

"Maybe."

This went on for some time with me holding the blathering idiot, questioning him, while he tried to resume walking.

Fortunately, an elderly man approached and asked what the trouble was. I turned, with gratitude, and asked him if there were soldiers in the village. He said no and explained that sometimes Japanese soldiers came by truck along the road and into the village. Thanking the gentleman, I turned my guide loose and we made our way to the river bank.

He called to a man in a small boat, and we were ferried across the river into a prosperous looking village. There were many geese and ducks on the river banks. I could well imagine them in a roasting pan, baked to a golden brown. The thought of dripping, succulent roast goose made me ravenous.

This wonderful dream was rudely shattered by my guide, who grabbed me by my coat and hustled me along a busy street and into a building. In spite of my height, neither the wonks nor the villagers noticed me. I looked like a low "coolie" by this time. I was dirty and had the full schedule of smells and varmints. They couldn't tell what color I was. I was pleased with my grimy appearance. It helped me to fit into the crowd.

The building we entered turned out to be a school, and instantly school was over. I was surrounded by a mob of curious young students. One youth awakened a teacher sleeping in one end of the room, and another fetched the headmaster. Hastily, I produced my pointee-talkee for the *syansheng* (gentleman or scholar). After satisfactorily answering several questions, I was established as an American marine officer.

Hot water was brought for drinking; cold water was furnished for washing. The latter sure felt good. Washing away several days of grime lifted my spirits. A pot of hot tea, *real* tea, brought a rosy glow. As I was munching on a piece of bread with some persimmon jam, the headmaster grabbed the bread from my hand, threw it in my shoulder bag, pushed the bag to me, and said: "Japs are coming down the road. Leave quickly." He designated one of his pupils, named Chin, as a new guide, and we left quickly out a back door.

In a few minutes the village was far behind us, and we were in the midst of tall wheat. We trotted for several miles until we reached low lying hills to the west. At the base of one hill was a farmhouse where we were given hot water to drink. After a short rest, we climbed the hill and walked along the crest of the range. My student guide pointed to a distant road and, gesticulating wildly, shouted, "Japanese trucks come!"

I was shocked but couldn't see any trucks or dust. Perhaps he meant yesterday or the day before. We didn't pause to find out. My new young guide was much better than the last one. He understood what I wanted to do.

We changed course to the southwest and saw slightly higher hills ahead of us. Late in the afternoon, we reached a small village and stopped for a rest and some tea. Our host provided Chinese cigarettes, which tasted like the cedar bark I had smoked as a small boy. Regardless of the taste, the nicotine gave me a lift and left me, a nonsmoker, dizzy. A bowl of hot wheat gruel made me feel much better.

For the first time, I saw evidence of the Kungchantang. On the wall of the hut there were three red streamers with Chinese characters. Their meanings were unknown to me, but my student guide gave me the vital information by reading off the names "Mao Tse-tung" and "Chu Teh." This meant I was, at last, in what I considered to be friendly territory.

I could begin to relax.

CHAPTER FOUR

Guerrillas

THE RED STREAMERS indicated the Kungchantang had been in this village. Were they still here or nearby? I certainly hoped so.

I needed sleep and rest. More importantly, something for my diarrhea. Food passed through me so fast it did little good to eat. My guide Chin had the picture by now. Laughing, he made a couple of obscene gestures and spoke with our host. The latter gave me a spoonful of a dark, thick liquid with a very strong, bitter taste. I downed it with a grimace. Hot tea washed away the thick, unpleasant feeling in my throat. Thankfully, my stomach relaxed. In a short time my lower troubled tracts and sphincter tightened.

Sleep was next on my list; I needed rest badly. My blistered feet felt like coals of fire. I stretched out on the k'ang, but before I could close my eyes, Chin burst into the hut shouting: "Lai, lai! Kwai, kwai!" (Come, come! Hurry, hurry!)

I jumped up and asked, "Na shr shemma?" (What is it?)

Chin excitedly replied, "Rbenren!" (Japanese!)

"Where?"

Chin pointed east. "Ding jin!" (Very near!)

"How many li?"

"Er li." (Two-thirds of a mile.)

"That's too damn close. Kwai, kwai."

So it was off again at a trot on a long night hike. After about a mile, Chin decided we could slow the pace. That was fine with me because I was hanging on by the skin of my teeth. Concentration was needed to focus my leaden eyes on Chin's back simply to follow him as I trudged numbly in his footsteps.

Chin was apparently familiar with the area. There was no hesitation in his choosing a course. We followed well-traveled paths, skirting the few villages along the way. In rural China, people stayed within their village walls at night for protection of life and property.

In this area where warfare and banditry prevailed, villages were organized for defense and guard posts were manned at night. All males were assigned positions for defense. Wealthier villagers furnished their own weapons — rifles and pistols. The poor used what was at hand — spears, pitchforks, hoes. With the villagers confined within their own walls, we had the path to ourselves.

We made fairly good time, despite my frequent squats. As we approached a village near midnight, we were stopped by the sound of a rifle bolt slamming shut and the harsh challenge by a sentry.

"Halt! Who is there?"

Needless to say, we stopped.

Chin replied, "One Kungchantang soldier and an American officer."

"Advance."

We moved several paces forward. The sentry repeated his first command: "Halt!" Again we stopped. A sentry, barely visible, pointed his rifle at us. He and Chin exchanged a volley of words, none of which I understood. Finally the sentry lowered his rifle and beckoned us to follow. Beating off the gathering wonks, he marched into a hut. Chin followed and I staggered in behind them.

A large man in ragged, black clothes wearing a blue military cap greeted us and motioned us to be seated on the k'ang. The only other occupant in the dilapidated room with mud and kaoliang walls was a big, black, mangy wonk, which was not pleased. He growled and bared his teeth at both of us. The man was no more friendly than his wonk.

It was an unusual scene — no wife, no children. Just the k'ang in the middle of four barren walls. Apparently the hut was a sort of guard house. The man indicated to Chin he was in charge of defense for the night. Chin did most of the talking. Our "host" and I engaged in conversation about me being an American. He became a little more relaxed after that exchange, and the usual white tea and gruel were provided. As we ate, the man seemed friendly enough, but not his big wonk.

That bastard kept watching me and growling as though looking for a chance to make a meal out of me. Chin and the man on duty kept talking, but I, tired and exhausted, dozed off. That was the chance for the wonk; he sank his big, yellow, dirty fangs in my right leg. I jumped to my feet yelling and kicking him off. Our host grabbed the dog by the scruff of the neck and beat him unmercifully. I thought we would have roast dog for breakfast. I could barely hear Chin shouting, "I am sorry! I am sorry!" above the howling of the wonk.

After the dog stopped howling and Chin stopped shouting, our host said what I took to be "I beg your pardon." He splashed water on the bite, but did not offer medicine for the wounds. The best I could do to prevent possible rabies was to encourage bleeding and wash the wounds again with water. Hydrophobia would have been a real problem.

Our host kicked the wonk outside and slammed the rough, heavy door. I thought the walls would fall down.

Chin and I were offered a place on the whei k'ang for the night. No second invitation was needed. There were no kaoliang stalks or straw to soften the bed, but they weren't needed. Exhaustion doesn't call for feather beds.

Long before dawn, Chin offered me hot tea and said, "Hurry, hurry." My first thought was that the Japs were again in the vicinity, but it turned out they were not. Chin just wanted an early start. My second thought was one of thankfulness for not having to get up for a nature call during my brief nap. My diarrhea was apparently plugged for the time being. The tarlike substance worked. I wished I had kept some of the bitter medicine for the future. My third thought, all too evident, was that the goddamn wonk supplied me with more fleas.

Chin kept saying, "Hurry, hurry!"

When I asked why, he said we had many li to walk.

I would have preferred more rest and some decent shoes. The old cloth shoes given to me three days ago were in shreds. When I pointed to them, the answer was the usual Chinese verbal expression for throwing your hands in the air in disgust: "Mei yuo fa tze!" ("There is no solution" or "that is the way it is.") No good argument could be used against such an expression. We drank a bowl of thin gruel quickly and left.

As we went out the door, the vengeful wonk lunged for me but was brought up short with a sharp, crashing blow to his head. We said our thanks and stumbled through the darkness, southwest.

At false dawn we entered rough, broken terrain. Daylight revealed large brown hills edged with green patches of wheat. Small streams and terraces were outlined by scraggly, scrawny trees. Over hills, down through ravines, and across fields of wheat, we plodded in a fairly straight line. That was unusual, as the Chinese almost always follow the wandering, footworn paths around hills and fields. Walking in a straight line meant Chin was in a hurry. On and on we went. Several times I asked if we could stop for food.

The answer was always: "No. Hurry, hurry!"

By late afternoon, my energy had been consumed. I was completely spent. Finally, after we had stumbled to the top of another hill, Chin pointed into the valley below and said, "Kungchantang."

"Friendly to Americans?" I asked.

Chin repeated, "Kungchantang," adding, "Three li. I no go." He turned to leave and said, "Dzaijian" (Goodbye).

I was saying, "Hen sye sye ni" (Thank you very much) as he left at a trot. He shouted over his shoulder, "Bubi kechi" (You are welcome).

His abrupt departure made me wonder if I was walking into a trap. Apparently he did not wish to have contact with the Kungchantang. There was something peculiar about his actions. Regardless of my wary feelings, I had to face the fact that I was alone in an unknown area and without water or food. There was only one thing to do — walk in the direction Chin had indicated. Because I had slept very little the last four nights and was limping from burning feet and fatigue, my pace was slow. Suddenly I was startled by three men who jumped up from behind bushes alongside the path and pointed rifles at me. Shock and adrenaline brought me fully awake and to attention. They didn't have to say anything. I threw my hands in the air and froze!

Slowly they moved toward me, stopping a bayonet's length away. Each examined me intently. Moving cautiously, they took position, one on either side and one behind me. One said what I took to be "move" as he motioned me with his rifle along the path.

"I am an American marine and your friend."

There was no answer other than a grunt, a jab in the back, and another motion with his rifle to keep moving. I moved. As we rounded a sharp curve, I saw two men armed with pistols standing near a small mound. My escorts motioned me to halt. Again I threw up my hands and stopped. One of the two men questioned me.

"Ni shr na yigwo de?" (What nationality are you?)

"I am an American marine, second lieutenant."

"Are you a pilot?"

Remembering that I had claimed such on entry into this area and knowing the Chinese penchant for detailed reporting, I replied yes.

With that answer they took my hands, pumped them vigorously, and asked if I knew Mao Tse-tung. When I said yes they said, "Very good. We are friends. Have you eaten?"

Of course I said I hadn't. I hadn't since Chin left me. They guided me into the village and we entered an unusually large house. Inside were several men. Some, apparently soldiers, were in blue uniforms. On the walls were banners with large Chinese ideographs. Between the banners were photographs of Mao and two other Chinese leaders whom I did not recognize. Several rifles were stacked in one corner. Two of the uniformed men wore side arms; I assumed they were officers.

Pointing at Mao's picture, I asked, "Mao Tse-tung?" The response was a pleasant chorus of "shr" (yes). I then mentioned the name Ch'en Yi, who took over the New Fourth Army after its original commander was killed in 1941. These statements brought smiles to many faces. Again, I identified myself as a second lieutenant, United States Marine Corps.

I offered my other evidence—the pictures of my fiancée and American money. This identification was waved aside. Judging from the actions and what few words I could catch, this group had known of my presence in the area since early that morning. Without my asking, white tea, gruel, and hard-boiled eggs quickly appeared. Having not eaten since early morning, I wolfed down everything offered.

The men continued to talk, apparently about me, occasionally pointing my way. Not sharing their conversation, I laid down on a bench and went to sleep. I couldn't have slept for more than an hour. When I awakened, it was still daylight.

One of the uniformed men with a side arm told me we should leave. "Kwai, kwai." I wondered, as I had many times before, if everything had to be done in a hurry. There was just time to drink a lot of white tea and eat a couple of hard-boiled eggs. I was told we would go to the headquarters of General Wong, many li to the south. One officer said we would move out quickly and be there the next night.

I doubted I could make such a hike with so little rest. These people were in a rush, however, anxious to get me off their hands, I supposed. My escort consisted of four soldiers in rumpled blue uniforms with bolt-action rifles.

In tow was a Chinese prisoner trussed in the traditional manner. His hands were tied behind his back and pulled up between his shoulder blades by a rope passing around his neck. Thus, any movement of his arms choked him. I thought the poor bastard would be shot as soon as we were out of sight of the village; however, quite the contrary happened.

As soon as we passed over the first big hill, out of sight from the village, our escort loosened the prisoner's rope and gave him one of their foul cigarettes. The prisoner walked along with us, a cigarette dangling from his mouth, talking as though he hadn't a worry in the world. At our first tea stop, the prisoner said something to one of the escorts, who reached in the prisoner's pocket and pulled out some money. Food and drink were bought for all with the prisoner's money.

This was the end of the fourth day and the beginning of my fifth night on the road. Again, we had the countryside and a well-beaten path to ourselves. We skirted some villages but properly answered the challenges of sentries at others and were permitted to walk through their district. In this area, villages were not as numerous as in the more prosperous farming sections.

The pace was not fast, but it was all I could do to keep up with my escorts. Nevertheless, I wanted them to know that an American marine could walk with the best of them. So I kept plodding along.

During the first part of this century, Chinese soldiers and guerrillas had a poor reputation abroad. All guerrilla bands were referred to as bandits and many actually were bandits. The latter groups were a terrible scourge for the peasants. I had learned to have a great deal of respect for the peasants while on my North China hunting trips. In addition to the bandit scourge, the government imposed very heavy taxes. Peasants had a damn hard life, yet they bore those burdens well.

Many Westerners conjured up rather pathetic images of Chinese soldiers. The latter were pictured going into battle with an opium pipe, blowing horns and banging on gongs, then fleeing at the first shot. The battle was to be won with money and intrigue, not warfare.

I learned quickly that the Chinese soldier was an extremely tough bird. He had great endurance and existed on very little. We Americans were to learn even more about their toughness and stamina later, in Korea.

It was a very long night. At what was probably some time after midnight, we stopped at a village for food and drink. Again, the elected spot was a small guard hut. There wasn't sufficient room for all of us on the k'ang. The prisoner was trussed properly and allowed to lie on the dirt floor with some of our guards. I rated the k'ang and was asleep immediately, but it was a damn short nap. We were awakened long before first light, then fed and watered. Afterwards we hit the trail.

With daylight (15 May 1945, my fifth day on the road), the guards became more cautious than during the previous night. The prisoner wasn't allowed any freedom. He was securely trussed before we approached each village. One guard would go ahead of our line of march to a dominating terrain feature. Sometimes he would motion for us to advance, but occasionally, he would hold us in place for a short time. I assumed he was looking for Jap or puppet patrols. The guards were especially cautious in the vicinity of two motor roads we crossed.

The guards' field sanitation discipline was lax. They drank from streams along the way. I guessed they had developed subclinical immunity to most diseases in the area, but I couldn't afford the risk and remained as dry as the Sahara Desert.

The soldiers did not attempt to conceal my identity as an American. In fact, they seemed to brag about it at places we stopped by pointing to me and exclaiming, "Meigwo feiji." Apparently, there was little fear of Japanese collaborators.

It was an extremely long day. Toward dusk I could hardly place one foot in front of the other. Because of my weakened condition from prison camp, plus loss of sleep and almost continuous walking, complete exhaustion was close at hand. My guards, noticing my doltish behavior and faltering gait, would take me to a nearby village and practically force white tea and food down my throat.

Apparently they thought all I needed was some fuel in my system to keep going. They were operating on the theory that the human body is like an engine. When the engine fails, all that is needed is more fuel and lubricant. Gruel was the fuel, and white tea was the lubricant. It was somewhat amusing, even to a footsore, very weary marine, and the treatment was effective. After each stop, miraculously my motor would begin to hum and off we would go into the night.

Some time before midnight, we came upon one of the wildest and most romantic scenes I had ever witnessed. We approached a large village that seemed to be aflame. It resounded with the strident clamor of hammers on metal and a powerful, spiritual flood of singing. I could not understand the words, but the music, I thought, was that of the French national anthem, "La Marseillaise." At least, it was the Oriental version of the music. Regardless of the content, it stirred my soul and brought up energy that I did not know I had.

After a rather perfunctory challenge, we entered the village to find a horde of men preparing for guerrilla warfare. One guard left with our prisoner, properly trussed, but returned alone. It was interesting to watch groups of ragged men marching and singing. Their weapons were many and varied. Some had rifles, from old muzzle loaders to a few more modern semiautomatic types. Others had spears, knives, and axes. Several "blacksmiths" were busy pounding out knives and bayonets on their anvils, which were made from pieces of rails from a railroad. Would that it had been possible to capture the scene on film.

Here was the birth, the very core, of the guerrilla movement. I first thought that surely this was the headquarters of General Wong. It would have been nice for a semiconscious, emaciated, and weary body to have had a place to sleep. But, no, we passed through the village and headed southeast. Without the prisoner, the guards set a faster pace. As the night lengthened, however, they also wearied and the pace slowed. I mechanically plodded on through fields and darkness, with sounds of the rebellion site behind us growing ever fainter.

Hobbling, staggering, and falling, I plodded through the night. Even my guards floundered along the paths. Tea and more tea. Food but not as much as I wanted. Stops were short, and then we trudged and blundered on through the darkness. I tried cigarettes for a lift to my failing energy, but they were no help. They made it worse. Too much coughing. I wondered in a vacuous stupor: "Why the hurry?"

Fighting the burdensome miles with a deep desire to sleep, I would fall to the ground, exhausted. The guards would pick me up and set me on my feet. They would find a village and pour more tea or gruel down my throat. Then I would manage to stagger along, torturing the blisters on my feet and trying to keep awake. I had heard of people walking in their sleep, but this was the first time for me.

The guards were now having difficulty finding the right paths, as clouds covered the stars. The leaders went into several villages and asked directions. There seemed to be no major path or road. Many small paths wandered this way and that way. We would try one trail and then another. It was long after midnight when suddenly we were halted by the warning snap of a closing rifle bolt.

All of us hit the deck. The guards answered the challenge with a flood of words. I heard the words *feiji* (airplane) and *chan shih* (fighter). We had blundered into the outposts of the guerrilla regiment we had been seeking for the last two days. We were led about two li to a low mud-brick wall and entered the outpost through a "feng sui" gate (a gate designed to keep out evil spirits). A guide took us to a large house that had the typical dirt floor and thatched roof but was in good repair. I laid down on the k'ang without invitation and, in the vernacular, crapped out.

I was awakened seconds later and told that General Wong would be coming soon. I fell asleep again before he entered.

The general was a short, middle-aged man with a round, pockmarked, worn-looking face dominated by keen, piercing black eyes. He had on the same type of uniform worn by my guards. There was no visible identification, but as he limped toward me and looked straight into my eyes, I knew he was the general.

My marine reaction was to salute. He returned my salute and asked if I was an American. Again I went through my litany of being Second Lieutenant "Mi," U.S. Marine Corps, and a few other details, such as my subterfuge of being a flyer.

He asked, "Have you eaten?" (I believe this to be the most considerate greeting in the world. You do not say "good morning," etc., in the Chinese countryside where food is scarce. You ask your visitor: "Have you eaten?" In my case, I learned to love this greeting.)

"No, I have not eaten."

The general turned to the blue-uniformed soldier with him — my guerrilla guards had disappeared — and issued orders. He sat down on the k'ang with me and continued to scrutinize me in my coolie clothes. I showed him my pointee-talkee, my U.S. money, and the picture of my fiancée. He appeared interested. Then he announced to my amazement that three other Americans were in a village several miles away and that they were "ding hau" (very good). That was wonderful news! It meant that all of us had safely made the jump from the train and found friends. He said I would see them that day (16 May 1945, six days and nights since escaping).

That was a happy thought but my body was still in distress. Four soldiers entered the hut with hot tea, steamed bread, and a tub of water and soap. What luxury! I knew the bath would feel glorious. A toothbrush and salt were more than welcome, as my mouth felt as though an army had been camping there for days. The choice between a bath and a meal was a hard decision. I took a combination clean/gluttonous route. I took off my clothes, sat down in the tub, and ate. The general stayed to watch. We talked a little as I greedily ate and blissfully bathed. Then both mind and body were content.

With my appetite satisfied and my body scrubbed clean, I was delighted to see a soldier enter with a fresh blue uniform and cloth shoes. What ecstasy—clean clothes and body and a full belly. My thanks rolled out to the general in as profuse a stream as my Chinese permitted.

He replied, Bubi kechi and motioned to a soldier, perhaps his aide, who produced a bottle and two very small cups. The aide filled the cups and handed one to the general and one to me. The general raised his cup and said, "gambei" (bottoms up). We drank a toast to American-Chinese friendship. The general and the soldiers left. The *bei gar* (alcoholic drink) hit me a minute later, and I collapsed on the k'ang for a long-delayed rest.

Before dawn, a soldier awakened me with a cup of hot tea. He guided me out in the dark to another large building. There I was surprised to see the general sitting with several soldiers around a long table loaded with bottles, plates, bowls, cups, and *food*!

This was not breakfast; it was a sumptuous Chinese feast. I had attended many banquets in my earlier days in China, but this was the best of all. For two or three hours we ate our way through dishes of fish, chao-tze (Chinese ravioli), stir-fried vegetables, noodles, sweet bread, and soup. All washed down with innumerable toasts to our friendship—China and America. A welcome rosy glow spread over me and washed away my fatigue, dulling the aches and pains of the last six days. By the end of the meal, I was inclined to stay there forever and hoped to sleep and sleep and sleep.

As we drank the last toast, however, I was told that we would leave immediately for Magistrate Ting's village to join the other three Americans. We walked to the end of the hutung (small street), where a soldier was holding a single horse. General Wong said, "The horse is for you." As the general was lame, I insisted that he ride. We then went into the "after-you-Alphonso" routine, saying: "You ride." "No, you ride."

After several such exchanges, I tried to mount. As it turned out, I was too drunk to stay on the horse. Surprisingly, General Wong seemed to be in the same fix. He couldn't stay on the horse either.

There was only one thing to do—walk until one of us was sober enough to stay in the saddle. After several hours of walking, both of us became tired, so we both got on the horse, the general in front and me behind, clutching the wooden cantle.

It must have been an amusing sight, as the accompanying soldiers could not resist some rather loud guffaws. The small Mongolian horse

Sketch of author in Chinese Communist guerrilla uniform, Anwhei Province, May 1945.

(pony) had difficulty carrying us and showed his displeasure by assuming a jolting gait. Each step ignited my aches and pains.

Late in the afternoon we approached a big, sprawling village. A large group of people came out to meet the general. He dismounted, and when I dismounted in turn, I became painfully aware that I was not used to riding a horse. Between the blisters on my feet and the pain in my butt, I walked like a hundred-year-old cowboy. Suddenly I was aware that there was an American in the welcoming group when a big "Yee-Hah" ripped through the air, followed by, "You ain't much of a Texas cowboy, you old sonofabitch!"

It was Bish, our old Flying Tiger.

CHAPTER FIVE

Reunion

B ISH RUSHED UP, yelling, "Where the hell have ya been? What took you so long? We thought you and Kinney had been caught by the Nips."

I grabbed Bish by the arm, "Hold still a minute and I'll tell you. What in hell are you doing here? Where are the others?"

"Well, Hi and Johnny Mac are around here somewhere. Both were here when I arrived two days ago. But where is Kinney?"

"I haven't seen him. He may be having trouble getting across the river. You know Kinney can't swim."

"And he claims to be a naval aviator?"

"Let's knock off the bullshit. I've got to find a place to rest my weary ass."

"OK. I'll take you to the hut where we're staying."

I turned to look for General Wong and his soldiers, but they had faded into the crowd. From somewhere in the mob there came a familiar American voice. "Hey, Mac! You old bastard. I didn't think you'd wake up in time to leave the train." It was Johnny Mac.

"Well, if it's not the old Mississippi gambler himself. I never expected you to make it around all the night soil pits. What's more, I thought sure the wonks would have eaten your 90 pounds by this time."

"It was not the wonks that bothered me, it was those long-eared razorbacks snorting around looking for something to eat." (Some villagers let hogs run loose as gleaners of the hutungs and fields. Those long-legged, flop-eared, gaunt-framed hogs bore a striking resemblance to the old razorbacks of Arkansas backwoods fame.)

I asked where Hi was. Johnny Mac said the last time he had seen him, he was trying to learn the commands to march some troops around the village.

46

Bish chimed in, "I see Magistrate Ting in the crowd watching the antics of us crazy Americans. Let's go over and see if you're to stay in the same hut with us."

I said, "I'm all for that. I'm petered out. But I'd like some chow before crapping out."

At that moment the magistrate came over with another Chinese gentleman in tow. He was introduced as Mr. Wu, a school teacher. Mr. Wu spoke some English. I introduced myself and the others and said, "All of us are second lieutenants in the U.S. Marine Corps."

Bish said, "I object! Tell him I am a member of the Flying Tigers."

"You tell him! You oughta be honored you were promoted to marine status. I don't believe Wu understands either 'Marine Corps' or 'Flying Tiger' in English. I'm damn sure I don't know what 'flying' or 'tiger' is in Chinese."

Mr. Wu said he was pleased we had come to his village. He also said that in a few days another man who could speak good English would arrive. Wu was not the best interpreter in the world, but he was doing a hell of a lot better than we could. As he continued to speak haltingly, we gathered that Mr. Ting was the "number one" in this area. In essence, the magistrate was a combination of judge, jury, and administrator for an area most of us would call a county. We also understood that this particular area was very important to the guerrillas because it lay astride one of their best routes to the eastern part of Anwhei Province. It also gave ready access to the Pukow-Tientsin Railroad. Lastly, this fertile area provided lots of food for the guerrillas.

It was a rather long session with Mr. Wu, and we were all weary. I suggested that we retreat to the hut for a rest when a small column of soldiers came marching past. There was a familiar voice in the rear of the column barking, "yi, er, san, sz" (one, two, three, four). It was Hi. He saw the three of us and in his excitement yelled "halt!" in English instead of Chinese. Then when the troops did not halt, one of the troopers commanded, "Zhanzhu!" (Stop!) This latter command had the desired effect. Hi ran over and launched the familiar questions at me: "Where've you been? What took so long? Any trouble?"

Johnny Mac said, "Slow down, Hi. Mac is weary and hungry."

Turning to Mr. Wu and Magistrate Ting, Hi asked for food for me. Wu told us that food would soon be ready and that we should go to the hut nearby and wait. We walked quickly into what appeared to be a hovel, and I looked around for a bed. As I was last to arrive, I was out of luck.

Wu said we could get another door-bed from a different hut for me. As we started to go outside to look for one, Kinney came charging through the door, grinning like a Cheshire cat. We all started bombarding him with questions: "Where've you been? You must've had trouble!"

Kinney tried to reply. "You guys sound like a flock of squawking ducks. For Christ's sake, one at a time. I'm hungry and tired as hell. Let's eat, catch some shut-eye, and talk about it all later."

Johnny Mac agreed. "OK. We each have a tale to tell and it'll take time. Let's eat and talk later."

Wu, who had been quietly listening to the chitchat, beckoned us to follow, and off we went to a larger hut.

For the first time, we were served rice along with the ever present millet gruel and some boiled cabbage. I love rice and can never get enough of it. In prison camp, rice portions were not only extremely meager, but the rice was dirty and full of chaff and hulls. Often small stones, rodent hair, and droppings were present. I think the Japs swept the godowns (warehouses) for our rations. Hi, Bish, and I, having been in the Orient for some time, were familiar with chopsticks, but not Kinney or Johnny Mac. They made an effort but had to rely on the pottery spoons furnished. There was little talking while we ate as though we would never see another morsel.

Later we were faced with the problem of finding two doors for beds for Kinney and me. Most of the outer doors to the huts were about two to two-and-a-half feet wide and five-and-a-half feet tall. They were hung on an L-shaped iron bar extending from the door frame and were easily lifted off their pivot points. To make a bed, the door was placed horizontally on stacks of mud bricks. This type of bed was used when there wasn't sufficient room on the k'ang for guests.

Such a bed was fine for us, as we were used to sleeping on prison camp wooden platforms. With the help of Wu and some soldiers, we appropriated two more doors and prepared for the night. Once we stretched out on our doors there was no noise until Wu called us for tea at daylight the next morning.

With tea and gruel in our bellies, we sat around to discuss the next course of action. Bish argued that there must be emergency airstrips in the area and that we should head for such a field to possibly arrange an airlift to Kunming (location of the Flying Tigers' headquarters). We all agreed that because of the many American air raids around our prison camp and Shanghai proper, some U.S. airfields must be within 300 to 400 miles of our location.

I said, "It's a hell of a long way to Kunming. Yenan is closer and there must be airfields in or around the headquarters of the Kungchantang (Communist) army. Why don't we head for Yenan?"

"You must be nuts! It would take a hell of a long time to walk to Yenan. In our condition we couldn't make it up the first big hill," Bish added.

Hi suggested that I had a good idea. We could rest and fatten up here and then head for Yenan. Maybe we'd be able to see the great Mao.

Bish didn't like that idea and said he didn't give a damn about seeing Mao. He wanted to get to the "land of the big PX" (U.S.A.) as quickly as possible.

Kinney thought we should wait right where we were until we could find out more about the situation and learn who could help us.

I agreed, but I said that if it would take only a couple of weeks to get to one airstrip or another, I thought we should go to Yenan. "I'm just as eager as any of you to get home quickly, but this is a chance of a lifetime. What the hell, we've all been away for several years, what difference does another week or so make?"

"You're nuts," said Bish. "Why Yenan?"

Hi explained, "Mac and I talked about this in camp and believe we could gain some valuable intelligence by going through the area here and visiting Yenan. There must be U.S. military liaison teams and airfields there."

Once again Kinney expressed his idea to wait until plans developed and to put off our decision until later.

There were nods of agreement as Mr. Wu entered the hut. We couldn't help putting the question of the location of a friendly airstrip to him. Wu said he didn't know of an airfield, but he thought the commissar would have that information. He explained, "We stay here two, three day and rest. Take medicine. Fix clothes."

We agreed with Mr. Wu that it was a good idea for all of us to get some rest and nurse our bruises. Hi told Wu that maybe we could find a little relief from the trots and the varmints on our clothes, get into fair shape in a few days, and then make the trip. Hi said he wanted to use the time to sharpen his Chinese.

Mr. Wu left, and realizing we had a little time, Johnny Mac said, "OK, now I want to know how all of you got off that goddamn train and how you got here."

Kinney suggested we take the floor in the order we jumped the train. "But first, Mac, you and Hi should tell us how you removed the bars and wire on the window."

Hi asked, "Mac, how did you remove the bars?"

"Well, it wasn't difficult. I was just scared the noise I made would alert the guards. The bars were very rusty but still a tough job for our small hacksaw blade. It took a long time to saw through them."

"You were in there a hell of a long time!" Hi said. "I was worried the guards were going to find out what was going on."

I told them I sawed through one end of each bar and then made a cut near the opposite end. By bending the bars back and forth, I broke them free and threw them out the window. Figuring I had been in the head long enough, I slipped back to my tick and left the barbed wire for Hi.

Hi took over the story and told how, about midnight, he moved his clothing around to make some sort of a dummy where he was sleeping. Then he checked with the three of us to see if we were set. He crawled into the head and slid under the blanket covering the small window. He said he tried to be quiet when he cut the wire, but it slipped out of his hand and made a hell of a bang against the side of the car. He opened a corner of the head curtain for a quick look at the guards, but there was no reaction.

Hi said he crawled out the window and hung onto the window ledge, waiting for Johnny Mac to appear. Fortunately, the train was going slowly. He could hear the guards becoming active and could see flashes of light around our end of the car. "I started running in the air," he said, "turned loose of the ledge, and continued to run on my way to the ground."

There was a steep embankment on his side of the track, so he turned away from the tracks and ran up the embankment. At the top, he stopped behind some bushes and checked his gear. Nothing was broken or lost. Luck was with him; he was uninjured except for a few scratches and scrapes from the bushes as he hurried up the bank. He oriented himself by the North Star and the Pleiades and started walking west. He walked all night, avoiding villages by the barking of the wonks. "I never cared for wonks before, but they were sure friends that first night."

Bish asked if he had seen any lights. Hi replied that he had seen lights once from a big village ahead, so he detoured a long way around that area. He found walking at night difficult because of the narrow paths and the different types of terrain. He didn't hurry as the train had kept on moving. As dawn approached, he found a wheat field off to one side of his path and lay down for a rest.

Hi described what happened when he tried to take a swig of water from his canteen. The flash of the sun on it must have caught the attention of a Chinese on the path. The man came into the field, apparently to see what was flashing, and found him. The man was startled but just nodded when Hi told him he was an American looking for Kuomintang or Kungchantang troops. Hi asked if any Japanese were nearby and the farmer said "bushr" (no).

After a little urging, the farmer took Hi to a village, where he exchanged his old prison rags for Chinese clothes. No one in the village could read his pointee-talkee, but his knowledge of Chinese was good enough to get across the idea that he wanted to find friendly troops. He spent the night there and, after breakfast, was guided here. "You know, I was fortunate to have jumped the train when and where I did," Hi concluded. "I really didn't have any trouble."

I chimed in, "You were lucky as hell."

"Lucky," replied Johnny Mac, "you were gilded with fortune. My jump from the train was not quite as charmed as yours. When the guards heard that loud noise made by the wire flapping against the side of the car, I thought it was all over. They flashed a light around our end of the car, but in a few minutes they settled down. By the time I made my dummy bed and snuck into the head, the train had picked up speed."

Johnny Mac said he glanced out the window and, noticing Hi was gone, jumped through the opening, doubled up, and hit the ground with a jarring thud. Despite the increase in the train's speed, he wasn't injured—just a few bruises and scrapes. He said that as he lay in the ditch, the train sped past him. "It was a damn good feeling to see that red light at the end of the train disappearing into the darkness."

Kinney asked, "How fast do you figure the train was going?"

"About 10 knots. But it was picking up speed as I left."

"You must have paid the same preacher I did," Hi quipped.

"Well, I don't know about that," responded Johnny Mac, "but I repeated a few prayers before the jump. They must have been effective. I had very little trouble in reaching here. My back hurt and I lost my package of food, but otherwise I was OK."

Johnny Mac told us that lying on his back, he oriented himself by the North Star. Then he got up and ran west. At the crack of dawn, he found a little gully off to the side of his path and took refuge for the day. Water was no problem, and he was too excited to miss his food. He said the day passed too damn slow. He couldn't sleep because he kept thinking some Chinese bandit was going to find him.

"Did you lose all your food?" Bish asked.

"Yeah, but as I said, I didn't worry about it. I did worry about the barking dogs. It made me think the Nips were trying to track us with dogs. That is, until the sound of barking dogs surrounded me. Then I remembered what Mac and Hi had told me about Chinese dogs guarding the villages. And I'd go around the noise."

Johnny Mac said that as darkness fell, he headed west and was startled by a couple of beasts that looked like big dogs as they shot past him. "I almost crapped in my pants until I heard 'oink, oink.' My God, I could have ridden either one."

Continuing his story, Johnny Mac spoke of the possibility of falling in the shit pits, but we all agreed that the stink was as good as a wall around them. The night dragged by, and when dawn came he was caught in the open without a good hiding place. When the first Chinese came in sight, Johnny Mac repeated the magic words "Meigwo feiji." The man seemed to understand, but couldn't read the pointee-talkee. Instead he motioned for Johnny Mac to follow and led him to a village where one of the villagers examined the pointee-talkee. He was given hot water and gruel. Later two men guided him to this place.

"All in all it wasn't too bad except for that feeling of helplessness being among people I couldn't understand and who couldn't understand me. Also, it was a shock to be in such a totally unfamiliar area. It shook me up a bit, being alone. I'm damn glad to be here, even among you bastards."

"Now, Johnny Mac, you know you're among a group of upstanding and virtuous American citizens," Kinney gibed.

"OK, Kinney," Johnny Mac replied, "let's hear about your arduous journey and how you captured the attention of the village queen."

Kinney said that Johnny Mac was not far off the mark, except for the last part about the queen. He said he'd try to stick to the differences between his story and the foregoing yarns. After Johnny Mac left, Kinney had waited a few minutes as the guards flashed their lights. After they became quiet, he had kicked me, as I had gone to sleep, and said, "It's time to go!"

"How in hell you could go to sleep just before trying to escape is beyond me," Kinney said.

He said he slipped into the head and crawled out the window. Hanging onto the ledge, he started to push off the side of the car but felt his feet brush some tall projection. He pulled up, hung there momentarily, then let loose, rolled down an embankment, and hit some rocks.

"Were you hurt?" asked Hi.

Kinney said he wasn't, but if he had let go from the window ledge on his first impulse, he probably would have hit what he believed was a railroad signal device, which surely would have creamed him. As it turned out, he wasn't hurt and began immediately to run, taking a right angle to the tracks. By the time the car with the extra guards and dogs swept past him, he was about 50 yards from the tracks.

After a short time, Kinney stopped, took out his compass, even though he could barely see it, and tried to get oriented. Hearing dogs barking close by, he thought the Nips were closing in on him. He took off and ran to the west. Uncertain about the direction, he thought the first compass bearing might have been influenced by his tin canteen, so he took off his shoulder bag containing the canteen, medicine, and food and laid it on the ground, walked a few feet away, and placed the compass on the ground. While trying to read the compass, he suddenly realized that the sound of the barking dogs was rapidly getting closer. Again he thought it was the Nips, so he immediately ran away from the sound of the dogs.

A few minutes later he realized he had left his compass and the rest of his gear behind. He knew he couldn't find the gear in the dark, and he didn't want to get any closer to the barking dogs. So he continued to run away from the sound of barking and what seemed to be the sound of men beating the brush with bamboo sticks. He ran in the opposite direction until he came to a wide river and flushed some squawking ducks and geese. His first thought was, "I'll be damned. I can't swim and now I'm trapped between a search party, the river, and the railroad."

Since dawn was breaking, Kinney hid in a nearby wheat field, knowing he needed to contact some Chinese for help in getting across the river. At dawn he saw several Chinese walking on a path nearby. He decided to approach one of the men carrying pots and pans on a *yei-ho* pole.* He walked up to him and said "Meigwo feiji" and pulled out his pointee-talkee. The man wasn't interested but pointed west and made chopping motions at the back of his neck as he continued walking.

Kinney tried the same approach on others passing by, but it only seemed to increase their efforts to get away. Finally a small boy beckoned Kinney to follow him and led him to a nearby hut. Inside was a man who could read the pointee-talkee. He motioned toward the river and then pointed to the words "Japanese soldiers" on the pointee-talkee. He, too, made chopping motions toward the back of his neck. After some time Kinney was given water and food and offered "coolie clothes." The boy then rushed him to a hiding place among reeds in a ditch, where he stayed hidden the rest of the day.

At dusk he was taken to another village, where he met a man who could speak a little English. Using the pointee-talkee, plus a little pantomime, Kinney let him know he wanted to go to Chungking. By the same long process, they bargained about the price of taking Kinney to Chungking. Finally they agreed on a price of $3,000 in gold (the equivalent of U.S. currency) for him and for each of his four accomplices.

"That's $15,000!" exclaimed Hi. "Who in hell would pay that kind of money for any of us?"

Kinney stated, "Well, at that point I didn't have any other choice. The next night the man returned and said, 'No can do.' 'Too many bad people out there,' he said, with a 360° sweep of his hand."

Kinney continued telling how for the next few days he was shuttled from village to village, where he was hidden during the day. During this period he was given lessons on how to say "Chiang Kaishek is number one." Later a new guide took him to what looked like an outpost. The men there wore blue uniforms and some had rifles. They encouraged him to talk or try to talk Chinese. The first thing he thought of were the words he had learned, "Chiang Kaishek is number one." As soon as he said it and had time to glance around, he saw a picture of Stalin and a banner with a star and sickle hanging on the wall. A bad mistake. The soldiers appeared very puzzled. He said he realized they were Communist troops. He thought the next step was the chopping block, but instead they gave him a place to sleep and a boiled chicken for a meal. "I ate the whole thing," he said, "and later regretted it."

**A yei-ho pole is a long pole carried on one shoulder with a bucket of night soil, grain, water, etc., suspended by rope at each end.*

He told how later he was given a donkey to ride to accompany the group. They went east toward the Pukow-Tientsin Railroad, stopping about a half mile short of it. They heard the sound of an approaching train in the distance and then a very loud explosion. The coolies with pack animals who had been with them left and rode toward the sound of the explosion.

Kinney said the group of soldiers and he rode northwest and by dawn reached a large mud-brick building which appeared to be the headquarters of the Communist guerrillas. About noon a column of guerrillas, plus the coolies and pack animals formerly with their group, who were heavily laden with booty from the wrecked train, passed them heading west. The cavalry moved out with this supply column, but Kinney stayed on at the headquarters that night.

The next day, walking west with a new guide, they met a Chinese who gestured excitedly as they approached. He stuck four fingers in the air, pointed west, and told them there were four American friends in the next village. "That information was great, but I couldn't imagine who the 'fourth friend' was. I was surprised as hell to see you, Bish. I wasn't sure you were coming."

"You knew I was interested when I showed you my map of China on the train," explained Bish.

"Yeah, but I thought since you were married that you would stay with the other married guys."

"I may be married, but I ain't dumb."

"Well, the married birds probably weighed the odds and decided that they were more apt to get home in one piece by staying on the train," said Hi.

"I guess they did," I said. "As all of you know, I'm damn anxious to get home in one piece, too. The four of us also weighed the odds and decided we had a better chance of getting home earlier and with all our marbles than going to the 'land of the flying red asshole'" (standard POW term for Japan, and specifically its flag).

"That may be true," replied Kinney, "but those bastards didn't have to try so hard to get me to change my mind. One of those guys tried to hold on to me to keep me from leaving the train. What a buncha shits! I have a girlfriend I'm eager to see, provided she hasn't run off with some draft dodger."

"Calm down, old boy!" said Hi. "Both you and Mac have just as much reason to want to stay alive as the married ones. But as you know we argued about this with many of them in Nanking. Remember, Colonel Ashurst was for us. He was the one who counted. Besides, we're all here, sipping hot water and eating pumpkin seeds, so what's our gripe? Let's hear Mac's tall Texas tale. I bet his biggest gripe was not having enough food."

"You're so right, Hi." So I told that when I jumped the train, the engineer must have thought he was driving "the Wreck of Old 97." He was making flank speed (maximum speed in the navy). As a result, I had broken or lost damn near everything when I hit the ground and rolled along the track in a ditch of water. I added that I hurt my back and my left shoulder and broke the little finger of my left hand in the fall. I described my fear when I noticed a Jap sentry post on the other side of the tracks, and told them how I had slowly crawled along the ditch until I reached a steep bank covered with bushes. I said I had crept up to the top and then took off to the west. "I couldn't go very fast, as my back hurt like hell when I ran."

For two days and nights I was without food or water, I continued. But on that third morning, desperate, I approached a farmer who took me to his home, fed me, and gave me Chinese clothes. I said that my story from here on was similar to Kinney's, except that I was on foot the whole time — no donkeys or horses around. "The Chinese literally walked my ass off. I almost forgot. I did have a ride on a pony with General Wong of the Communist guerrillas for the last few li before we reached here. Tell you more about it later."

"Hell, it sounds like you had a picnic," gibed Kinney.

"Well, I could have added some gruesome details, but, you know, Texans are always modest."

"Texans modest?" questioned Hi. "Wow, now I've heard it all. Think you can top all those tales, Bish?"

"Well," began Bish, "an old Florida cracker can spin some tall ones. After you birds left, the guards must have heard something, because they flashed their lights around a long time. Seemed like they suspected trouble, but your dummies were better than the dummies we left on the train."

"Aw, come on, Bish, and give us the story without the comedian touches," said Johnny Mac.

"OK," continued Bish. "When I started for the head, a couple of the yardbirds caught hold of my arm and warned me about going, saying the rest would be beaten and suffer a loss of food for days. All of us had heard that bullshit before."

James P.S. Devereux, a marine officer of Wake Island fame who was a major at the time, later reported there was little maltreatment to the remaining prisoners of war after the escape:

> The next night the train jerked suddenly to a stop. Enraged Japanese officers clambered in with drawn pistols and swords, squealing in rage as they counted heads and spouted threats. . . .
> Colonel Otera [the Japanese commander of the camp] was so outraged that he announced he was placing himself under arrest. Elaborate precau-

tions were taken to prevent any further escapes, the windows were wedged and an officer with a drawn sword took his post in the guard's [sic] section of each car.*

Colonel John A. White wrote:

> Early in the morning at the stop for a nature call, we, in the other cars, heard of the escape and marveled at their courage and daring. The Japanese reacted swiftly but not as savagely as we might have suspected. An immediate head count disclosed that these five, all from the same end of one car, were the only missing prisoners. The guards showed their anger only by making us pull down the blankets which allowed the undetected getaway. They did not retaliate in any way, even against those in the section of the car as the escapees. Evidently, the train commander knew the war [sic] progress in the last two years. . . . Someday, he might be held accountable for any cruel, inhumane and illegal punishment. . . . Among ourselves, we discussed the escape many times, asking, "Why didn't I do that?" . . . Again, honestly, I, as well as many others, did not have the same spirit of adventure as those five.**

Bish's story was very similiar to mine. As I had said, "Old 97" was tearing up the tracks when he left the train. He was damn glad it was going fast because as he looked out the window, the train whipped over a bridge just before he jumped. Again, like me, he fell in a ditch of water, which softened the blow some, but still left him dazed. He didn't lose anything but a hardtack biscuit we had been given for supper. By the time his marbles were straightened out, the train was gone.

Bish crawled up a bank into some bushes, located the North Star, and took off for the west. He kept moving. Fortunately, the next morning at daybreak, a Chinese peasant saw him and recognized him as an American. His newfound friend also understood those special words *Meigwo feiji* and took him to his hut. And, as the saying goes, "fed and watered" him.

Bish was given some Chinese clothes and one of those Chinese straw hats which covers most of a person's face. "With that hat," he said, "and with a little mud smeared on my face, I could have picked up a yei-ho pole and you would've thought I had stepped out of one of Pearl Buck's books. I'll bet I looked like any shit coolie that ever hit the road."

I said, "Bish, you should wear those clothes all the time. They suit you."

Bish responded, "You should talk. You look like a descendent of Genghis Khan in that uniform you're wearing. And your beard reminds

---

*J.P.S. Devereux, Brigadier General, USMC (Ret.). Wake Island (Canoga Park, Calif.: Major Books, 1978), pp. 252–53.
**John A. White, Colonel, USMC (Ret.), The United States North China Marines (Millbrae, Calif.: John A. White, 1974), p. 156.

me—when in the hell do we get a shave and a haircut? My face feels like number-one sandpaper."

"But," Bish continued, "first let me finish my tale. We traveled at night and slept in huts during the day. I was here on 14 May, four days after leaving the train. It wasn't a bad trip, except for the damn flies, lice, and fleas, and the constant smell of the shit pits, plus a few other minor details. By the way, I see Mr. Wu motioning for us to come to the chow line."

Our tales completed, we made a mad rush out the door.

CHAPTER SIX

Sweet Dreams and Sweet Potatoes

T HE NEXT TWO DAYS at Magistrate Ting's village were for rest-
ing, gaining strength, and trying to decide our next move. I
wondered what had happened to General Wong; I hadn't seen him
since I had joined my friends. I thought he must have returned to his own
area and left our disposition to Mr. Ting, who was evidently awaiting instructions from higher echelons.

Those restful days were not without activity. We choked down charcoal and opium to control the trots. Hi and Johnny Mac produced iodine
from their unbroken stash bags for cuts and flea bites. Our clothing was
boiled to get rid of the lice and nits. (If that hadn't worked, we'd have tried
searing the seams of our clothes with a red-hot iron rod—a method I had
seen used in North China.)

Baths with soap were great. The soap was a close cousin to the old lye
soap of pioneer days. It did a thorough job of scaling off the remaining
prison camp crud. My skin felt as though I had been curried, but it felt so
good being clean I wanted to jump in the air and give a big "wow."

The real crowning touch was the performance of a barber. Mr. Wu
said the barber was a prisoner of war, a puppet soldier of the Japanese. I
was apprehensive about having him shave me with a straight razor, even
with an armed guard standing beside us. When a straight razor is next to
your carotid arteries, there is not much difference between an accidental
and a deliberate slip of the hand.

My fears amounted to nought. The barber was a marvelous craftsman.
He shaved each of us from the top of our heads to the bottom of our feet.
Thus we got rid of more nits and lice. We inspected each other, monkey
fashion, to ensure that our lousy fellow travelers had disappeared. Most

Americans have not known lice, which is just as well. They bite, suck blood, and carry typhus. Lice have been the nemesis of many armies, always riding with the "Four Horsemen of the Apocalypse." The whole-body shave was delightful. To have the inside of one's nose and ears shaved was not only unique but pleasantly titillating. I thought it should become an adopted procedure in the States.

Clean clothes and bodies make good spirits. Vivacity and humor, long dormant, swelled within and burst into the open with the festive shaving. The unending flow of food added to our pleasure. Our benefactors seemed determined we would have enough chow to gain strength and become physically well. For the first time, we had boiled and mashed sweet potatoes. Noodles, hard boiled eggs, steamed bread, and millet gruel came in a continuous stream. Never before nor since have I eaten so much in such a short time. Our health and disposition improved rapidly.

Most of our time was spent eating or sleeping. Bish and I were placed in a separate hut to make things a little more comfortable. The first day, immediately after a big, big lunch, I lay on my door-bed half asleep.

In reverie, I began to dream of days past and particularly of my fiancée, Jean Paterson. I had nicknamed her "Skip" when we dated at the Naval Academy.

Almost five years had passed since I last saw her. Very few letters came to me in prison camp, but I learned later that she had written many. It seemed that the Jap guards in prison camp delighted in deliberately los-ing mail, not distributing it for months, or destroying it—in short, anything to irritate prisoners of war or deny them solace. I received one picture of Skip and about six or seven 25-word, censored letters from her in the course of three-and-a-half years in prison camp. Her picture was my main solace and inspiration. As I mentioned before, it had also assisted in identi-fying me to the Chinese as an American.

Half asleep, I took the picture from my pocket and gazed longingly. She is a beautiful woman, I thought. I hope she is waiting. Does she know if I am alive? Although many POWs allowed our captors to take pictures of them and make audiotapes for broadcasting and propaganda, I did not believe in doing either. Neither did my buddy, Joe McDonald, of whom I will speak later. He and I hid in the outhouse or barracks attic when such activities took place. In fact, Joe's kin never heard he was in prison camp. An obituary was written for Joe in the Reno, Nevada newspaper and a tombstone was placed in a Reno cemetery for him. He moved it to his back yard after the war. It was a great showpiece.

I assumed Skip received word I was alive when the diplomats returned home on the Swedish ship *Gripsholm* in the fall of 1942. I knew of the *Gripsholm*'s sailing, since Major Edwin P. McCauley, USMC, on active duty with the Peking marines, went back to the States on the *Gripsholm*.

We never could figure how only one marine from North China was selected to return home. Was it because of the Boxer Protocol? How different it would have been if the Japs had honored their part of the 1901 agreement and sent us all home. Apparently our State Department did not insist that the Japs honor the agreement.

I wondered if Skip had received any of the few 25-word postcards we were permitted to send? Why would she wait on a bird who was probably off his rocker by now? I deliberated on the old epigram: "Absence makes the heart grow fonder." Or is it the reverse: "Absence makes the heart grow fonder for somebody else"?

"Come on, Mac," I thought. "Get the lead out of your ass, self-pity out of your mind, and get going."

Many camp mates were always reminding or haranguing me about the low probability of a woman remaining faithful to an engagement commitment, considering my predicament. My reply was: "First, she is a lady and will keep a promise. Second, she has three pretty sisters who could well fill the bill." Don't relinquish the castle before you meet the foe was my position.

It occurred to me that it might be a good idea to awaken Bish and talk to him about our return to the States. He would have some ideas because he was married and had a child he had not seen. I decided, however, that such a talk would only stir up some feelings in Bish that he didn't need right now. We would have plenty of time to discuss personal affairs and plans for the future. It was better to leave such subjects alone for the moment.

Thinking of letters brought to my mind a humorous incident in the prison camp. One POW received a letter and a snapshot from his wife. He was immensely proud of the picture of his wife and his prize horse and saddle. The only problem was that both the horse and the woman were just plain, damn ugly. What does one say when shown such a picture? Most of us just stared in silence. One of our more diplomatic fellow inmates came to the rescue. Confronted with the picture, he gazed intently and said, "That's a damn good-looking saddle."

I laughed aloud, remembering the incident, and returned to a more pleasant half-dream of my first date with Skip. It was a blind date on Valentine's Day 1936, plebe year at the U.S. Naval Academy. We went to see *The Mikado* by Gilbert and Sullivan with its all-male, midshipman cast. I really didn't watch much of the show because this was my first date in almost a year. (The present Naval Academy is not like the old "Canoe U.") I was too busy staring at my date.

It was love at first sight for me. For the next three-and-a-half years we dated. She attended nearby University of Maryland and came to Annapolis for occasional weekends and Saturday night dances. Even at that early stage of our first date, I wondered if she would continue to see me. I was a country boy from Lorena, Texas, and not exactly a polished, sophisticated chap, but I believed the Academy had rubbed some of the raw edges off me. I spent most Christmas and September leave periods in Skip's family home and came to know many of her friends at the University of Maryland. She had a wonderful family who fortunately accepted me and made me feel welcome, although her three younger sisters did heckle us quite a bit. Those good times seemed remote, but still warm and comforting.

On our dates in Annapolis, we existed on ten-cent hamburgers. In those days a midshipman's spending money was miserly—two dollars a month the first year, four dollars the second, until finally in our first class (senior) year, we received ten dollars a month. Dating meant hamburgers and nickel Cokes for nearly four years; but we'd splurge once in a while on movies that cost a quarter.

We became engaged 1 June 1939 upon my graduation and commissioning as a second lieutenant in the Marine Corps. Unfortunately, a then existing screwy law dictated discharge from the service in the event an officer married before two years had elapsed after his commissioning. I wanted the career of a marine, so I stuck with the law.

To be honest, I chose the Marine Corps because I believed it would give me more time ashore with Skip than the Navy would. I also liked the blue trousers with red stripes, the esprit de corps, and the tradition of Major General Smedley Butler, who won two Medals of Honor. As often happens, the unexpected results were more important than the expected. After a year in the Marine Corps' Basic School in Philadelphia, I was assigned to the North China marines.

I was stunned! My application had been for either Quantico or San Diego, the embryonic location of the Fleet Marine Forces. North China was a choice assignment for any officer at that time. It was a plum for my career but a crashing bolt of lightning to my romance.

After Skip and I talked about the assignment, we decided she would come to Peking in June 1941, when the two-year waiting period had elapsed, and we would be married. Again, the fickle finger of fate intervened. In October 1940, all military dependents in the Far East were sent back to the States, and American civilians were requested to leave. That was the end of our plans for a wedding in Peking in June 1941.

Thinking back, Peking would have been a more delightful experience had Skip been with me, but I still enjoyed every moment. Bachelor life has its advantages also. I was stationed in Tientsin for a couple of months before I was transferred to Peking. In that wonderful old city, I began to appreciate China and the Chinese way of doing things. Lieutenant George R. Newton and I had a house in the old Russian Embassy compound within two blocks of the main gate to the marine barracks. The latter were right next to the American Embassy and the Ch'ien Men Gate in the

Great Tartar Wall around the city. We were within a few blocks of the Forbidden City. (The Ch'ien Men Gate leads to what is now Tiananmen Square.)

As I lay half-awake, I thought I was standing at the gate to our Peking house waiting for the *mafoo* (stable boy) to bring my horse, when I heard: "Mac! What the hell is wrong with you? You're snorting like an old race horse on the home stretch." It was Bish, standing over me.

When I finally woke up, the surrounding mud walls threw me for a loop. Momentarily, I couldn't figure out where I was or what was going on. The fatigue of weeks and years held my mind at bay. I was still back in Peking.

"Where in the devil are we?"

"The Astor House dining room in Shanghai," replied Bish.

"Oh, for Christ's sake! Knock off the comedy. I was peacefully dreaming when you rudely interrupted me."

"Well, it's not time for chow. But you were making so much racket I had to wake you."

To fill in the time before our evening meal, Bish and I wandered around the village. The villagers showed little interest in us, but young children followed us, aping our movements and having one big time. We noticed that boys up to six or seven years didn't wear pants. All girls above toddling age wore trousers. Female toddlers wore ever-readies. The streets (really hutungs or alleyways) were filled with men and boys. Only very young and very old females were present. Occasionally, we would see a middle-aged female scooting into her hut as we came into view. I hoped they were not frightened. They shouldn't have been. Three-and-a-half years on very poor rations doesn't make a man priapismic. Actually, we were viewed as *yang kuei-tzu* (foreign devils). Good to keep a distance.

As we turned down a small offshoot to the main hutung, we came upon an elderly woman sitting in the doorway of her house. As we approached, she turned a wizened face toward us, gave us a cursory glance, and then looked back at the shoe she was working on. Her long black hair streaked with grey was pulled back into a tight knot. Her black trousers and loose blue shirt showed signs of wear but were clean and neat. She had on straw sandals, so perhaps the shoe she was making was for herself. Our presence did not seem to bother her at all. She had probably seen too many "East-Ocean" (Japanese) foreign devils to be afraid of us.

In the countryside most cloth shoes were homemade from scrap cloth left from other endeavors. In the cities people bought factory-produced shoes. Cloth shoes were generally worn in the winter for warmth or for dress (with home-loomed tube socks), while the very comfortable and cheaper straw sandals were worn the rest of the year.

The old lady had a pile of flattened rags by her side. She had before her an old cloth shoe for a model. As we watched, she carefully placed rag upon rag and tacked them together, building a loose pad about a half inch thick. The pad was trimmed to conform to the model's sole. Then she took a three-inch needle, threaded it, and began to sew the pad to make a hard sole. The pad was placed on a small wooden block with a hole through which the needle could protrude. She pushed the needle through the material and the hole with a stone. Once the needle was through the cloth layers, she gripped it with her teeth and pulled the thread tight. (She must have used her back teeth, as she hadn't very many in the front.)

Johnny Mac had joined us by then and asked me if most of the farmers in China made their own shoes. I said I had noticed that a few miles from a big town or village, people became very self-sufficient. Here it appeared that the thread she was using was sisal. It was strong and helped to make a long-wearing sole. We could see with the many stitches she was making that the thread would take most of the wear.

Bish asked how the people made cloth. I said that I had seen a few spinning wheels and hand looms in the countryside, but the industrial world had poured so many cheap goods into the country that home industries had suffered greatly. "The way I see it, this war with its blockades has rekindled cottage industries," I remarked.

Johnny Mac said he thought there must be lots of either cottage looms or textile mills in the New Fourth Army area for them to make uniforms and be able to furnish us with clothes so quickly.

"We can find out by going to Yenan," I reminded them.

"Mac, quit saying such damn fool things before you convince yourself and the rest of us," laughed Johnny Mac.

The old lady looked up questioningly at us, and Johnny Mac came through with his extensive Chinese vocabulary. "Ding hau. Meigwo feiji." (Very good. American airman.) The old lady smiled, displaying her few remaining teeth, and with a thumbs up salute replied, "Ding hau."

We were leaving when Mr. Wu came around the corner and said he had been looking for us because it was time to eat. As always, we were easily diverted by the prospect of food. So far, the effects of gorging ourselves had not been too devastating. A return of the trots was normal when we were eating so much after years of near starvation. Regardless of the trots, we could not, or at least did not, refrain from eating, eating, and eating. If I was not eating, I was thinking about it.

While we were shoveling it in, Mr. Wu came by with a man who introduced himself as Mr. Shih Yu-shan, a school teacher from a large village. Clearly, his English was superior to that of Mr. Wu. He didn't need much encouragement to talk about the area and the difficulties his people had suffered. Between the comments of Wu and Shih, we could get a fair grasp of the meaning of their speech. Both indicated that many Japanese forays in the area, followed by bandit raids, had left little of value in their county. Only when the New Fourth regulars or guerrillas were present did law and order prevail. They said the peasants planted and harvested crops as quickly as possible. Livestock was kept to a minimum because large numbers of farm animals encouraged Japanese raids.

Although interesting, Mr. Shih's information was not sufficiently beguiling to keep my eyelids pried apart. Hi, who was having trouble too, fell from his perch on a stool. Bish and Johnny Mac were "sawing timber" long before Hi fell. Kinney saved the day by alternately standing and sitting to stay awake. Finally Kinney suggested that Shih meet with us the next morning for a little tour of the area.

Early the following morning (18 May), Shih gave us a taste of how a guerrilla camp was organized. He indicated that although it was only a small operation and storage place, it was very important. The guerrillas were organized along the lines of the regular army with squads, platoons, and companies. He said we would learn more about the organization later but explained for now that Mr. Ting was part of the civilian administration of the *hsien* (county). His job was to take care of all matters not concerned with the military. Mr. Ting, as a member of the Kungchantang party (Chinese Communist party), was responsible to the party and maintained close liaison with the military.

There were more cottage industries in the village than we had supposed. Most enterprises were concerned with the manufacture of clothing. But salting and drying food for preservation was also done here.

"Mr. Shih," I asked, thinking of food again, "how do you preserve or dry sweet potatoes? At home in Texas, we stored white potatoes in a storm cellar, but sweet potatoes would rot too quickly."

Shih said that the area was not ideal for growing sweet potatoes because they require well-drained, sandy soil, but they were still a major crop. He added that dried sweet potatoes were easily stored and transported and that when potatoes were harvested, all members of the household participated. The potatoes were cleaned and sliced thin, and the slices placed in the sun to dry thoroughly—a very simple operation. The dried slices were then stored in baskets in the driest part of the house. Later potatoes could be boiled or ground to be used as flour.

Johnny Mac said he thought ground sweet potatoes would make good sweet potato pie. He went on: "Reminds me of Ole Miss pie. Now that was good eatin'."

"You Rebels always think your Southern cooking is the best," said Hi. "Have you ever tried good Yankee pumpkin pie? It beats that Southern stuff all to pieces."

"Stop braggin'," said Kinney. "Mr. Shih, why are dried sweet potatoes of such importance here?"

Shih explained that for guerrillas and the army, such food is light in weight and easily stored and carried. It can be eaten dry or cooked and is, of course, nutritious. He said that it was the primary winter food after most of the other food had been eaten. He explained that it helped to extend ground millet, kaoliang, and wheat in cooking.

"Hell, I thought Chinese lived entirely on rice," said Bish.

"Not much rice is grown in this county," Shih explained. "Millet, wheat, kaoliang, soybeans, sweet potatoes, and peanuts are our big crops. All farmers have vegetable gardens with cabbage, onions, garlic, radishes, and beans."

He said he thought we had had enough agricultural lessons for one day.

I agreed and said I was going back to the hut to soak my feet some more in salt water.

Bish said salt water had sure helped his feet. His blisters had broken and there wasn't any infection. He asked Shih if there was any saltpeter around here.

"No, I don't think so," replied Shih. "On the other side of the railroad there may be some since gunpowder is made over there. Tomorrow we will be going east and will cross the railroad to the New Fourth Army headquarters."

Kinney asked Shih if we would be walking or riding horses.

"What difference does it make, Kinney?" asked Bish.

"I want to know whether to sit in the salt water or soak my feet in it" was Kinney's reply.

So it was off to the huts to soak our feet and think of what was to come. I personally wondered if vinegar wouldn't have been better for our feet but was content with what I had. With my feet in a wooden bucket of salt water, my thoughts drifted back to our discussion of sweet potatoes, and that train of thought led me back to events in the prison camp.

My second day in the prisoner of war camp in Woosung, China, during February 1942 was windy, cold, and rainy, a very miserable day—typical Shanghai winter weather. The day before, we had marched to the camp from the railroad station in a cold, driving rain. I was still wet, a partial icicle not yet completely thawed. I was standing in the middle of the barracks shed assigned us, wrapped in all the clothing I could find, plus my thin cotton blanket, wondering what in the hell I could do to get warm.

There were many people in the room, and we crowded together to provide body heat against the chill. I saw some Americans dressed in civilian summer clothing with their thin cotton blankets clutched around them. One of the men was pushing through the crowd in my direction. I didn't pay much attention to him at first. I assumed he was from Wake Island because the previous evening we had been told that marines and civilians from Wake Island were also assigned to this camp. The man had a ragged beard and stopped directly in front of me. He peered at me from beneath his thin blanket, grinned, and asked, "Do you know me?"

Words exploded from me. "Yes, you old sonofabitch! You're Joe McDonald from Reno, Nevada." I was surprised and delighted to see him, even under the existing conditions.

Joe and I had been good friends at the U.S. Naval Academy our first year. He left the academy and I had not seen him since 1936. After leaving Annapolis, he went to the University of Nevada. He graduated from the university in 1941 and decided he wanted to see more of the world. So he signed on for a job with Morrison-Kneudsen, a company with many construction projects in many different countries. Joe ended up on Wake Island instead of at one of the exotic spots like Tahiti he had hoped for. On Wake, he formed a lasting friendship with T.C. Landreth, also known as "Mouse."

Mouse had started to Tahiti with two friends, but funds ran short. His friends returned to the States while Mouse took a job with Morrison-Kneudsen, which placed him on Wake in 1941. Thoughts of tantalizing maidens and exotic places were squelched by the Pearl Harbor attack. At Woosung, Mouse became one of the early contingents sent to Japan, and Joe and I lost a great scrounger.

Suddenly the wretched conditions in the camp seemed better to me with Joe's appearance. Joe and I thought along parallel paths and could work together if there was any chance for improving conditions.

Joe's birthday was 8 September and mine was the ninth. Throughout our stay in the prison camp, we had a birthday party at midnight 8-9 September to celebrate and held it in the *benjo* (toilet). At one end of each barracks was a benjo that was about 12 by 25 feet with a door at each end. There were ten defecation holes; each hole, about 12 by 18 inches, was placed over a large, three-foot diameter earthenware pot writhing with maggots and covered with flies. These pots were emptied about once every two to three weeks by night soil coolies. A long urinal trough was located on one side. Urine ran directly onto the ground.

Needless to say the place smelled to high heaven, and, in general, was most loathsome. However, doors at each end of the dirt corridor provided some privacy and security. Further, the guards seldom, if ever, went into the place. Accordingly, Joe and I decided it was the safest place to have a party.

We scrounged, saved, and stole food items for that purpose. Sweet potatoes were highly prized. Joe worked in one of the Japanese barracks and was always able to steal potatoes from the Japanese for our parties.

Our birthday main course consisted of baked sweet potatoes. Bricks were heated in the camp galley and then buried with the potatoes in the dirt corridor. After three to four hours, they were the sweetest sweet potatoes one could eat.

It is not the surrounding environment that controls the situation, but the internal. We ate, sang "Happy Birthday," and laughed, disregarding our smelly location. After the war, Joe and I had many happy times talking over those benjo parties.

I was amused thinking of my crazy dreams, half-dreams, and reveries of the day. I lifted my feet out of the salt solution, dried them on my shirt, and gave thanks I had had such sweet dreams of Skip and sweet potatoes all in the same day.

Let come what may tomorrow . . .

CHAPTER SEVEN

Vignettes

MR. SHIH gave us the Chinese equivalent of reveille by pounding on a big brass gong. The reverberations would have awakened the dead. He reinforced the resonations with shouts: "Food ready! Come eat!"

Bish grunted, turned over, and mumbled to himself.

"Come on, Bish," I said. "The waffles are getting cold."

"Go to hell!" growled Bish. "It's too early to get up."

Mr. Shih repeated his call for breakfast.

Hi stuck his head in the door of our hut and reminded us that today we would head for the New Fourth Army headquarters.

Johnny Mac, joining Hi, added: "Tell Bish he'd better hurry if he wants to get a choice of which mule he rides."

I splashed water on my face, threw some at Bish, and took off for the chow line. Bish was right behind, hurling dire threats with every step. The others were eating when we arrived. It was still dark, and the peanut oil lamp didn't give much light, but we didn't need much to find the food.

Mr. Shih was standing by the table and gave each of us a piece of string, an aluminum bowl, a spoon, and a pair of chopsticks. He told us they were ours to keep and said we should take them along because we would need them on the long journey ahead. Then, demonstrating as he spoke, he showed us the hole in the edge of the bowl and in the spoon handle. He used the string to tie the spoon and bowl to his belt. He said that we should stick the chopsticks in our socks and advised us to tuck our pant legs into our socks to keep the fleas out.

We thanked Magistrate Ting and Mr. Shih for their help and hospitality during the last few days. Mr. Shih replied for both of them: "It's our duty to help those who fight the East-Ocean devils."

After breakfast, each of us gathered his few possessions, tied his food bowl and spoon to his belt, stuck chopsticks in his socks, and was ready to go. As we walked out the door, Mr. Shih gave each of us a "sausage roll" containing millet and sweet potato flour, which we slung over one shoulder like a bandoleer. This was to be our food, if needed, over the next two days.

Our transportation to the east side of the railroad turned out to be mules and donkeys. I was very surprised to see four mules and several donkeys lined up and waiting for us. Oxen and donkeys were common farm animals in North China. Practically every household had a donkey, and many had an ox. The oxen were used for plowing and were venerated as pets. Donkeys pulled the threshing or grinding stones and small carts; they also served as pack animals for transporting goods. Mules were expensive; hence only the wealthier families owned them. They displayed the prosperity of a family.

Having been raised in Texas, I was familiar with mules. They're a lot smarter than horses. For instance, a team of runaway horses will plough through a barbed wire fence, but a team of mules will not. Further, mules don't require as much care as horses. At home we used mules for plowing fields, pulling wagons, and, occasionally, hunting birds. They make good mounts for hunting in rough terrain because they're not as skittish as horses. But mules as saddle mounts for several days? I wasn't too sure since they're not good-gaited animals. Regardless of my thoughts, we were stuck with mules, and one of us was stuck with a donkey. The mules were not as large as the old "Missouri mules" with which Johnny Mac and I were familiar. Neither were the donkeys as large as the old breeding jackasses we used to produce mules by coupling them with mares. Perhaps the farming experience Johnny Mac and I had would come in handy.

When we sighted the donkeys, there came some cries of objection.

"Hell, I know I can't ride that jackass," came an outburst from Hi. "My feet'll drag the ground."

"That donkey is the right size for you, Johnny Mac," exclaimed Kinney.

"Well, not on your life," scoffed Johnny Mac. "Even though I probably weigh the least, I don't want to ride that animal. Mac, you're the cowboy, you ride it."

"No, not me. My feet'd drag like Hi's."

Bish suggested we ask Shih to hold five sticks in his fist, and whoever got the short stick would ride the donkey, which Bish had named Tojo. Mr. Shih dutifully broke five straws and held them out for us to draw.

Bish lost. "I demand a rematch," he said.

"Cut the bitching," responded Kinney. "You've named your mount well, so get on Tojo and let's get going. Shih and Wu are beckoning us to hurry."

We walked over to Shih, who said he'd have to leave now, but he explained that Mr. Wu would accompany us to the commissar's house in

Ho-tan, a large village west of the railroad. He said there would be horses there on which we could cross the railroad to the east side because mules and donkeys were too slow to use for the crossing. He added that there were many Japanese and puppets guarding the railroad, but that there would be many partisans to ensure our safe passage. We were concerned when he said it would be a fast night march and that fighting might occur. He said that he was leaving us here and that in Ho-tan another man would join us as an interpreter. His last words were: "It is a long way to Yenan. Have a good journey. Goodbye."

"Good God, Mac!" exploded Johnny Mac. "Have you been telling these people we want to go to Yenan?"

I laughed and ignored that one.

We mounted and rode out of Ting's village, with Bish griping at every step the donkey took. Four uniformed, armed partisans walked in front. Mr. Wu, on a donkey, led our mounted group. Four other partisans followed, leading the remaining donkeys loaded with sacks of grain and hay.

Each saddle was simply a cotton pad held in place by a rope girth. Wooden stirrups were suspended from a loop of hemp rope thrown across the pad and held in place by one's feet and balance. There were no bridles, only bitless halters. This tack led to two problems. First, if the animal moved at a speed beyond a slow walk, we had difficulty remaining aboard. (Mules have no mane to substitute for a pommel.) Second, without a bit a mule is difficult to turn or halt. Mr. Wu seemed to have no difficulty controlling his mount, but we did.

When Bish tried to make his donkey move faster, the beast simply sat on his hind end and Bish slid off. Johnny Mac, trying to turn his mule to help Bish, lost his balance and fell off. The rest of us almost fell off too from laughing so hard.

"What's so damn funny?" Bish demanded.

Hi couldn't resist saying, "First time I ever saw anyone fall off a sitting ass."

Wu called back. "Come, hurry, hurry. Long way to go."

I thought "hurry, hurry" must be the only words many of these Chinese knew.

Bish and Johnny Mac remounted, and we started again to the east. Progress was slow; mules and donkeys take their time. The soldiers with us broke into a song which Wu said was the "New Fourth Army Marching Song." It was in the Eastern five-note octave scale rather than the Western eight-note harmonic scale we use. Still, it sounded pretty good to us. The mules and donkeys became calmer, and we rode along without talking. Perhaps each was thinking about his good fortune at having left behind the vagaries and hardships of prison camp.

My thoughts turned to my capture and the beginning of the war with

Japan. I was sent to Shanghai on 22 November 1941 as a diplomatic courier for the rump U.S. Embassy in Peking. (The "real" embassy was in Chungking.) My job was to take diplomatic mail to Shanghai and return to Peking with diplomatic mail. Departing Peking by train on 22 November, I arrived in Chingwantao, the port city for North China, and boarded the SS *Adriadne Moller*, a British vessel which arrived in Shanghai early on the morning of 26 November 1941.

At the time I left Peking, we were aware of an impending move of the North China marines to the Philippines, but were not cognizant of any immediate threat of war with Japan. In Shanghai, after conversations with the American and British consuls and my friends in the Fourth Marines there, the crisis became more evident to me.

Twelve of my classmates from the Marine Basic School class of 1939-40 went to Asiatic duty stations. Eight went to the Fourth Marines in Shanghai, two to the Philippines, and four to North China. Ultimately, 12 were with the Fourth Marines in the Philippines and two of us in North China. Of the 12 whose last duty station in 1941 was the Philippines, six were either killed or died in Japanese POW camps. One officer, Charles H. Bennett, survived the Japanese prisoner of war camp to return home. Another officer, William F. Harris, Fourth Marines, survived the Battle of Corregidor, escaped, swam to Luzon, and made his way to the island of Morotai in what is now Indonesia. There he was recaptured by the Japanese.* Later he was killed in the Chosen Reservoir battle during the Korean War. Two lieutenants, Jack Hawkins and Michiel Dobervich, USMC, escaped from the Davao POW camp in Mindanao.** Kinney, Hi, and I were the only other ones to escape and make it home before the war ended.

The Fourth Marine Regiment was scheduled to leave Shanghai the following morning, 27 November. Its departure date on the *President Madison* had been suddenly advanced by two days. The U.S.–Japan negotiations in Washington, D.C., indicated possible conflict with Japan, but not in the immediate future. Still, I was concerned that such a conflict might catch me halfway between Shanghai and North China. I requested the American consul in Shanghai to ask my commanding officer in Peking for a change in my orders—to be detached and ordered to the Fourth Marines. Whether the message was sent I do not know, but I never received a reply. (Colonel Ashurst said later he never received the request.) My standing orders directed me to return to Peking.

That meant the next step after obtaining the diplomatic mail from the U.S. Consul was to find transportation back to Peking. Requests to the U.S. consul to obtain rail or ship transportation did not produce results. I wasn't

*Edgar Whitcomb, Escape from Corregidor, (Chicago: Henry Regenery, 1958).
**Colonel Jack Hawkins, Never Say Die, (Philadelphia: Dorrance, 1961).

in favor of rail transportation. In the past few years, some American personnel had been taken off trains by the Japanese and held incommunicado for several days. It appeared the only hope was to travel by ship, but visits to several shipping lines brought no success.

On the morning of 27 November, I went to the Shanghai Bund to see friends in the Second Battalion, Fourth Marines, depart. It was a dismal sight. The sky was covered with low-lying clouds, creating a chilly, gray, and gloomy morning. Cold rain added to the discomfort. Lieutenant Colonel Donald Curtis, the commanding officer, his officers, and his men were surrounded by a very tearful crowd—remnants of the American, French, and British colonies. The only cheerful note was a band playing "The Marines' Hymn." I spent the remainder of the day searching for transportation to North China.

The morning of 28 November dawned clear but cold. A very large crowd lined the streets to say good-bye to the remaining marine contingent. With Colonel Samuel L. Howard, commanding officer, Fourth Marine Regiment, his staff, and the regimental band leading the parade, Lieutenant Colonel Curtis T. Beecher and his First Battalion marched down Bubbling Well Road to Nanking Road to the Bund. The Fourth Marines band played a medley of marches— "Stars and Stripes Forever," "Dixie," and "Semper Fidelis"—providing some cheer to the exodus.

Well-wishers waved American flags, and Chinese exploded firecrackers. Somewhere near me a piper played "Scotland the Brave." The band from Jimmy James' "Mandarin" (the marines' favorite nightclub and restaurant) on Nanking Road joined the parade at the rear of the column and played good American swing. Another band from Shanghai's famous "Blood Alley" in the French Quarter of the International Settlement also joined the parade. (It was in "Blood Alley" that marines, soldiers, and sailors from all over the world drank, caroused, and fought.) Tears flowed in buckets from the unhappy sweethearts and girlfriends—White-Russians, Europeans, and Chinese—as the bands combined on the Bund to play "Auld Lang Syne." The marines embarked on the *President Harrison*, which steamed slowly down the Huangpo River bound for the Yangtze River and the Philippines.

It was the end of an exotic and licentious era in Shanghai. For marines, it had begun when the Fourth Marines landed in Shanghai in 1927 to protect the citizens in the International Settlement from the forces of the Chiang Kaishek's Kuomintang in the south and the rampaging warlords in the north.

Before World War II, to live in Shanghai was to experience the heights of hedonism, provided one was not Chinese. The city was known throughout the world for its iniquitous ways. Its social life was without comparison. Extravagant parties were regularly held, and the hundreds of bars and cabarets seldom closed. Gaiety held sway among the foreigners. Money could buy anything from opium to very young girls. Both whiskey and life were cheap. Chinese beggars lined the hutungs, and it was the regular duty of the police to remove any dead Chinese from the streets each morning. All was not golden.

After I left the tear-laden crowds at the Bund, I had to find a way back to North China. Attempts to get the American consul to help were in vain. I then went to the British consul and asked for help. His advice was to head for the "boondocks" outside Shanghai. I would have liked to take his advice, but my orders prevented such action. Finally, the British vice-consul told me I would need an exit permit from the Japanese to board a vessel for passage to North China. (The Japanese had occupied and controlled North China since the Marco Polo Bridge incident at the small village of Liukouchiao near Peking in July 1937.) He also provided me with a pass to go through the Japanese lines at Soochow Creek into Hongkew (an area of Shanghai known as "Little Tokyo" that was controlled by the Japanese) and to the headquarters of the Japanese Landing Force (JLF, their term for marines). I thankfully proceeded, hopeful I would have some luck.

The next morning, as civilian dress was prescribed for diplomatic couriers, I was not wearing my uniform. As I crossed Soochow Creek, I must have looked conspicuous among the Chinese, wearing a Texas rancher's Stetson and cowboy boots. The Japanese gendarmes at the bridge did not question my credentials, however, and permitted me to proceed into Little Tokyo.

As I entered the JLF headquarters, a pretty young Japanese woman at the reception desk looked up and asked, "What may I do for you, Tex?" I was astonished.

"Where did you learn English?"

"At the University of Southern California."

We chatted for a bit about the United States and why she was in Shanghai. She said that even though she was an American citizen, she was also a Japanese citizen by reason of her Japanese ancestry. She had returned to Japan in 1940 to visit relatives and was immediately "drafted" as an interpreter and secretary. After this explanation, she got down to business. "Now, to repeat, what may I do for you?"

I told her I needed a permit to leave Shanghai, another to enter North China, and transportation to Chingwantao.

"Well, I can provide you with the permits to leave and enter, but at present there is not much shipping from here to Chingwantao. Give me a day or two and I will see what I can do for you."

"I'd appreciate anything you can do to help me return to North China as soon as possible."

"Come back tomorrow afternoon. I'll have the permits for you to leave

Shanghai and enter North China and perhaps some information on shipping."

"Well, thanks for your assistance. I'll be back tomorrow about 3:00 P.M. But I wonder if you'd care to join me now for tea?"

(It was nearly time for afternoon tea, and I hadn't had lunch. Besides, she was a good-looking girl and an American.)

"I appreciate your offer and would enjoy talking with you," she replied. "But it wouldn't be good for me to be seen with an American outside the office. I hope you understand why I must regretfully decline."

"Yes, I understand. Sorry relations between our countries won't allow friendly association. I'll see you here tomorrow."

The next day, I went back to the JLF headquarters and received the exit and entry permits but, unfortunately, received the word "no shipping." For the next three days I haunted the offices of the American and British consulates and the JLF headquarters in Hongkew for information on shipping. For several days in a row, there appeared to be little hope of obtaining transportation. Finally, the afternoon of 3 December 1941, my pretty Japanese friend had good news. I could book passage on the SS *Herleik* for Chingwantao, leaving the next day.

My friend was as pleased as I was with the news and even had a pot of tea and some sugar cookies for us at her desk. In fact, I spent almost two hours there while she made the arrangements, bought the tickets with American money I produced, and smoothed the way for me to embark the next day, 4 December. The ship was scheduled to arrive in Chingwantao on 8 December 1941. It was a pleasant and successful afternoon.

I informed the U.S. consul of my arrangements and requested that the embassy in Peking be notified to send a representative to meet me in Chingwantao.

The SS *Herleik* was a small tramp steamer owned by Norwegians but sailing with Panamanian papers and flag to prevent seizure by any of the Axis powers. I embarked the next morning, but the *Herleik* did not sail for Chingwantao until late in the afternoon on 4 December.

Captain Olson and I, his only passenger, relaxed in his cabin, drank coffee and brandy, and smoked Burma cheroots all the way to Chingwantao. His radios were not working, so we sailed in silence with no knowledge of the outside world. This did not prevent us from discussing the impending crisis, however, which we did from stem to stern.

On the morning of 8 December, when we were about 50 miles from the harbor, a Japanese destroyer took position 500 yards off our stern and trailed us into Chingwantao. Without communication, Captain Olson didn't know why such action was taken but considered it unusual. We steamed into the port and tied up at the Kailan Mining Administration (KMA) dock. (The KMA was a British coal company with mines in North

China.) Thanking the captain for his courtesy and hospitality, I gathered my diplomatic mailbags and luggage and stepped down the gangway to the pier.

I was met by a Japanese officer and two soldiers. I showed them my permit for entry into North China. The officer looked at the permit and said, "OK." At the end of the pier, I was met by Hubert F. Ferrell of the American Embassy and a marine car and driver. We proceeded to the railroad station and together took the next train to Peking. Before we boarded the train (at about 10 A.M.), our marine driver told us that there was an unconfirmed rumor of war between the U.S. and Japan. Mr. Ferrell had not heard anything to that effect, nor of any specific trouble. Neither had our driver heard of any conflict. As there was no indication of war, we proceeded to carry out orders. Many Japanese officers and soldiers saw us but did not pay any attention to us, nor did they attempt to hinder us from boarding the train.

About 11 A.M. a Japanese officer and two soldiers got on board the train and examined our passports and travel permits, a common procedure in North China. Around noon, at an unscheduled stop at a remote station, another Japanese officer with several soldiers entered our car and attempted to force us off the train. Again we produced our passports and North China travel permits. The officer said our permits were "no good." We insisted they were good and refused to leave our seats. They left as the train started to move. At Tangku, a port on the Hai Ho River for small boats bound for Tientsin, a White-Russian passport inspector who was working for the Chinese denied any report of trouble between the U.S. and Japan. He added that the North China marines would be leaving for the Philippines on 10 December (an earlier date than we had known).

We continued the journey without further incident until just before arriving in Peking. At about 3 P.M., a Japanese officer sat down beside us and when the train pulled into the Peking station, he got up when we did and followed us closely. As we exited the train with the diplomatic pouches, another Japanese officer with several soldiers surrounded us and directed us in English to proceed with the pouches to the Japanese gendarmerie headquarters. The officer refused to discuss the matter in English. Not knowing Japanese, I argued with the officer in Chinese to no avail. To reinforce his words, several rifles and bayonets were pointed at us. We were detained at the gendarmerie headquarters and questioned for about two hours. Finally, when asking directly the reason for such treatment for an American marine officer and diplomatic courier, we were informed that a state of war existed between the U.S. and Japan. I was astounded. Why hadn't we been accosted or detained earlier by the Japanese on the long trip from Chingwantao?

I requested permission to take the diplomatic pouches to the U.S.

Embassy in accordance with international law and procedures, but the request was denied. I made a claim of diplomatic immunity on two grounds: first, as a diplomatic courier; and second, as a member of the U.S. Embassy Guard with protection as a diplomat under the Boxer Protocol. The Japanese refused to recognize that either claim provided diplomatic protection, however. We were given a receipt for the diplomatic pouches, and Mr. Ferrell was allowed to accompany the pouches to the Japanese Embassy.

I was forced to return to the marine barracks, where I found that the state of war was all too true. Fortunately or unfortunately, practically all supplies and ammunition of the North China marines had been packed and moved to the Chingwantao docks in preparation for our scheduled move to the Philippines on board the *President Harrison*. Marines stationed in Tientsin and Chingwantao, as well as Peking, were a part of the North China marines.

The bones of the prehistoric Peking Man were among the marines' gear on the docks.* These remains were delivered to Colonel W.W. Ashurst, USMC, by Dr. Henry B. Houghton, president of the Peking Union Medical College, for transportation to the Philippines aboard the *President Harrison*. The bones were packed in a special crate and taken by train to Chingwantao. En route the crate was guarded by marines. According to one story, the crate containing the bones was taken to the marine compound in Chingwantao and stored in a locked room. Another story reports that the special crate was either placed on the docks or left on the train with other marine gear. Regardless of which story is correct, the crate containing the bones of the Peking Man was captured by the Japanese and has not been seen since. Paleontologists and anthropologists regret the loss of Peking Man (*Sinanthropus pekinensi*), who walked the earth about 700,000 years ago and was of great value to those studying the evolution of man.

Tens of thousands of Japanese troops had occupied North China since 1937 and were stationed in and around Peking, Tientsin, and Chingwantao. Many of those troops were deployed to circle the marine compounds and the U.S. Embassy grounds on the morning of 8 December 1941. Looking back, since nearly all of our weapons and ammunition were crated and on the docks at Chingwantao, I believe that Colonel William W. Ashurst, USMC, commanding officer, made the right decision that morning when he surrendered the North China marine forces of some 200 marines to the Japanese. For him and for all of us it was a very bitter pill to swallow, however.

Jolted into reality, I heard Bish yell: "Mac, wake up! Don't fall off that mule."

*Harry L. Shapiro, Peking Man (New York: Simon & Schuster, 1974), pp. 151–57, 178.

My reverie was over. Peering ahead, I saw a small village immediately in front of us.

Mr. Wu announced as we entered the village, "I trade our food for hot food, OK?" There was a chorus of "hell, yes!"

We dismounted and walked in circles to relieve the pain of riding virtually bareback for six hours. Our walking resembled that of grizzled old cowhands. The partisans took the stock to be watered, and Wu took our group to a small hut for midday gruel. We ate, quickly mounted our steeds amid groans of anguish, and continued to ride toward the east.

As we rode, the late afternoon sun cast long, grotesque shadows of us and our mounts. On foot our partisan escorts trudged wearily as the lengthy march took its toll. Our mules trod calmly behind Mr. Wu's donkey. The pack donkeys strained under their loads but patiently plodded along. Despite aching butts from the long ride, we remained in blithe spirits because our feet were getting a rest. Mile after mile of fields of waving wheat and kaoliang were interspersed with groups of mud-brick huts. Naked children were playing about, wonks were barking, and farmers were working in their fields.

The sun was warm. My mule's motion was lulling, and the cadence of his hooves was hypnotic. I was almost sound asleep when the peaceful respite was shattered by Mr. Wu, who informed us that we were close to a village where we would spend the night. He added: "Maybe you'll be glad to walk a little?"

Shaken out of my lethargy, I slid off my mule before Mr. Wu finished talking. There was a loud chorus of "yes" from us all.

Bish added: "I'll be glad to if I can."

Mr. Wu interrupted, saying, "I no see soldiers or horses. Maybe we spend two nights here?"

By this time we had entered the village, and the usual swarm of children and dogs greeted us noisily. Among the children there stood a tall, slim, gangly man.

Mr. Wu pointed to him and introduced him as our new interpreter, Hu Ping.

Mr. Wu told Hu Ping our names and repeated them several times to ensure he understood.

Hu Ping added his bit: "Me new interpreter. My name Hu Ping, speak good English."

We moved into a hut with Hu and prepared our beds, the usual placement of doors on stacks of bricks. Later, after we had eaten and the evening progressed, it became evident that Hu's knowledge of English was quite limited. He grasped a well-worn Chinese/English pocket dictionary, pointed to words, and tried to pronounce them. It became late as Hu Ping tried to perfect his knowledge of English in a few hours. At last we sprawled out for some sleep. Tired from all the palaver and the long ride, I tried to go to sleep quickly, but Hu Ping beat me to it. His snores resounded within the hut and literally shook the roof. The only solution was to move outside to the threshing area and sack out there for the rest of the night.

CHAPTER EIGHT

Marine Embassy Guards

A FTER BEING ousted from the hut by Hu Ping's snoring, I looked up at the stars, thankful it was not raining. I was more thankful to be away from the Japanese and among friendly people. I couldn't help but regret, however, that my China days had taken such a drastic turn.

On 9 December 1941, the day after World War II had started for us in Peking, a thick blanket of snow covered the ground. It was cold as hell. A strong north wind swept down from the Gobi Desert and through the marine compound. It chilled further my already bleak spirits brought on by our surrender.

Escape appeared impossible from a walled compound surrounded by several thousand Japanese troops. All my household gear and clothing had been packed, prior to my going to Shanghai in late November, in preparation for our movement to the Philippines. Among the many boxes stacked on the dock of Chingwantao was most of my clothing. I was short of clothes for warmth and comfort, and my spirits were lower than a snake's belly.

The only gleam of hope lay in the possibility that the Japanese would honor the Boxer Protocol and consider the Marine Embassy Guard as having diplomatic status. Such standing would bring repatriation along with our embassy neighbors. The communication we had with embassy personnel encouraged that belief, but it turned out that such was not to be the case.

On that cold, snowy day, I was regretfully sure that it might be a hell of a long time before I returned to the States. As I pondered morosely, I wondered: Where was that euphoria I felt upon my arrival in Peking a year and a half ago?

An admonition of Samuel Johnson states: "He who would bring home the wealth of the Indies must carry the wealth of the Indies with him."*

*The Oxford Dictionary of Quotations, 2d ed. (London: Oxford University Press, 1953), p. 274, §4.

79

So it is that when traveling one must carry knowledge with oneself in order to bring home knowledge. This was cited to us constantly at the U.S. Naval Academy. Contrary to that sage advice, I, like many others, arrived in China with relatively little knowledge of the country or its inhabitants. Accordingly, I was somewhat overwhelmed by its beauty, fabulous structures, and history. Despite the filth and poverty surrounding its elegance and splendor, Peking was described as the epitome of the captivating charm of China. Once settled in Peking, I became submerged in the ambiance of the mysterious Far East.

What was the charm of China for me? It wasn't the wind-driven Gobi dust in summer or the frigid ice and snow in winter. Neither was it the dreary spectacle of people living and dying in abject poverty and squalor. It was very difficult to understand the conditions under which most of the Chinese, particularly the peasants, survived. I doubt that anyone who hadn't seen the deplorable conditions of the Chinese peasantry in 1940-41 could understand their plight.

Natural disasters such as floods, plagues, and droughts, combined with starvation, pillaging bandits, and exorbitant taxes, pressed the peasantry to the depths of deprivation. A peasant's life was of negligible value. Female infanticide was common. When hunting, I often saw dead female babies, half eaten by dogs, lying on river banks. Male babies meant extra laborers and income, females only an expense. A child beyond the age of ten was said by the Chinese "to be out of reach of the dogs," because wild dogs often dug up buried small children and ate them. Yet, of course, the peasants married and had children to perpetuate the species. The strength of China lay in the latent toughness of its people, their will to survive, and their eternal cheerfulness despite such dire adversity.

My association with the peasants was the foundation of China's charm for me. Often during hunting trips I'd spend a day or a night with a Chinese family on the banks of the Suin Yi River northwest of Peking. One particular family (a man, his wife, and two small children) lived in a hut constructed of kaoliang stalks daubed with mud and topped with an insecure thatched roof. They were cheerful despite their lack of food and clothing. My first visit was on a cold, snowy day, and I hadn't brought food with me. They shared their meager meal of gruel with me and furthered my comfort with warmth from their k'ang.

On subsequent visits I always took extra food and a little vodka. The oldest child, a boy of six, and his father acted as retrievers of the upland birds or waterfowl I shot. The father would take off his clothes and plunge into the icy river to retrieve ducks. I don't know how he endured the cold. In pheasant season the boy was an excellent "pointer" for birds. The man, his son, and the mother would pluck and dress the birds, keeping the feathers and innards as a reward. Their pay on one of my hunting trips was

A sketch of a Chinese peasant's home made of cane stalks and mud in which the author frequently stayed while hunting in North China during 1940 and 1941.

probably more than they made farming in a month. I enjoyed my visits, not only for hunting and the opportunity to expand my Chinese vocabulary, but for their friendship. I found other peasants just as cooperative and friendly when I traveled or hunted elsewhere. Their friendship and cheerfulness meant more to me than the beautiful sight of the gold-tinted roofs of the Forbidden City glowing in the early morning or late evening sun.

The Forbidden City, surrounded by its pink walls, lay a quarter of a mile from our marine compound. It was a world apart from the rest of Peking and China. The Forbidden City and its surrounding areas, bounded by the Tartar Wall, were distinctly different from the city of Shanghai. Although we in Peking lived a sybaritic life like many in that great city of commerce, our lives were more sedate and ordered. It is a gross understatement to say that it was a devastating psychological shock to the North China marines to be dumped from the heights of plush living to the degrading depths of a Japanese prisoner of war camp.

Peiping (northern city) or Peking (northern capital), as we called it then, consisted of five separate "cities" surrounded by walls. In the very center lay the walled Forbidden City, formerly the residence of the emperor or empress and the royal retinue. The Imperial City, another walled area encompassing the Forbidden City, was the residential sector for officials of the regime.

The Tartar Wall surrounded these two cities, the walled Legation Quarter, and a large nonofficial residential sector for Chinese and foreigners. The Tartar Wall was about 15 miles in circumference, 40 feet high, and 35 feet wide. At the top it was wide enough for the use of chariots in the past or modern vehicles today. On the south side of the Tartar Wall was another Chinese "city" enclosed by a 25-foot-high wall on three sides. All of the 15 gates on the Tartar Wall were topped by richly decorated towers. Today all of the walls, with the exception of the one around the Forbidden City, have fallen from lack of repair or have been demolished by the Communist regime.

In general terms, the main streets of Peking were wide and ran between the Tartar Wall gates at right angles to each other. Off those central streets was a maze of hutungs (alleys) twisting and turning in many and devious directions, confounding most Westerners. The word *hutung* comes from *hu*, meaning Mongolian, and *tung*, together. In the days of the emperor, the word referred to streets in the area where Mongolians and other aliens were permitted to live.

The hutungs had delightful and useful names, such as "Dried Fish Street" or "Donkey Market Street." Westerners never ventured into the hutungs on foot, but always in rickshaws because it was too easy to get lost. The rickshaw boys were as familiar with the hutungs and their hidden shops and restaurants as are taxi drivers with our own cities. It was in these hutungs that the Westerner could get a taste of how Chinese city dwellers lived or find sought-after Oriental treasures.

Chien Men Gate is now an entrance to Tiananmen Square. Chien Men Gate was in the middle of the south Tartar Wall before the latter was demolished by the Communists. Before the establishment of the Chinese Republic in 1911, it was the main entrance used by the emperor and his retinue when proceeding from the south Chinese "city" to the Forbidden City. The Temple of Agriculture, the Temple of Heaven, and many other temples were located in the south city. It was in the "Temple of Heaven" that the emperor prayed for a prosperous new year.

The marine compound, the American Embassy, and the Legation Quarter were located immediately east of Chien Men Gate and north of the old Tartar Wall. Within the walls of the Legation Quarter were foreign banks, shops, residences, and foreign legations and embassies.

Going south through Chien Men Gate, one found a large shopping area which was dear to the hearts of Western women. There one found streets named for goods sold by shops on that street—Silk Street, Silver Street, Brass Street, etc. I spent many hours on those streets, particularly Silver Street, where I frequented "Old Friend," an alluring silver shop of renown. There I purchased specially designed pieces of silver for what I hoped would be a part of my future married life.

I can truthfully say that I thoroughly enjoyed the life in the Legation Quarter. The activities within it were eons away from those in the surrounding city and countryside. The people living within the quarter were privileged characters. No Chinese, with the exception of servants, lived within the area, although they were not barred from entry. Our personal, social, and official lives seldom reached far beyond the walls of the Legation Quarter, except for recreational incursions into the Chinese city and countryside. Many old-timers will remember the sites of social activities or sporting events, such as the Peking Club, Wagons-Lits Hotel, the hotels Du Nord and Pekin, the race course, and the Western Hills. My favorite recreational activities included hunting birds in the areas northwest of Peking and playing polo on the French *glacis* east of the Legation Quarter wall. Other preferred sports included riding the wonderful little Mongolian ponies on fox hunts and horse racing near the small village of P'ao Ma Ch'ang west of Peking. Such events were major social functions.

Bird hunting in China was almost beyond belief. Very few, if any, of the peasants had guns. Weapons were expensive, and there were laws against peasants possessing weapons. Pheasant, snipe, partridge, bustard, and a type of wild pigeon were plentiful. The hills to the west of Peking were the best areas for upland bird shooting. In the fall and winter, flocks of ducks and geese covered the skies, rivers, and adjacent fields. One could have blindly pointed a shotgun in the air, fired, and killed ducks. Geese flocked to the winter wheat fields in large numbers to flick the snow aside and eat succulent green shoots. My favorite duck and goose hunting area was on the Suin Yi River northwest of Peking.

It was there that Colonel Ashurst, Warrant Officer (Gunner) William A. Lee (winner of three Navy Crosses in Nicaragua), Lieutenant George Newton, Master Sergeant Henry (Hank) B. Stowers, and I spent many off hours hunting. I was hard pressed to match the bird kills of Colonel Ashurst and Bill Lee, as both were distinguished marksmen, but I usually managed to bag a fair share of the game.

We used a unique system of dividing the game on these expeditions. It would be divided into equal piles according to the number of hunters. Then each man drew a straw to determine who received the first pile, etc. Thus there was never room for complaint about who had the best position for shooting.

On one hunting trip there were huge flocks of geese on the opposite side of the river from the side where Hank Stowers and I had hoped to set up shop. The weather was cold. Snow was on the ground and ice along the river banks. Regardless, Hank and I decided we'd take off our clothes and wade across to the feeding geese. At our location the river was wide, so we thought it would be rather shallow. We bundled our clothes, tied them to the ends of our guns, and started across, with me leading the way. The water never came above my shoulders but Hank was much shorter. Looking back when we reached the middle of the river, all I could see was Hank's nose sticking above the water. Fortunately, we made it to the other side safely. Hank swore he would lead the way the next time. We towelled ourselves dry with our wool shirts and proceeded to bag an unusually large number of geese. Despite our success, we were reluctant to wade the river again, but it had to be done. Hank led the way.

At another location on the river, a man operated a rowboat as a ferry. On one occasion when we were using the ferry, Bill Lee took out a small can of Copenhagen snuff and took a big "dip." The ferryman saw this and, probably thinking it was candy, asked for some. We tried to tell him it was tobacco and would make him sick, but he thought it a poor explanation for not giving him candy. Finally Bill relented and gave him a big pinch and warned him not to swallow it. The ferryman thought this was extremely funny. Ignoring our warnings, he swallowed the tobacco juice, and within two minutes, turned green and became violently ill. We took the oars to cross the river. Once on the other side, the ferryman recovered enough to say, "I thought you foreign devils were lying. Now I know you spoke the truth."

The Chinese built deadfalls (traps arranged so that a heavy object would drop on the prey, killing or disabling it) or used nets to capture birds. Those methods were not very successful, however. They had a unique way of killing bustards. They would sprinkle grain soaked in an alcoholic beverage on the ground for those big birds. When the bustards ate enough of the grain, their equilibrium was not sufficient for flight. The hunter would then simply walk up to the birds and club them. I never tried that method; it seemed unsportsmanlike conduct to me.

The Horse Marines in Peking had been disbanded in 1938, but we still had a large number of their mounts, Mongolian ponies. One of my assigned duties was that of provost marshal (PM). As the PM, I was entitled to three ponies and received ration allowances for them. The ponies were to be used to ride through the city and warn foreign residents of impending danger (which never occurred on my watch). The idea, a holdover from the Boxer Rebellion, was to warn foreign residents in Peking of impending riots or rebellions by the Chinese. When warned, the Europeans were to take refuge in the walled Legation Quarter, where they would receive protection by the U.S. Marines and other foreign troops stationed there.

We kept the ponies in shape, not regretfully, by playing polo and participating in the fox hunts at P'ao Ma Ch'ang. Lieutenant Newton, Mario Prodan (a buyer for Gumps in San Francisco), Rusty Fette (manager of the Fette Rug Company), and I comprised the polo team for Peking. Lieutenant

William P. Hogaboom, USMC, played on the team in the fall of 1940 but went to the Philippines in the spring of 1941. We played the French, British, and Tientsin marine teams on the French glacis of the Legation Quarter. It was great fun, although I never had a high handicap.

The subject of polo brings to mind the vagaries of fate. In the spring of 1941, Colonel Ashurst was ordered to send one second lieutenant to the Philippines. Since Bill Hogaboom and I were the only second lieutenants, we rolled "liar's dice" to see who would go. I lost. On the way over to the office to inform Colonel Ashurst that I would go, Bill stopped and looked quizzically at me.

"Mac, you like to hunt more than you like polo. I like polo more than you do and it's played the year around in the Philippines."

I replied: "That's right. But there's pretty good hunting in the mountains down there."

"Well, would you mind if I went rather than you?"

"It makes no difference to me. You've got it if you want it."

"OK. I'll go. You stay here and enjoy your hunting."

With those few words the courses of our lives were drastically changed. Bill was one of many of my classmates killed in the Philippines.

I missed Bill after he left Peking. He and I had participated in the "fox hunts," which were big social events in the fall and winter. They consisted of following on horseback a paper trail laid down by the master of the Hunt Club. Occasionally there was a real fox to chase. Obstacles such as hurdles and water hazards, plus following a poorly marked trail at a dead run, made the hunt interesting. We called it a proper hunt because we had the traditional stirrup cup, and many of the riders wore their pink coats. I won the right to wear a "pink coat" in early November 1941; I guess I had arrived socially.

Sometimes we participated in a gymkhana, which consisted of performing various riding stunts and contests. One stunt was to try and spear a big potato swinging on the end of a rope while we rode at a full gallop. Another was to play musical chairs by riding fast around a circle of chairs and jumping off our mounts into a chair when the music stopped. My favorite competition at the gymkhana was the camel races. We rode Bactrian camels, which were in plentiful supply in North China. They made for rough riding, but they were fast. Often they would try to bite the rider. More often they would spit on him.

George Newton and I enjoyed the gracious living accorded Westerners in China at that time. To take care of home chores, we had a cook, a coolie who did the "dirty work," such as stoking the large stove to heat the house, and a "Sew-Sew Amah" (a woman to wash, iron, and repair our clothes). Newt and I also each had a "number one boy," a "boy" being a servant, whose job was to lay out our clothes, arrange for cocktail or dinner parties at our quarters, boss other servants, and do odd jobs. One of the odd jobs was to ensure that any Chinese beggars who died near our gate, either inside the wall or outside, were removed immediately. (If the police found a dead person near our wall, we became responsible for the funeral expenses.)

An interesting aspect of the number one boys was their unfailing ability to have a meal prepared for any number of people at the drop of a hat. Newt and I, being bachelors, had not accumulated any dinner service to speak of. When we had a few people for dinner, our number one boys would borrow dishes and silver from nearby households to accommodate the number of people invited. Often guests would sit at our table for dinner and eat from their own plates and silverware. It was a very congenial community. All the number one boys joined together to borrow whatever was necessary in the way of food or utensils to ensure a good party.

It was understood that practically all Westerners and Chinese of means had to have a private rickshaw to avoid *tou lien* (losing face). There were several reasons for this. The "for hire" rickshaws were usually dirty and their pullers likewise. Tuberculosis was rampant among those pullers, as well as other contagious diseases. Using a public rickshaw meant one would lose face, a fate always to be avoided. The private rickshaw boy kept his two-wheeled vehicle scrupulously clean, with its brass paraffin (kerosene) lamps shining like a full moon. The cost of all the above mentioned help was extremely low. Each of us paid our number one boy around 40 Mex per month. The exchange rate for Mex, as we called Chinese money, varied from about 15 to 17 Mex for one U.S. dollar. We paid our number one boys more than the usual, as both were married and had children. They also obtained "squeeze" or "cumshaw" from the other servants as expected in the chain of command. We paid the cook and the rickshaw boy about 30 Mex, the coolie and the Sew-Sew Amah 20 Mex each month.

The number one boys did very well financially. They brought merchants to the house, and if we bought something, they received cumshaw from the merchant. As both Newt and I bought many items, the cumshaw must have amounted to a goodly sum. Our number one boys also did all the shopping for locally purchased food, another source of cumshaw. Additionally, they earned money from the sale of empty cans. We bought canned beer at our marine exchange and canned food at our quartermaster store. Being a number one boy for Americans also gave considerable "face."

I must not forget "Dai Foo Jeeber" (Doctor Jeeber). "Jeeber" was a word used by marines to designate a barber, manicurist, etc. Doc Jeeber came to the house twice a month to cut my hair, trim fingernails and toenails, and treat blisters, corns, etc. He did all of this for 15 Mex a month. Such wages may seem extremely low, but in 1940 and 1941, we paid our servants a great deal more than the Chinese paid theirs.

My favorite number one boy was "Charley," who was in charge of the Marine officers' mess. He had worked for marines since the Boxer Rebellion in 1900. Charley's main duties were to keep our small messroom clean, maintain a hot pot of coffee, and shine shoes. I was always enthralled and amused when Charley would squat down to shine my shoes and look up at me and say: "Lootenant, do you know Holcomb?" (At that time "Lieutenant Holcomb" was Major General Thomas Holcomb, USMC, commandant of the Marine Corps.) Charley would then rattle off a litany of many marine officers who had served in Peking since the Rebellion, along with some choice anecdotes about each one. The last time I saw Charley, he was wearing my old Naval Academy overcoat, which I had given him the previous year. The overcoat swept the snow as Charley serenely walked out the main gate of the compound after our surrender.

To return to the topic of expenses of living in Peking, our rent was $20 a month and food came to about $40. The basic cost of living for me was around $50 to $60 a month; education, entertainment, clothes, etc., amounted to another $40 or $50. To learn to speak Chinese, I hired a professor from Peking University as an instructor. Since both he and I had to work during the day, he came to the house and had breakfast with me several mornings a week. He did not speak any English, so we had great fun with abstract words.

Even with an income of only $183 a month, I was able to save some money with which I purchased silver, rugs, and linens. Items such as these were very reasonably priced. It was a pleasure to shop in China. The merchants would arrive with their goods at our house. We would have tea and haggle or bargain, sometimes for an hour or two. As soon as the merchant stated his asking price, we would counter with an offer half or less and then bicker back and forth. The merchant seemed to enjoy the process as much as we did. Fortunately, foreseeing the approaching war, I sent all my prize purchases home to the States in May 1941.

Officers and diplomatic personnel were not the only ones who savored the benefits of the exchange rate and the availability of servants. All of the marines learned to live in the manner of the "finest duty in the Corps." The enlisted men had Chinese boys to clean the barracks, shine their shoes, make up their sacks, *blanco* (scrub and whiten) web gear, etc. The one exception was the task of cleaning their rifles. At inspection, the excuse "the room boy did not clean my rifle" was not acceptable.

The primary mission of the Marine Embassy Guard was to provide security for the Legation Quarter and the supply line, the railroad to Chingwantao. This task was to be accomplished jointly with marines in Tientsin and troops of certain other occupying powers. Foreign troops stationed in North China were a direct result of the Boxer Rebellion in 1900. A secondary mission, none the less important, was to show the flag. The presence of the guard demonstrated that the U.S. had national interests to protect in China.

Those missions mandated emergency drills, tactical problems, and continual practice with weapons to maintain a marine's level of proficiency with the rifle and other small arms. Weapons were fired on a range outside the city. Local Chinese manicured the rifle range for the privilege of selling bullets they had dug out of the rifle range "butts" (mounds of earth behind the targets to stop bullets). Merchants who sold joss sticks near an old Buddhist temple on one side of the range had found a strategically good place for their wares. There the marines bought and burned joss to appeal to the Chinese gods for a high score in shooting. To qualify for a sharpshooter's or expert's badge meant a few extra dollars of pay.

Five days a week there was an inspection and drill on Breckenridge Field behind the barracks within sight of the Chien Men Gate. Saturday morning there was a formal parade and an inspection by the commanding officer. Weapons and indoor tactical instruction followed the regular drills. Two or three times a month, hikes were scheduled, and, occasionally, tactical problems were carried out outside the city. Each marine stood guard duty every three days. A formal guard mount was conducted each morning except Sunday. Sentries were posted around the embassy, our compound, and on the Tartar Wall adjacent thereto. On cold, windy, and snowy days, the roving sentry on the Tartar Wall had tough duty.

In early 1941 we received orders from Washington, D.C., not to carry ammunition outside our compound, despite the presence of bandits in the area. Apparently the purpose of the order was to avoid possible conflict with the Japanese troops in the area. There had been altercations between marines and Japanese soldiers in the local cabarets.

Consequently, an officer in charge of a unit on a hike was on the horns of a dilemma. There was the chance of being court-martialed, either for a defeat by bandits or for carrying ammunition, thus disobeying an order. At the time it appeared to me that it would be better to be court-martialed for carrying ammunition to defend oneself against bandits rather than being defeated by them. Consequently my unit carried ammunition on a hike. I believe Colonel Ashurst knew but preferred not to take action.

Liberty call was sounded for off-duty sections at 1500 (3 P.M.) five days a week and at noon on Saturday. Sunday was a free day except for the duty sections. There were worlds of choices for recreation. If a marine was a "shack pappy," he headed for his shack on one of the many winding hutungs. Otherwise, he could stop at one of the enlisted men's clubs. Before noting some of the absurd prices, remember that in 1940 and 1941 a private's pay was $21 a month, with ten cents subtracted for medical care. Our post exchange sold uniform items and the usual personal care items. Cigarettes were 50 cents a carton.

There was an NCO (noncommissioned officers') club and a privates' club, where Johnny Walker Black Label sold for 95 cents a fifth. Beer, stateside beer, was ten cents "gold," local and Kirin (Japanese) beer, about six cents. Soft drinks and hamburgers were about three cents. A good meal at either club was around 15 to 25 cents. Dances were frequently held at both clubs and at Johnson Hall, our indoor gymnasium. The dances were very popular with the men and their girlfriends. At the numerous cabarets within the old Tartar section and at the very popular "International Cabaret," numerous Chinese and White-Russian girls provided entertainment.

A marine on liberty could also take one of the Mongolian ponies and ride about town or go to the racetrack at P'a Mao Ch'ang during the racing season to try his luck. Tours to the Western Hills and the Summer Palace were popular. In the winter, skating at Pei Hai (North Lake) was a favorite pastime. Summer was a good time to visit the Forbidden City or any of the many temples about Peking. In Central Park one could sit on a bench, sip tea, and ogle the pretty Chinese girls in their split skirts.

On Sunday there were many churches one could attend. Marines remaining in the compound during liberty hours still had a wide choice of activities: swimming, workouts in the gymnasium, use of our well-stocked library, some extra shut-eye, or studying Marine Corps Institute correspondence courses. The curriculum ranged from the study of agriculture to steam engineering. Many marines took advantage of such courses.

In addition to the foregoing, intramural sports were played the year around. Baseball, basketball, track, swimming, etc., absorbed much of the energy of young marines. Our smokers, featuring wrestling and boxing, were very popular with the marines and their guests. We competed with teams from the Tientsin marines, embassies, other local Western military units, and various Chinese universities. One of my more embarrassing moments came during a basketball game at Yen Ching University. I jumped to shoot a basket and my shorts fell to my ankles—to the great delight of the student audience. Talk about losing "face"!

One of the more poignant experiences in Peking was to stand on the Tartar Wall overlooking the Peking railroad station and watch a train leave with the marines going stateside. Girlfriends (Chinese, Korean, White-Russian, and other nationalities) of the marines leaving gathered to engage in a sobbing wake for the departure of their "rice bowls." The wailing would diminish as the train chugged out of the station and the girls began to compare notes on the replacement marines who would arrive the following day. The "shack pappy" marines leaving would have written to some of their stateside buddies who were destined as replacements and recommended "Susie Wong," "Nina Orjonakidske," etc., as excellent "shackees."

The next day, at the railroad station, a more joyous scene would occur.

Author at White Dagoba, Pei Hai, Peking, China, July 1940.

When the train with the marine replacements steamed into the station, the girls would be there seeking W.T. Door, Joe Blow, etc., marines who had been recommended by their former partners. Similarly, W.T. and Joe would be looking for Susie and Nina. Once they found each other, it was not immediate bliss, however. The new marines were confined to the compound for a week while being indoctrinated in the pitfalls of the Far East.

The happy "shack partners" would be brought together by the provost marshal and instructed in their respective responsibilities. The girls would receive a physical examination at a local hospital for any possible wayward bacteria. If such were found or if the girl had a record of using drugs, she was blackballed. In short, her "rice bowl" was broken. The terms "broken" or "loss of rice bowl" meant the loss of livelihood.

The Peking Marine Guard had an extremely low rate of venereal disease. Further, we never had any trouble with drug use, although all types of drugs, including opium, were readily available. Several reasons may explain the foregoing. First, China duty marines were very carefully selected. Second, discipline was taut and morale was high. Third, any marine who got into trouble would find himself on the "Hendy Maru" (the marine transport SS *Henderson*) bound for the States. And fourth, a shack pappy was kept "in line" by his girlfriend, as infraction of the rules by the marine meant the loss of her rice bowl.

Those who served in the Peking Embassy Guard in the "old days" (prior to World War II) were a special breed, and they never have forgotten their wonderful times in the Far East. They wore their China khaki with pride and spun tales which have grown better and bigger as the years pass. The group with which I served and became a prisoner of war of the Japanese has had reunions almost every year since the war. Hardships make good and fast friends.

But back to my bed on the threshing floor. I was awakened early by roosters crowing and a big dog sniffing to see what was lying on the ground. Mr. Wu and Hu Ping arrived to see if I was OK.

Mr. Wu asked, "Are you sick?"

"No, I was just enjoying the cool air."

"It's time for food and then we start for Ho Tan," said Mr. Wu.

Hi came out of the hut and said: "Mac, you were wise to move out of the hut last night. I had a hard time sleeping with the noise in there."

Hu Ping smiled and said, "We eat now."

"Boy, I'm ready," I replied, and I said to Hi in a low voice: "We'll talk about the snoring later."

There was no more conversation as we walked eagerly toward the hut, looking forward to whatever there was for breakfast.

CHAPTER NINE

Radios and Crystal Sets

W
HILE EATING breakfast, we started talking about the noise Hu Ping made. None of those in our hut could sleep the night before because of his very loud snoring. Laughingly, Hi suggested that we call Hu Ping the "Big Snooze." We readily agreed. Hi asked Mr. Wu to explain to Hu Ping his new name. But just then a partisan trooper rushed into the hut and cut loose with a volley of words. Neither Hi nor I could understand what he was saying. We heard the words *rbenren* (Japanese) and *meigworen* (American) and, by his excitement, gathered that he had an important message.

When the outburst was over, Mr. Wu said that we must change our plans for crossing the railroad. The trooper had reported several Japanese patrols between the railroad and this village. One large group was about 15 li (five miles) from here and headed in our direction. Many Japanese soldiers were patrolling along the railroad. They must have believed that we Americans were in this vicinity. Spies or traitors here might have betrayed our location. Mr. Wu reminded us that they would be rewarded by the Japanese if we were caught. Wu said we would head north to a larger village (Ho Tan) where there were many partisans. We would leave our mules and donkeys here to be returned to the last village. He added that the partisan would relay our change of plans to the troops gathering for the crossing. He thought that since we Americans were dressed in blue uniforms and were walking, we'd look more like partisans to those we passed. He said we would take little used paths so that fewer people would see us.

Hi asked, "How about giving us rifles?"

"I'd sure feel a lot better if we had weapons," Johnny Mac added.

Wu replied, "We don't have enough rifles to give you." Bragging, he added, "Our soldiers can shoot well. They will guard you. I hope we don't have to shoot. Our ammunition is not plentiful."

I had noticed that each of the four partisans with us had a very limited supply of ammunition. Each had two clips in his belt, maybe ten rounds each. Their bolt action rifles had unusually long barrels, which made the weapons a bit unwieldy. Those weapons appeared to be copies of the old Mauser 7.92mm, model 88. That model was known as the "commission rifle" because many were made and sold to the Chinese in the early 1900s. The Chinese had copied and produced that model by the thousands in the old Hanyang Arsenal. (The arsenal was located in Wuhan, formerly Hankow, the capital of Hupeh Province.) It was easy to spot the Chinese model, as it had a straight bolt handle, unlike the handle on most bolt action rifles, which curves down from the breech opening. With only four weapons and 40 rounds, our firepower was not impressive.

We quickly drank our gruel, grabbed our gear, and left the village. With two soldiers in front and two bringing up the rear of our column, Mr. Wu and Hu Ping set a fast pace. I was thankful that we were in somewhat hilly country with a scattering of woods, rather than the flat agricultural plains of Shanghai. At least we had good possibilities of dodging enemy patrols. The hills also blocked distant observation, a factor in our favor.

We had attracted little attention along our route. Still, we couldn't be sure that reports on our location weren't being passed on to the Japanese. We were interested in putting as much distance between ourselves and the patrols as possible.

There was little conversation. The pace was rapid, and it took too much energy to talk. We were still in poor physical shape, despite all the food we had eaten in the last few days. Toward midday, our speed slackened as we approached a small village, where we hoped to stop for white tea and gruel.

For the first time we didn't eat in a hut or with the villagers. The partisans made several small fires from grass, straw, and twigs, and we used our aluminum bowls to boil water and make millet gruel. Ground millet seed is similar to corn meal and doesn't take long to cook. Without salt the gruel tasted like target paste but provided welcome energy.

I had noted in my hunting trips in North China that common salt is a highly prized item. It was a government monopoly and served at times as negotiable tender. Most salt was brought from the seashore, where seawater was placed in paddies and allowed to evaporate to obtain salt. Up to this point in our travels, I had noticed only a few cases of goiter, which results from a lack of iodine. In the hilly interior of China, goiter was quite common, however, as the salt there contained little or no iodine.

As we waited for our gruel to cook, thoughts of the previous night and the snores of Hu Ping were revived.

Hi said, "I'm completely petered out. I didn't sleep last night. The 'Big Snooze' kept me awake all night."

Wu asked, "What do you mean, the 'Big Snooze'?"

Hi went into great detail about snoring and how Hu Ping had snored so loudly that no one in the hut could sleep. I'm not sure Hu understood all the talk about snoring, but he heard his name mentioned and entered into the conversation.

"What mean, 'snore'?" he asked, as he pulled out his well-worn dictionary.

"You make noise when you sleep, so we call you 'Big Snooze,'" Hi said.

Hu responded, "You call me 'Big Snooze.' Why?"

Bish answered, "You make big noise when you sleep. Like this." And he made a loud rasping noise.

Hu repeated Bish's imitation of snoring and laughed boisterously. He pointed to himself and said, "Me, 'Big Snooze'!" Again he laughed, clearly revealing his missing two front teeth. We laughed with him, glad he was pleased with his new name.

Responding to Wu's call that it was time to go, we bolted our gruel and started the afternoon's journey at a dogtrot. By the middle of the afternoon, I was damn glad I didn't have a rifle. I doubted I could have kept up the pace if I'd been carrying one. It was hot and dusty. Our dirty faces gave us the appearance of local partisans. With the heat, even the soldiers were beginning to sag. My dysentery returned with a vengeance, delaying our progress from time to time.

At a short stop for tea, Kinney asked Wu why he was so sure Japanese patrols were in the area. Wu said their people gave good reports, which were essential to guerrilla operations. He explained his idea of intelligence as the ability to know everything that happens in your area and said that it simply means survival. Operating as the guerrillas do behind Japanese lines, they had to know at all times the actions and movements of the enemy. He said Anwhei and North China had the best-developed system of roads, canals, and railroads in China. But he stressed that the Japanese, with their modern transport, could move quickly in this area, adding that knowing the Japs' movements helped his troops to respond swiftly and counter the enemy's advantage. He said, "The *lao-pei-hsing* (common people or masses) keep us informed of all things happening in our area. That was how we were able to bring all of you together quickly."

Bish wanted to know how they were organized to get such information.

Wu explained that they organized the people into groups of tens, hundreds, etc., which provided for good control. He said Chinese like to act in groups, as opposed to the western trust in individual action. Each group was responsible for keeping adjacent groups informed of any happenings in its area. Messages were passed from group to group by runners or signals, and radios were used in large group headquarters. He further explained that it was a simple system. The common people were organized in a similar way to the army. Wu said that we would learn more about it later when we got to the New Fourth, but that now it was time to go.

We resumed our trot to the north. It seemed we had been going in circles ever since we had joined the guerrillas. We had gone west, then south and east, and now we were heading north. As the railroad ran in a generally northwesterly direction, I thought surely we were very near the tracks. The faint, low moan of a steam whistle confirmed my suspicions. I was startled and turned to ask Hi if he had heard it. Before I could speak, Hi ran up to Wu and asked: "Did you hear that train whistle?"

When Wu said yes, Hi countered with: "Are we going in the right direction?"

Wu said that we might be too close to the railroad, and we turned westward. "Soon we should pick up a guide to take us to our village."

I was not fully convinced we were heading in the right direction and neither were any of the others. We were in between two railroads, the Pukow-Tientsin Railroad to the east and the Wu-hu–Pang-fou Railroad to the west, with the Yangtze River to the south. Were we boxed into a rather small triangle? Distance is hard to judge when you are not familiar with landmarks. Perhaps we were further to the south of our jump-off point than I thought. The day had been hot and the pace tiring. Worry seemed to have taken over. I would have enjoyed a little rain. What's more, rain would have provided us with additional cover.

As we walked up a small incline between two hills, riflemen appeared on either side and motioned us to come forward. Wu told us to remain where we were, and he went up to one of the groups and apparently, with much dialogue, explained the presence of foreigners. Both groups came down to see us. They looked at each of us carefully, with rifles pointed toward us, and then returned to their positions, leaving one man to guide us into the village.

We were met at the edge of the village by several armed partisans and the leader of the village, Commissar Chang.

Naturally, the first question I asked Commissar Chang through Mr. Wu was: "Will we cross the railroad from this village?"

Wu, interpreting for Chang, told us that we would spend the night here and then move to Ho Tan tomorrow, where more partisans were waiting to help us in the crossing. Chang said that there were many Japanese soldiers posted along the railroad. It was his hope that his men could blow up a train and get some needed materials. He said the explosion would also divert attention from our crossing. He added that we needed horses to cross quickly. The horses had not arrived, and we must wait for them. Wu told us we had "much" time to wash and eat. He said that afterwards the commissar wanted us to visit his home and listen to his radio.

After bathing in a nearby shallow stream and eating everything in sight, we reluctantly straggled over to Commissar Chang's home. We were tired. Further, not only I but both Bish and Hi were having a recurrence of dysentery. The commissar met us at the door and gave us a welcome swig of *mao tai*. I could feel that small swallow bounce off the bottom of my feet. Wow, it was strong! It set the tone of the evening, marred occasionally by Bish, Hi, or myself dashing for the outside.

Chang's radio was an ancient set powered by wet cell batteries of the nine-volt type, similar to an automobile battery. He used earphones most of the time, but had a speaker shaped like an old-fashioned hearing aid horn. None of us was an expert with radios, although Hi, Kinney, and I had had some radio experience. I was the assistant communications officer in Peking and had studied electricity and radio at the Naval Academy. We worked with the set for an hour or so and heard some English spoken amid the constant clatter of loud static. The Russian radio station in Shanghai, to which we had listened with a crystal set in the prison camp, was audible, but there was only a brief identification announcement in English. No war news.

Wu, translating, told us that Commissar Chang used his radio to keep track of Japanese movements and the progress of the war, however, he found it difficult to keep his radio working as the battery often failed. I asked him how he kept the battery charged. Wu, after consulting with Chang, went to another room and returned with a hand-cranked generator, saying the commissar said it worked very well, but the battery did not last long enough.

I suggested that we might be able to make a crystal set for the commissar so that he could listen to Shanghai and possibly other stations. That would save the battery set for shortwave reception. This brought a response from Kinney: "Mac, surely you remember the difficulty we had building crystal sets in prison camp. I doubt we could do it in the short time we have here."

Hi's and my room in POW camp had been torn apart many times by the guards in an attempt to find radios and other such contraband. They never found anything, but beat us each time, just for the hell of it.

At this point Wu suggested we stop working with the radio and return to the hut and get some sleep. He told us we would have a long walk the next day that could possibly extend through the night. He added that even if we got horses, it would be a rough and tiring journey and that there would probably be a firefight when we crossed the railroad.

We thanked Commissar Chang for his hospitality and returned to our hut. Fortunately our snoring friend, the Big Snooze, was bedded down in another hut.

Kinney's remark about all the trouble we had in the prison camp trying to build a crystal set was the trigger for a flood of memories. If there was one thing in the prison camp we wanted almost as much as food, it was information about the progress of the war. Until the marines left the North China area in late January 1942, we operated a shortwave radio and heard news from the U.S. We also received other information from friends about the debacle at Pearl Harbor and the continuing successes of the Japanese.

But when we arrived at Woosung (about 20 miles north of Shanghai) on 1 February 1942, we were cut off from our sources of information. The prisoners shared three common thoughts. How long would the war last? How long would we be in this hellhole? And to Hi and me, the most important, what were the chances of escaping?

The Woosung prisoner of war camp was located in the vast flat plain surrounding Shanghai. Wrapped around the camp were two electrified barbed wire fences. One was close to the barracks and another one farther out. Both were manned by guards. In winter the almost continuous icy rain falling from low, leaden skies increased the weight of the dismal news trumpeted to us daily by the Japanese. Gloom deepened after two unsuccessful escape attempts by some fellow prisoners in March 1942. We just couldn't believe or understand the successive string of victories the Japanese boastingly reported. Such success seemed impossible. How could we determine the actual progress of the war? We needed information to counter sinking morale and to use for escape possibilities.

Many North China marines still believed that they would be repatriated along with the American diplomats from Peking. This thought and hope was nurtured and reinforced by the visit of a Japanese colonel from Peking in early February 1942. He talked with Colonel Ashurst and Major Edwin P. McCauley, USMC (ret.), who had been on active duty as our quartermaster. The general tenor of the conversation was that the visiting colonel would occupy Major McCauley's home in Peking and take care of it for him until the war was over.

The primary result of that visit was that Major McCauley was repatriated from the Woosung prisoner of war camp in the summer of 1942. He went home with the diplomats via the *Conte Verde*, transferring later to the Swedish liner, the *Gripsholm*. I have no explanation for Major McCauley's good fortune. The only concrete thing a few of us received from the Japanese colonel's visit was a swig of Scotch from the bottle he brought Major McCauley.

A fortunate group was also repatriated from the Woosung camp in June 1942. It consisted of Warrant Officer Paul D. Chandler and four enlisted marines. Those five men had been left in Shanghai by the Fourth Marines to maintain radio communication for the American consul. For some reason the Japanese classified those marines as diplomatic personnel because they were servicing communications for the American consul.

In late February 1942, Japanese General Hata visited the prison camp. This also encouraged the repatriation belief. In a backhanded, Machiavellian celebration of their numerous "victories," the general presented a weak-powered radio to each barracks. The radio could receive only two frequencies on the standard AM broadcast band from two stations in Shanghai, the Soviet and Vichy French. No news of the Pacific war was broadcast other than Japanese propaganda. It was Hata's idea of the Oriental "drip system" of torture—continuous doses of bad news. One hour of listening time per day was permitted and was tightly controlled.

It did not take long for two of our Peking radiomen, Technical Sergeant Charles D. Pierce and Sergeant Frederick Balthasar Mohr, to convert our gift radio to a shortwave set. Hi, Kinney, and I listened to the set, as did Pierce and Mohr. Each time we surreptitiously listened to KGEI in San Francisco and occasionally to BBC in New Delhi. We would change the set back to receive the standard broadcast band. The news from those two stations was not encouraging, but at least we could compare that news with the Jap propaganda. Before we left Peking, Pierce dismantled a shortwave radio that he later smuggled into the Woosung prisoner of war camp. Almost simultaneously with General Hata's visit, Pierce reconstructed that shortwave set. It was operated for several months by Lieutenant George Newton. George kept his set in a wall cell (a box hidden within the wall) in the room he occupied with marine captains James R. Hester and John (Jack) A. White.* Hi, Kinney, and I had it a little easier. We only had to hide a couple of vacuum tubes and transformer coils, which were plugged in each time we used our set.

What were the risks? The biggest risk was that some turncoats in the camp would report us to the Nips. Second was the frequent and unannounced inspections by the Japs. Third was the probability that some of the POWs who could not refrain from talking about the newscasts loud and long would be overheard by the guards.

What would happen if we were caught? The results we knew would be drastic. How drastic kept all of us guessing. There were only two posted penalties in our camps: death or exile. These penalties were to be imposed for "escaping," "rushing for your own goods," and assaulting a guard. Beatings for minor infractions or at the whim of a guard were quite common, but usually were not too severe. Both Hi and I, however, were harshly beaten into unconsciousness on at least two different occasions. (These beatings and the use of the "water cure" will be detailed later.)

In view of the risks, some of us were very careful to whom we told specific news. For general consumption, we mixed scuttlebutt with the actual news in order to lead some of our own talkative people astray. Another

*White, North China Marines, p. 116–121.

tactic was to delay several days before spreading the news. Sometimes we also tried to indicate that the news came from some of the guards or the Japanese newspapers. Fortunately, Captain James F. Climie, USMC, could read Japanese. Additionally, Liu, a Chinese crewman off the U.S.S. *Wake*, was able to obtain some information from Chinese and Japanese newspapers.

Despite our efforts to mislead "Quislings," the Japanese apparently knew we were receiving information and confiscated the barracks radios they had given us. This happened about the time of the battle of Midway. Fortunately, George Newton was able to continue operating his set. Pierce, meantime, had been able to obtain and set aside enough material to construct another set. We continued to rely on the set George was operating until we moved from Woosung to Kiangwan on 6 December 1942.

We were able to smuggle the parts of both sets into the new prison camp at Kiangwan. Pierce reassembled George Newton's set, which he kept and operated in the camp canteen. The second radio was not reassembled and activated until much later. Hi and I kept the parts in a wall cell in the outdoor toilet. We thought if Pierce's set was discovered we would have a reserve. It was baffling to us that the Japanese relied upon Pierce to keep some of their own radios working. Thus he was able to obtain additional tubes when the original ones in our radio ceased to function.

When Pierce was shipped to Japan in the summer of 1943 as a member of a work party, Mohr took his place as the maintenance man. He worked in a Japanese military garage and was able to obtain many parts we needed. He continued to keep and operate the set in the small canteen run by Corporal James Hardway, USMC.*

The Japanese apparently knew a shortwave radio was being operated in the camp, despite all the precautions taken by the operators. As previously mentioned, we knew there were "turncoats" in the camp, but could never determine their identities. Actually no marine was ever suspected. Some of the civilians who apparently cooperated with the Japs were invited to special functions. They, needless to say, were not popular with the rest of us.

Despite all our efforts to mislead many people about the source of news, the Japanese increased both the frequency and intensity of their searches. Mohr became disenchanted with operating his set and gave the responsibility to Peking Marine Sergeant Victor F. Cirrachi and PFC Merlyn J. Soucek from Tientsin. They continued to operate the set until their departure from the Kiangwan camp for Japan. As far as I know, they dismantled the set and took the parts with them.

White, North China Marines, p. 118.

When we moved to the Kiangwan camp, Kinney and I wanted to build a crystal set to listen to stations in Shanghai. We thought the information would serve as a backup for the clandestine shortwave set in the event it was discovered. Besides, it would give us something to do and also test our ingenuity.

Two things hampered our project to build a crystal set. First, there was the problem of finding suitable material for a diode. Second, where would we find other items such as the wire, a magnet for the earphone, and sheet metal for a capacitor? Fortunately for our project, the Japanese, ever in need of skilled labor for their war effort, ignored the Geneva Conventions and forced prisoners of war to work in areas which supported Jap military campaigns. This meant the enlisted marines, merchant seamen, and Wake Island civilians were marched out each day to work on Japanese military projects. Some marines, at great risk to themselves, stole material and brought it into the camp for us. In early 1943 Marine Supply Sergeant Michael J. Schick of Tientsin established contact with local Chinese at his work site and developed a system for buying various items and obtaining Chinese *yuan*. Without the bravery and ingenuity of these marines, our efforts to build a radio would have been in vain.

At Kiangwan the Japanese established several camp maintenance shops between the inner and outer electric fence around our barracks. The sheet metal shop proved to be very valuable for both our radio endeavors and our escape. Two sheet metal workers from Wake Island operated the sheet metal shop. Soldering irons, combined with their expertise, answered many of our prayers.

To our good fortune, some of the items needed for a crystal set materialized with the receipt of Red Cross food boxes about the middle of December 1942. A small can containing a few ounces of Nescafé was the answer for making an earphone. The can itself was the container and the thin metal top seal served as the vibrator for the earphone. All we needed was a magnet.

The search for magnets was a long one. First, we took thin strips of iron, cut them to size, and tried to magnetize them. We made a coil of regular electric wire and, using a light bulb for a resistor, let the current flow through the coil to establish an alternating magnetic field. Kinney and I sat for hours under the prison water tank chucking those thin iron strips through the coil. The idea was to catch the current and the magnetic field at the peak of the hysteresis loop and thus establish permanent magnetism in an iron strip. We found magnetism in some strips but not of sufficient strength for our purpose.

Again we turned to Mohr and the marines working in the Japanese automobile shop. Mohr brought us a magnet and a spool of thin, insulated copper wire. The latter was used for the primary and secondary coils for signal input and the tickler on the diode. I was thankful Kinney and Hi had the patience to wind the coils.

Two more difficult steps remained. The first one, to make a variable condenser, was easily solved by using three pieces of sheet metal stolen from the Japs' maintenance shop. The second one, to make a diode, proved more difficult. Lead solder was obtained from the same shop and sulphur from our sick bay. The trick was to melt these together to form galena, or lead sulfide. A charcoal fire and a clay pot accomplished the task.

Once the crystal set was assembled, we played with the wire tickler over the face of the galena crystal to obtain a signal. By varying the slide over the secondary coil and the spacing of the condenser, we could magnify the signal and tune in different stations. It turned out that we could only receive two stations which broadcast in English, the same we received on our vanished gift radios. We called it a success, however.

Once Kinney and I had constructed one crystal set, it was fairly easy to make a second one. Hi and I built another but used it only occasionally. We believed the operation of one set was sufficient. We kept the second crystal set and the extra shortwave set built by Pierce hidden. The crystal set was stored in a wall cell in our room for infrequent use, but the extra shortwave set was hidden in the wall of the toilet for emergency use only.

Using KLIM cans contained in the Red Cross food boxes, we also made watertight containers for burying radio parts. Some tools, including those set aside for escaping, were hidden in wall cells in the outdoor toilet near our building. As a precaution, other material was placed in watertight cans and buried in various spots around the grounds. The Japanese never looked for contraband in the toilets; the odor was too strong, even for them, accustomed as they were to crude facilities. On several occasions when we expected detailed searches, we resorted to hiding radio parts in water-proofed cans and lowering them into the ordure in the large earthenware jars of the toilet. It was a disagreeable task, but the radio parts were safe.

During one of the many detailed searches of our room, Lieutenant Morisako, a Japanese guard whom we called "Mortimer Snerd," found under my sack a device that Hi and I had made. It consisted of an iron wire bent into a semiloop with its two ends stuck into a wooden frame. Dangling from the iron bow were five "snake catchers" made of wire, string, and cloth. The device had been made to help position the foot of a U.S. Army Air Corps first lieutenant, for healing. He was a pilot of a B-25 shot down on a raid in the Wuhan-Hankow area, and he had been wounded in his right foot.

The idea behind the "snake-catching device" was to place the wooden part behind his heel and attach the "snake catchers" to each toe. By twisting the wires to tighten them and thus pull on his toes, his foot would gradually be stretched into a normal position while it healed. The trouble was he would have had to wear it all the time to be effective and that was impossible.

To return to Lieutenant Morisako—he grabbed the snake-catching device from under my straw tick and jammed it on his head and danced around the room, yelling, "Radio, radio!" Of course Hi and I burst out laughing at the ridiculous sight and were clobbered by the guards as a result. Many years later, recalling the memory of Morisako behaving like an idiot, we were always highly amused.

As the war wore on, the Japanese became more and more thorough in their searches. With the Allies' landing in France and severe Japanese losses in the Pacific theater, our guards became rather frantic in their search activities. Consequently, we had to be extremely careful with radio operations. In view of the increasing crescendo of American military operations, Hi and I couldn't resist pulling out the hidden second short-wave set to listen to KGEI. After a few weeks, Major Luther A. Brown told us Colonel Ashurst had given orders for any radio sets to be buried because conditions in the camp were becoming too touchy for such operations. We saluted, in effect, and said, "Aye, aye, Sir."

We buried the shortwave set and reported back to Major Brown that it was buried. He said, "Good." But he did not say not to dig it up. We let the set remain buried about a week, dug it up, and resumed operations. Orders are orders, but they can be interpreted in different ways if the need arises.

We continued to operate that set until we received word of the impending move to Japan. Then it was dismantled and the parts placed in KLIM cans to be used in Japan by us or by others if we escaped. The crystal set was abandoned. I assume the shortwave went on to Japan with the others after we escaped.

As I drifted off to sleep, I wondered if we had been caught with the shortwave sets, would we have been executed or exiled? I would have been in favor of exile. It couldn't have been much worse than Kiangwan.

Chapter Ten

Firefight

T HE NEXT MORNING, 20 May 1942, when I awakened, I felt as if I was in exile. Low-lying, dark clouds scudded across a menacing slate gray sky. Fine, drizzling rain blurred the landscape, and mud was knee-deep. Boy, I thought, what a hell of a day for a fast walk to our takeoff point for crossing the railroad. Good for cover but bad for us in our weakened physical condition. As I had so many times when exposed to cold rain in the prisoner of war camp, I fervently wished for a raincoat. But why was I thinking of mundane comfort items? Better think of the problems that lay ahead.

Up to this point, I had been too busy and euphoric over our apparent success in escaping to be apprehensive of recapture. Now stress combined with abject discomfort and weariness brought on vivid fear of recapture. Our dependence on others for safety and well-being had not engendered confidence. In addition, I wondered why we were going back east when American or Nationalist Chinese airfields were, in all probability, west of us. We knew that we had to get to an airfield. Why were our Communist guides taking us back east?

Added to this, I felt naked without a weapon. Rifles and pistols are integral to being a marine. In the "Old Corps" a marine was issued a pistol or a rifle, and it was his to keep as long as he remained in the corps. You took your weapon wherever you went. You practically slept with it. You knew the serial number and functioning of that weapon better than your name. You took better care of the weapon than you would your girlfriend or wife. One could excuse a marine for many things but never for a dirty weapon. Your life depended on it.

The idea of possibly being in or near a firefight without a weapon was not only unsettling, it was downright repugnant. Neither Wu nor "Big Snooze" had a weapon. And the knowledge that there was a shortage of weapons did not make me feel any better. My companions expressed the same concerns.

Our physical weakness compounded such thoughts. Hi, Bish, and I were still having trouble with dysentery. None of us had regained much strength. All the food I was eating was going straight through without stopping even for a moment. We were glad to have made it to this point, but weak and weaponless, what were the possibilities of losing all? If we were killed, would our deaths be reported to American forces? Visions of my fiancée and family receiving such news flickered through my mind.

I was sinking into a blue funk when Hi looked out the door of our hut and said: "Hell, it ain't the best day for us to travel, but neither is it good for the Jap patrols."

"I agree. It's gonna be a long, wet walk to our rendezvous point. These cloth shoes aren't much good in rainy weather, but they beat the hell out of those wooden clogs we wore in prison camp mud. I hope to God I can walk for 24 hours in the rain without giving out. How 'bout you?"

"Frankly, I'm petered out, too. This crapping every few minutes is about to drive me nuts."

"It wouldn't be so bad if we had a few pieces of dry paper to wipe our asses with. This wet straw is a losing game."

Just then Wu peered in the doorway and said cheerfully: "Rain, ding hau! Let's go meet partisans, get horses, and cross railroad. Rain give us cover. Jap soldiers no like bad weather. First I have medicine for your sickness."

After gulping down the offered liquid, I thanked Wu and told him that I hoped the medicine would help us make better time. Then voicing our concerns, I asked Wu why we were going east when the airfields must be west of us.

Wu said he was told to guide us to the village of Ho Tan and from there to cross the railroad into eastern Anwhei. He said he thought it would be better to go east, since the headquarters and some main elements of the New Fourth Army were in that area. He also said that once we reached the New Fourth Army headquarters, we would be told what to do next.

Bish asked Mr. Wu if we could get some straw rain capes and hats and added that he didn't want to catch pneumonia at this stage of the game.

Wu explained that many Chinese farmers put a thick mat of straw over their shoulders as a rain cape. He said that rain sheds off the mat as it does from the straw roofs of huts.

I had seen such rain gear used and said that the straw raincoat was similar to our boat cloak. You drape the mat over your shoulders and fasten it around your neck. A conical hat of straw completes the outfit. It works fairly well for a short time but not for extended periods. A man wearing such garb looks like a walking shock of wheat or kaoliang. Sometimes,

A Chinese peasant's raincoat and rain hat, both made of cane stalks and straw, which the author used as camouflage while hunting in North China in 1940 and 1941.

when hunting geese and ducks, we used straw capes as blinds. They're excellent for cold or snowy weather, too, because they're warm and shed snow easily.

Kinney pointed out that they'd be damn good camouflage for us. Wu explained how many of their soldiers wore the straw rain gear when near enemy troops or when enemy aircraft were operating. The straw blended well with surrounding wheat or kaoliang fields. He added, however, that we didn't have time now to look for straw mats because it was time to start for our meeting point.

The usual breakfast of hot millet gruel warmed my spirits, which were sagging from the prospect of a long march in the rain. Each of us was given two small loaves of *mian bao* (steamed bread) to stick in our shoulder bags for lunch. I tried to figure out a way to keep the bread dry, but to no avail. By the time we passed through the gates of the village wall, I had bread soup in my bag.

As he had done yesterday, Mr. Wu set a rapid pace. It was difficult to walk fast, as we slid in the mud with each step. Passing through a small village, we stopped and our escort cut short walking sticks for us from the few surviving trees. Those sticks helped to keep us from sliding off the tops of dikes around the fields. Mud sticking to our cloth shoes created earthen snowshoes and increased the difficulty of walking. As the day wore on, I found it difficult to lift mud-caked feet and place one foot in front of the other.

Although it was late May, the rain was cold. I coughed and wondered if my old ailment of lung worms was returning. In the prison camp, many of us were infested with worms of various types. Hookworms were the most common. One particularly nasty manifestation of such an infection was coughing up worms and having to spit them out. Many forms of ascariasis (a disease caused by intestinal nematodes that migrate through the lungs) were endemic to China. I decided not to look at my spittle until we reached a medical facility.

Rain came in sheets. My energy was fast disappearing, and I longed to stop and rest in one of the many villages we passed. I thought how comforting it would be to dry our clothes by a warm fire and wait for the rain to cease. Hi, Bish, and I had been away from the land of the big PX for five years. One more day wouldn't make much difference. We could cross the rail lines another night.

I made the suggestion to Wu. He must have been thinking the same thing. It took him a few minutes to say: "No. Everything is ready for the crossing tonight. We must go quickly because New Fourth Army *chan shih* (fighters) will meet us in a village near the railroad." (The Communists preferred the term *chan shih*, meaning "fighter," to the word *ping*, meaning "soldier," which in the past had a disreputable meaning in China.) Wu said that the chan shih would have horses for us and be ready to guide us to the crossing point. He encouraged us with the news that a band of partisans would join us to protect our crossing.

About the middle of the afternoon, we arrived at a village where we were met by Captain Wong of the New Fourth Army and Mr. Pei, the local schoolmaster. (The organized Communist forces had officers and noncommissioned officer rankings. It was difficult to tell the rank of a fighter, however, because none wore rank insignia. Although the officers and the men wore the same uniforms, all ranks knew by name who was senior and in charge.) I was very happy to see that Wong had Mongolian ponies for us to ride. It would be colder riding in the rain than walking, but we all needed to conserve what little energy we had left for the dash across the rail lines.

We were taken to the local school, an old abandoned Catholic mission. The Japanese had destroyed much of the stone structure, but students and teachers had repaired part of the building for use as a school. In this immediate area, almost all of the villages within ten miles or so of the railroad had been raided recently and temporarily occupied by the Japanese. They made frequent raids throughout this section to obtain livestock and food, as well as to keep the partisan groups off balance.

In general terms, when the Japanese made sporadic raids, the peasants hid everything they could and faded back into the interior. The partisan forces did the same, and, additionally, harassed the rear of attacking columns and destroyed small patrols. Civilian movements often duplicated the tactics of the partisans. Chinese, ever mindful of their past, recalled that Sun Tzu had proclaimed such tactics around 600-500 B.C. These tactics, which were later adopted by Mao Tse-tung as basic strategy, were the following:

1. When enemy advances, retreat.
2. When enemy halts, harass.
3. When enemy seeks to avoid battle, attack.
4. When enemy retreats, pursue.*

The forays of the Japanese were indicated by the destruction of the mission and the makeshift housing in the area. Many huts had been destroyed, and only the fire-blackened walls were standing. When we entered the school, there were no fires for warming our bodies or drying our clothes, but at least we were out of the rain. Cold, boiled water and peanuts supplemented our waterlogged bread for lunch. I would have given my soul for a cup of hot tea.

Several students and teachers came and asked questions about the war and education in America. Education in that district of China was very minimal. That was understandable, considering the fact that very few books were available and even fewer supplies, such as ink, paper, etc. As

*Sun Tzu: The Art of War, trans. Samuel B. Griffith, Colonel, USMC (Ret.) (Oxford: Clarendon Press, 1963).

we tried to answer their questions with Wu interpreting, Captain Wong became restless, "chomping at the bit," and said, "Kwai, kwai!"

Wu repeated Captain Wong's plea to hurry, but Mr. Pei insisted we take a look at his school. He was very proud of what he and his students had accomplished. The desks and other equipment were excellent examples of ingenuity. The desks and benches were made of mud-straw bricks and very little lumber. The benches served as beds for students, the desks as storage for their minuscule possessions. Students made their own rough paper from straw and were very proud of something that passed as ink. In addition to their studies, students performed maintenance on the school building and grew most of their food. They had a busy schedule.

Mr. Pei was chagrined that only a few females were attending school. He said it was very difficult to break with the peasants' tradition of educating only males. The Communists were encouraging girls to attend the school, but results were slow in coming. As a finale, Mr. Pei asked us to appear before the assembled students and sing our national anthem.

None of us could carry a tune and we knew that we could never scale the high notes of the "Star Spangled Banner." We decided to sing "The Marines' Hymn" instead. As the student body stood at rigid attention, we went from Montezuma to Tripoli to guarding the Pearly Gates. Some might think it was a sacrilegious substitution, but it was, and is, the best substitution anyone can make. Besides, we established a tradition for the remainder of our walk across China.

Rain was still falling as we mounted horses for the trip to our rendezvous and the railroad. I was sure it would have been warmer to walk, but Captain Wong insisted speed was essential. We moved out at a gallop. Our normally surefooted Mongolian ponies found it difficult to stay atop the levies in the rain and mud. Several ponies fell, but no one was seriously injured. Still, I wondered what would happen if one of our party was badly injured. The only medical facilities we had seen were the "barefoot doctors."

The barefoot doctors were farmers or partisans who had been trained to perform low-level medical services. After a few weeks of training in first aid, treatments of simple ailments, and sanitation, they spent about half their time performing medical duties and the other half at their regular jobs. In the larger villages, traditional doctors practiced their drug, herbal, and acupuncture methods. At the beginning of World War II when my household goods were confiscated by the Japanese, I lost one of the many ancient Chinese items prized by foreigners, a small jade carving of a naked woman. In earlier times the Chinese doctors could not or would not examine a naked female patient. It was the custom for the woman to point to places on a similarly carved figure to indicate where her pain existed.

Although I had observed the use of traditional Chinese medicine, particularly acupuncture, I was not impressed with the overall results. The one exception was their herbal remedies. The Communists, in their desire to modernize China, downplayed the significance of their traditional medicine. In this area there appeared to be no real attempt to integrate Western and traditional Chinese, sometimes demonic, medical practice. Perhaps this was inevitable, as there were little or no Western medical supplies available.

Toward dusk, the rain stopped, the clouds lifted, and patches of blue blossomed overhead. The steam rising from the ponies' wet hair intensified the odor of sweaty horse flesh. We humans were not fortunate enough to be so warm. Our wet clothes stuck to our skin, revealing the bony structure of thin bodies. My spirits rose as we approached the rendezvous, however. Perhaps once on the east side of the tracks, we would know our immediate future.

As darkness fell, we came to a halt, confronting a group of huts surrounded by a high, earthen wall. I assumed this was the long-heralded village of Ho Tan. Inside the wall on a narrow street waited a drenched band of guerrillas. I estimated a hundred or so partisans were gathered in and about the village. It was a wild-looking group. They were armed with every imaginable weapon—rifles, pistols, grenades (similar to the old German potato masher), and boxes which I took to be primitive land mines.

The leader of one group was particularly vicious looking. A large scar extended across his right jaw, his nose, and an open socket where his left eye had been. I had little doubt about the fighting ability of the group, but I did have doubts about their organizational and tactical prowess.

Such doubts were somewhat dispelled as Mr. Wu, interpreting for Captain Wong, reported that the captain had told the leaders of the groups our plans for the crossing. There were specially trained fighters posted to guide each group to the desired location. Local partisans were to be stationed about a half mile to the north and south of our crossing site on the railroad.

The group to the south had explosives to blow up the locomotive as it approached from the south. Captain Wong believed that the train was carrying many supplies they needed. Posted sentries would signal which train was carrying the desired supplies. He said blowing up the engine would serve as a diversion for our crossing to the east.

Wu said he would have given us American weapons if they had had extras. He further stated they would leave this village and assemble about half a mile from the railroad at midnight. Mr. Wu and Captain Wong planned to lead the way across the rails. We would follow closely with our horses in single file. We should go quickly to the rails, go slowly across the rails so the ponies wouldn't stumble, and then move at a run to the east. The signal to start would be the sound of the explosion blowing up the engine.

Kinney said: "These people must do this often." He reminded us that the guerrillas blew up a train shortly after he met them and before he joined us.

Thinking of Captain Wong's instructions, we went to the hut of our local host, where Wu and a local man had made a small fire. We crowded around to dry our clothes. There really wasn't enough heat to dry our clothing, but it felt damn good. Fuel for fires was hard to obtain. Although there were coal fields in Anwhei Province, I saw little evidence of its use for cooking or heating homes. In some of the villages, merchants had coal and charcoal for sale. Most of the peasants used by-products from their crops, weeds, and grass for fuel, however. It was only the rich peasants who used charcoal or coal.

Later we went to a larger house for our evening meal. As we entered, I was startled to see a coffin beside a long table. All of us were too surprised to ask questions before food was placed on the table and we were invited to sit on the coffin and eat. Each of us sat down gingerly and ate.

Inside the coffin was the father of our host. The old man had died a month or so before our arrival. Our host, following ancient Chinese tradition, was waiting for the propitious day to bury his father. The day and place of burial were always selected by a geomancer to ensure that the *fengshui* (the spirits of wind and water, according to a necromantic belief) were in harmony.

According to ancient belief, if the dead were not buried at the proper time or in the proper place, the wind and water spirits were disturbed, placing the living ancestors in danger. In fact, it was believed the whole area was endangered. Long, lingering feuds among families and communities existed in cases where it was believed that the spirits had been displeased by the misplacement of graves. In the past, much of the arable land in China was occupied by graves, thereby contributing to the eternal shortage of food. We sat lightly. We were in accord with our host's wishes, as we did not want the fengshui to be disturbed.

Fortunately, the coffin was tightly sealed, and we were told the corpse had been more or less pickled in *bai gar*. Except for a few twinges of necrophobia and conventional inhibitions, we enjoyed a hot, filling meal of stewed vegetables and millet gruel. Hu Ping appeared more upset than we Americans. He kept glancing uneasily at the coffin. Wu and Captain Wong engaged in animated conversation. Apparently their talk was about the railroad crossing, because Wu would glance our way from time to time as if to say "all is well."

As we waited for the signal to mount our horses, there was a chance to catch a little sleep. But unlike the night I went to sleep on the train, my nerves were too tight to rest. Like me, none of the others appeared to want to sleep. We were anxious to be on the road, wondering what was in store.

Possibly to calm myself, I started talking to Wu. I asked why coal was not used very much in this area. We had been told there was plenty of coal in Anwhei.

Wu explained that the Japanese controlled most of the coal-producing areas. The coal their people mined had to be used for industries such as production of weapons. He said that coal was also very expensive and cost too much for the farmers to use.

Hi added that one way to use a small amount of coal reduced to dust was to make coal balls. He told how we used coal balls in prison camp to cook food.

Wu wanted to know how we made them, so Hi explained that it was like making mud bricks. You mix clay or earth, coal dust, and a little water and just make a round ball about six inches in diameter with your hands. You stack the coal balls and let them dry for two or three days. Hi reminded us what a tough and tedious job it was, particularly in the winter. Six or eight prisoners of war had drawn the unfortunate job of making coal balls every day for our cooking.

"Now, Hi, don't get into telling him of your attempt to make a coal ball machine," Kinney said.

Hi said, "Ask Mac. I had that thing just about ready to work when we left camp."

I added that it was a hell of a good idea. If we could have gotten that thing to work it would have saved the men from a lot of sickness. Those poor bastards sitting out in the cold making coal balls suffered all winter from colds and flu.

Wu asked Hi if he would please make a drawing of the machine for him. Hi dutifully went to work with a piece of charcoal and tried to sketch the machine on a piece of rough paper. Before he could finish, a partisan came into the hut, spoke to Captain Wong, and left hurriedly. Captain Wong announced that it was time to go.

It was about midnight. We mounted our ponies and rendezvoused with a guide a short distance from the tracks. According to Wu's whispered words, the Japanese puppet sentries along the track had been "removed," and the flank guards were in their assigned posts to the north and south of our position. One train passed without any action. I wondered how the partisans knew which train contained the supplies they wanted, but it didn't really matter to me as long as we were able to cross to the east. It was nerve-racking to stand quietly for what seemed to be hours, holding my pony while waiting for the signal to go.

My wondering was cut short with an explosion to the south—the signal to cross the tracks. We didn't need an order to mount and ride. We jumped on our ponies and tore off at a dead run. We ignored the caution to cross the tracks in single file and at a slow pace, as the crackle of rifle

fire to the south was a spur for speed. The cracks and thuds of bullets landing nearby gave an additional boost to our haste.

As our ponies ran across the tracks, the firing moved closer. The stut-
ter of a machine gun was heard to the south. Flames lit low-lying clouds
to our right. To our left rear (north), additional rifle fire was heard. We urged
our ponies to top speed into the inky blackness of the east. The tempo of
rifle fire slowed and was finally completely drowned by the thunder of a
swiftly gathering storm.

Torrents of rain fell again, decreasing what little visibility we had. The
rain was good for the partisans in the fight at the railroad, but we needed
visibility. Except for momentary impressions as lightning flashed, I couldn't
see the horse or rider in front nor those behind. Our mounts jumped and
bucked at particularly close claps of thunder. An electrical storm is not the
best time to be riding in completely open country. I thought fleetingly of
the old wild West cowboys riding in the rain to head off a stampede. We
needed their yellow slickers.

In the darkness the horses simply followed one another, head to tail,
on a narrow, zigzagging trail. It was rough terrain, and the hills were steep
and slippery from the rain. Several of the ponies the partisans were riding
slipped and fell, but none of the escapees' ponies fell. We spent most of
the time clutching tightly to their manes.

As we sped through the night, I was reminded of a similar night ride
in Texas. It was during a bad drought in west Texas in the summer of 1931.
I was living with an uncle and aunt on a large farm (a section and a half)
25 miles northwest of Muleshoe, Texas. We had a small herd of cows and
14 horses. In the dog days of August, we ran out of water for our stock in
a drought. My uncle asked the manager of the old XIT Ranch across the
road from us if we could water our stock at the ranch's earthen water tanks.
The answer was a definite no.

As there was no alternative to watering our stock, for several nights
we opened gaps in the ranch fences and drove our cattle and horses
through for water. It was always a wild ride. As soon as the cows smelled
the water, they took off on a dead run across prairie-dog towns and badger
holes. I prayed with every jump of my horse that he would not step into
one of those holes. He didn't, thank God. All we could do was to try to keep
up with the herd until they had water and then drive them back home. Fortunately, our incursions were never challenged.

I was praying, as I had in Texas, while my pony skidded and plunged
through the darkness. My safety resided in his four hooves. I was pleased
when after a few hours, word was passed to dismount and walk. We
discovered then that the Big Snooze and some of the partisans were no
longer with us. Captain Wong said that we were not going to look for them
or wait on them. We had to get distance between us and the railroad.

Thereafter, we alternately trotted the horses for about an hour and then dismounted and walked for ten minutes or so to rest our mounts. Thus passed the night and most of the next day.

We wondered what had happened to the Big Snooze and the missing partisans. They probably had had the good sense to hole up in some hut and wait for the rain to cease. Our group stopped at a small village at false dawn for white tea. I was hungry as hell and would have liked to rest a bit, but Captain Wong had different ideas. He was anxious to move away from the railroad. We quickly mounted again and rode on to the east, but at a slightly slower pace.

About the middle of the afternoon, the rain stopped and we arrived at a partisan headquarters. Colonel Chang, the commander of partisans in that area, met and escorted us to a hut. Wu told him we were exhausted because we had been walking or riding ponies for almost two days, and we needed both food and a place to sleep. Immediately we were ushered into a nearby hut. We took off our wet clothes and hung them about the hut in hopes they would dry. With no encouragement and without clothes, we lay down on door beds to catch some sleep. I had barely drifted off when there were shouts and curses from Bish. I glanced up and saw him running naked out the door. I jumped up and followed him outside to see what was the matter. By that time the rest of our gang, all naked as jaybirds, had run out to see what was happening. Consequently, we soon had the entire village gawking at those crazy, naked foreigners.

We grabbed Bish and quickly went back inside the hut. "What in the hell is the matter with you?" I asked.

Out of breath, he answered, "I lay down on my back to sleep and all of a sudden there was a thud of something falling on my bed. I looked down between my legs and there was a snake staring back at me. What did you expect me to do? Grab that snake and hug it? I let him have the bed."

Hi said: "Bish, you are out of your goddamn mind! You were dreaming. There are no snakes in this part of China. The Chinese have eaten all of them by now."

Bish defended himself. "That's your idea, but I saw a snake lying there between my legs, looking up at me as though we were good buddies."

I conceded: "OK, OK. We'll look for the snake."

We scoured the room for the snake but no luck. The snake must have been just as startled as Bish. Apparently it had fallen out of the thatched roof of the hut. Regardless of Bish's fright, we certainly furnished a good deal of amusement for the villagers. They continued to take turns looking in the door and laughing at those stark naked, mad Americans. Fortunately, Captain Wong appeared and put the villagers to flight.

We had barely gotten over the snake episode and back to sleep when the Big Snooze appeared and awakened us. He and three of our accompanying partisans had arrived after dark. Big Snooze claimed that he had fallen from his pony and the partisans had stopped to help him. His claim was believable, because we knew he was not the best of horsemen. In fact, on horseback he resembled Sancho Panza accompanying Don Quixote in search of windmills. Fortunately, the Big Snooze was not injured beyond a few bruises and scratches. He met us with a big smile.

The next morning, 22 May 1945, a group of stretcher bearers brought several wounded men through the village. We were told that they were wounded in the clash around the train site the night of our crossing. They were being taken to a medical facility in the vicinity of the New Fourth Army headquarters. The problem was that no one seemed to be sure where the headquarters was located. We found later that the Communists' idea of a headquarters unit was not the same as ours. Their headquarters was spread over several widely separated villages and frequently moved its location. Such tactics were designed to deceive the Japanese but often confused their own people.

It may seem strange that a Communist army could exist so close to and even within strong Japanese positions. Again, the Chinese Communists' idea of an army was not even similar to ours. In the vastness of China, wide gaps existed between Japanese-controlled areas, as well as among the Nationalist forces. The Japanese controlled the railroads, main vehicular roads, and the important waterways. Communist partisans controlled large areas between the Japanese-held lines of communication and urban locations. Similarly, Chinese Kuomintang units controlled areas not occupied by the other two forces. Fronts in China were very fluid. Control of areas alternated among the three political groups as the Japanese advanced or retreated. Any regions not so controlled by the political groups were often ravaged by bandits. One could never be sure who was controlling a specific area. Therein lay the danger for the movement of small groups such as ours.

Wu said we would leave the next day and search for the New Fourth headquarters. He also said another interpreter would be arriving before we left, as he had to return to his village to the west of the railroad. We asked if it would not be dangerous for him to travel alone and cross the tracks. He replied that there were always gaps between the sentries along the railroad. There was little danger for a single Chinese who tried to slip across the tracks, especially at night. We hoped that our new interpreter would be as good as or better than Mr. Wu. We still would have the Big Snooze, whose English was improving ever so slowly.

About the middle of the afternoon, Wu said to Hi and me: "I have been amazed at the amount of food you eat. I wonder about your treatment by the Japanese and the food you had in the prison camp. What did you have to eat as prisoners of the Japanese?"

New Fourth Army stretcher bearers, central Anwhei, May 1945.

Hi said, "Mac, you want to go first or should I?"

"Take it away. I'll fill in a few gaps here and there."

Hi explained that the food consisted of three teacups of rice and three small bowls of a very thin vegetable soup each day. Most of the rice was very coarse and contained a large number of small stones. One had to be careful eating to avoid breaking one's teeth. Fortunately, some of the rice was not polished and provided a few vitamins. One of the worst tricks the Japanese pulled was that the amount of food was based on the number of working prisoners each day. The ration for every ill or nonworking prisoner was cut in half.

Since all our food was cooked by prisoners in one place, we simply lumped the daily ration for all prisoners together and divided it equally. The problem was that since the rations were so small to begin with, if many prisoners were sick or not working, food was not sufficient to hold body and soul together.

I added my version, telling about a shipment of Red Cross food boxes that arrived in December 1942 and thereby saved many from illness or starvation. In the following 24 months, each man received one Red Cross box of food about every two-and-a-half months. Without the Red Cross food, our death rate would have been much higher. Unfortunately, we did not receive all the food the Red Cross sent. The Japanese rifled the packages and took a large share of the shipments. They would have taken more except for our commanding officer, Colonel Ashurst. He refused to sign vouchers for the food unless all the boxes noted on the vouchers were delivered to us. The vouchers were supposed to be sent to the Swiss consul in Shanghai.

I indicated that there were three highlights to our saga about food. First, the Red Cross packages were God-sent. Second, the prisoner of war officers worked a small garden and grew vegetables. Unfortunately, the Japanese took a lot of those vegetables, and we prisoners received less than half of what was grown. Third, an American civilian in Shanghai by the name of Jimmy James gave the prisoners a big Christmas dinner in 1942. "That dinner was good for both body and spirit," I said. "A great morale boost when we seriously needed it. None of us will ever forget the generosity of Jimmy James and his restoration of morale in the camp."

Jimmy had operated the "Mandarin," a high-class restaurant/nightclub on Nanking Road in Shanghai, and a good restaurant, "Jimmy's Kitchen." Both had been well attended by members of the Fourth Marine Regiment. (After World War II, the North China Marines tracked Jimmy down. He had returned to the States and opened chili restaurants, first in Tyler, Texas, and then in Dallas. Since 1958 the North China Marines, former prisoners of war, have held annual reunions; Jimmy James was always invited and attended until his death in 1991.)

Wu told us the Japanese had not treated us as well as the Communists treated their prisoners of war. He said they gave their prisoners the same food and supplies their fighters received. "We will see some Japanese, Nationalist Chinese, and puppet prisoners when we get to our headquarters."

I told Mr. Wu that there was one more very important item about food I wanted to mention. In the early days at our camp in Woosung, we had a small garden for vegetables, founded and engineered by Marine Warrant Officer John Hamas of Wake Island. The problem with that garden was the lack of fertilizer. To obtain some animal fertilizer, other than human, I had turned to my old friends Joe McDonald and Mouse.

They were occupied in trying to construct a drainage system around the camp that would include the drainage of urine from the big earthenware pots in the outdoor toilets. Since the local Chinese farmers emptied the pots only once a week or so, they often overflowed. Further, if the pots were not drained, the splash problem for prisoners was terrible. I helped Joe and Mouse construct crude surveying instruments with a carpenter's level, a stick marked in inches, and a rope marked in feet. The instruments worked fairly well, but digging the required ditches was difficult and tedious, because the fall was only about an inch in a hundred or more feet. Joe and Mouse then constructed similar drainage systems for the Japanese in the adjoining compound occupied by a Japanese cavalry regiment. Therein lay a source of fertilizer for our garden.

With the permission of the camp commander, Colonel Yuse, (known to us as "Colonel Useless"), Joe and Mouse took a hand-pulled, two-wheeled cart to carry their tools to the cavalry compound daily and brought back horse manure. The horses were fed corn and/or beans, and each time Joe and Mouse brought back fertilizer, they would rob the horses of some of their food, put the corn or beans in the bottom of the cart, and place the manure on top. The trick was to separate the beans or corn from the manure when the cart came back to the prison compound. That was partly my job. Even if we didn't manage to get the corn or beans completely clean before cooking, boiling killed most bacteria anyway. Joe, Mouse, and I had several delightful meals of beans and corn and managed to provide some extra food for others.

Hi said: "I remember eating some of those savory beans, but I never knew where you got them. Even at this late date, I feel ill thinking about eating them, but at the time they were damn good. And that fertilizer helped grow vegetables on John Hamas' patch of ground."

"Beans are always good, regardless of the flavor," I replied. "I don't know about you and the others, but I'm still tired, even after all our sleep today. So I'm off to bed. Tomorrow may be another rough day."

Wu agreed and said, "The others are already asleep."

CHAPTER ELEVEN

Beatings

S LEEP DID NOT come easily. I could not get my mind off the conversation with Mr. Wu about food and the bean episodes with Joe and Mouse. One particularly vicious event clogged my mind. I had cooked some of the "horse beans" in a tin can and was walking out of the toilet with the can in my hands. (We did our clandestine cooking in the toilet.) Bam! A crashing blow hit my head. My brain seemed to explode. Flashes of light merged with sparkling spots, dazzling my sight.

I was knocked down, and glancing up as I fell, I saw Ishihara and two Japanese soldiers. Ishihara, one of the camp interpreters known to us as the "Beast of the East," was poised, ready to swing again. Both hands grasped a long, wooden pole over his head. I rolled to one side to avoid the blow, but one of the soldiers kicked me back into the club's path. I tried to get up and get away, but each time I did, Ishihara would hit my head with the club and knock me down.

Then blows pummeled my shoulders and back. The presence of two Japanese soldiers pointing bayonets at me discouraged action against my assailant.

As the Beast struck me repeatedly, he kept yelling: "Why you no salute me? Why you 'rush' for your own goods?" (One of the rules of the camp was "Do not rush for your own goods," whatever that meant.)

"You American 'Molines' think you so big and strong. You think you better than Japanese. I show you who's best. You must salute me all the time." Ishihara kept swinging the club as hard as he could, striking wherever he could: my head, my back, and my arms. I curled up into the fetal position in an effort to make the blows less painful. Then he tried to kick me in the balls. Finally, I shouted, "OK! I salute you!"

Ishihara yelled, "You better, you goddamn 'Moline.'" Momentarily the blows stopped. I glanced up to see the Beast's contorted face. Spittle foam

Isamu Ishihara, interpreter at Woosung and Kiangwan POW camps, known to the POWs as the "Beast of the East," 1942–1945.

formed around his mouth. I thought he had finished beating me and started to get up, when again stars and lights flashed before me. That was the last thing I remembered.

As I gained consciousness through a fog, I thought I saw nearby Dr. Bill Foley, a U.S. Navy medical officer who had been attached to the Tientsin marines. Cold water hit my face. I turned slightly and saw a Japanese officer standing over me with a bucket.

I thought it was the Beast so I tried to stand up but immediately fell. My legs wouldn't support me. As my eyes focused, I recognized Bill and asked, "Where are my beans?" Bill said later that I kept asking about my beans. He hadn't seen me carrying beans so he thought I'd lost my mind.

My head hurt like hell. The throbbing pain was concentrated in big knots on the top of my head. Dazed as I was, I felt the bumps to see if there was blood. My hand came away wet, but not red. No blood.

Someone again doused me with water. I instinctively tried to cover my head with my arms. Bill asked, "Mac, can you hear me? Don't try to stand. I'll see if any bones are broken." He felt my arms and legs and my head and pushed on my chest. "I can't find any broken bones but I want you to lie there and take several deep breaths."

I breathed deeply several times and was relieved to feel no sharp pain—just that agonizing pain in my head. I told Bill that I felt OK except for "this goddamn splitting headache."

Foley said I should stay there until he could find someone to carry me to my bunk; he later told Hi I might have a concussion. He then turned to Dr. Shindo, the camp officer of the day, and said, "What can we do about that mad son-of-a-bitch Ishihara? He'll kill someone."

Dr. Shindo did not reply to Bill's question.

(Isamu Ishihara became our chief camp interpreter in May 1942. He was a slim, fairly good-looking Japanese with mustache and a full head of well-oiled hair. He dressed meticulously in an officer's uniform, wore a long, wide sword, and carried a loaded riding crop. Both the sword and the riding crop were used frequently to hit prisoners. He was very proud of the fact that he spoke pretty good English, but he was an arrogant bastard who believed that he was born to rectify all the character flaws of Americans, real or imagined. Having lived in Honolulu several years before the war, he believed himself an authority on Americans. He was sure all Americans were dimwitted and racially biased sonsabitches.)

Foley returned with a couple of other prisoners who picked me up and carried me to my bunk. We were met by Hi, who asked, "What in the hell happened to you?"

Foley explained that he had been talking with Dr. Shindo when someone came running to tell him Ishihara was beating me. He added, "I don't know why. As we all know, that bastard is liable to do anything."

Hi said Ishihara had been searching our room and was looking for me. He usually hit us with his riding crop or with the flat of his sword whenever he searched our room. But for the record, this was the first time I had received a severe beating (August 1942). Hi believed Ishihara suspected we had forbidden items in our room and was mad as hell because he couldn't find any.

Major Luther A. Brown (the officer next senior to Colonel Ashurst) came in to see what was happening. Foley told him that he had checked me and had found no broken bones but recommended I remain quiet for a couple of days.

Major Brown asked me why Ishihara had beaten me.

I told him about the son of a bitch saying "You no salute me!" and that I hadn't even seen the bastard until he'd knocked me to the ground. I added that it was news to me that we had to salute those moronic interpreters.

The major said he'd report this to Colonel Ashurst. He added that he had complained to Colonel Yuse before about Ishihara, but Yuse hadn't done a damn thing about his objections.

When Major Brown left with Dr. Shindo, Foley said, "There isn't a hell of a lot I can do for you, Mac. These 'sons of turtles' (a Chinese curse) don't give us any medicine to work with."

I was sore as hell for about two weeks and mad as hell at Ishihara. Hi and I talked about doing something to the Beast, but our common sense prevailed. We just became more cautious about what we did and where our infractions took us. We tried to keep carefully hidden the few unauthorized items we had. We also tried to avoid Ishihara, which was not always possible in the close confines of the prison camp. The Beast often made the morning and evening inspections when prisoners were counted. He also made random inspections of the barracks. We had to rely on a little luck.

Although I was now free from the prison camp and the Beast, I couldn't stop thinking how I would cheerfully kill the bastard if I ever saw him again. Not only because of his atrocities but also because he destroyed my can of beans. The thought of the food we had just eaten was calming, however, and the rustle of the wind in the thatched roof lulled me to sleep.

The morning of 23 May came too early for me. I wanted to sleep longer, but I also wanted breakfast. The latter was more appealing. I quickly doused my face and hands with a little water, awakened Hi and the others, and left our hut. In a few minutes we were all gathered around Mr. Wu for morning tea and gruel. Wu greeted us, "We wait here for a new interpreter."

While waiting, I mentioned I had been thinking about some of the troubles we had in the prison camp. Mr. Wu was interested and asked us to tell of some of our difficulties with the Japanese. He said he would keep a record, and our assailants would be punished after the war.

When such a question about atrocities was (or is) asked, I find it difficult to know where to start and when to stop recounting experiences and the atrocities we endured. There were so many incidents of brutality and cruelty that one can only tell a few without boring his audience. Even that is difficult. When such memories are brought to the forefront, they shatter one's peace of mind or become what is now known in the post-Vietnam era as "post traumatic stress disorder."

I told Mr. Wu that Ishihara surpassed all others in his inhuman acts toward prisoners. There were many random ruthless acts by numerous guards and interpreters, but Ishihara's brutality seemed to be a deliberate, planned program. I said that one of the reasons for Ishihara's anger was that we tried to preserve our dignity and esprit de corps. The fact that we marines maintained our organization and discipline within the boundaries set by the Japanese prevented more frequent atrocities in our camp.

I thought one of the many reasons the Japanese mistreated prisoners was that they did not recognize surrender as legitimate. It was a known fact that they discouraged surrender of their own combatants under any circumstances. Further, if a Japanese soldier did surrender, it was considered his duty to commit suicide.

If a Japanese soldier did not commit *seppuku* (ritual suicide), he would return home in disgrace to his family and his community. In short, by surrender, a combatant became a nonperson to the Japanese. Mr. Wu nodded in agreement to my theory.

I continued my complaints about the Japanese by mentioning the "rape of Nanking" and other atrocities they had committed that demonstrated their low regard for the value of life. They treated members of their own armed forces in a rather brutish fashion. We all had often witnessed the striking of a Japanese soldier by an officer or noncommissioned officer. Often the blows or punishment were dealt with a stick or the flat of a sword. Mistreatment of European or American prisoners of war indicated to all Asians the superiority of the Japanese. Atrocious acts against the officers and noncommissioned officers in our camp were a deliberate attempt to destroy any semblance of military discipline and the esprit de corps we maintained. In that endeavor, they failed miserably.

I explained to Mr. Wu in general terms that legitimate orders of the Japanese camp commander were enforced by our own marine officers and noncoms. However, there were many orders given by the Japanese that were enforced only by the threat of dire consequences if not obeyed. On several occasions, Colonel Ashurst simply refused, even when confronted with the penalty of death, to order his command to carry out certain orders. One incident, previously cited, was when Colonel Ashurst refused to sign vouchers for nonexistent Red Cross food packages. The one which is most vivid in my memory, however, was when Colonel Otera, the camp commander in Kiangwan, gave the order for marine officers to become "night soil coolies" and carry human ordure to fertilize a farm. Colonel Ashurst said, "They will do so over my dead body!" The "night soil coolie" order was dropped.

I continued to explain that among the enlisted men on outside details, orders to perform most tasks were passed down the line via the noncom ranks. A master gunnery sergeant of Wake Island and a sergeant major of

North China were the top "honchos" or leaders when outside the prison camp. There was only one incident which was out of line among the marines. A marine, after receiving a dressing down by Major Brown about some infraction, said, "Goddamn the Marine Corps!" whereupon the major knocked him on his ass. Discipline was maintained not by blows, however, but because our marines had been well trained and wholeheartedly believed in the Marine Corps.

Hi added some of his own thoughts about the beatings, saying that as a prisoner of war, you can't just sit on your ass and wait for things to happen. He told of how he and I, as soon as we were in either the Woosung or Kiangwan prison camp, set about making ourselves as comfortable as possible and getting together material for our escape.

For instance, hot water was scarce. At first we experimented with heating water by sticking two bare, 120-volt electric wires into a wooden bucket of water. Such a method heated water, but it drew a hell of a lot of current. This method, soon adopted by other prisoners, used so much power that the Japanese threatened to cut down on the number of hours we would have power in the barracks.

Hi told of how we effectively countered that threat by getting one of the civilian electricians to install a jumper around the electrical meter. Frequent inspections by the Jap guards prompted us to remove and replace the jumper daily. That was a problem. To avoid the excessive use of power with our bare-wire heating elements, we and others constructed "hot plates," hoping they would use less power. At first, the hot plates were crude devices made of mud and clay with coils of any type of wire we could steal. But soon many hot plates were being made, and they became more elaborate and used excessive amounts of power.

Finally, the Japanese caught on to the fact that there was considerably more power being used within the camp's electric grid than their meters recorded. Further, blackouts were occurring, which meant no power on the electric fences. This really got to them. The aftermath of that discovery was raids on the barracks and intensive searches for both hot plates and radios.

I continued the story, telling how regardless of what Ishihara was searching for, he always found something in our room he did not like and would give us a few whacks with his riding crop. We had resurrected an old 20-gallon tank which we cleaned and placed in our room so we would have wash water, without having to go outside in the cold winter weather, to wash our hands or clothes. Next, we retrieved some pipe and built into the wall of our room a small urinal which drained into an ad hoc septic tank outside the barracks wall. It was a luxury not to have to make that 30-yard dash through icy winter winds to the privy to urinate. Eating primarily a liquid diet—thin soup, rice, and "tea"—made many such trips necessary.

The Japanese did not like seeing the comfort we got from our endeavors and tore out such installations when they found them, only to have us rebuild and hide them again. Hi remembered what happened when the Beast found one of our hot plates. He said he had tried to forget the whole thing and added he had been knocked out early in the fray and wanted me to tell the story.

So I went on to tell how we had been working on our hot plate in November 1943, and both of us left our room to attend some formation called by the Japanese. Instead of hiding the hot plate in the wall as usual, we stuck it under Hi's bunk amid some junk, thinking our nemesis, the Beast, would be at the formation. These formations were frequently held to announce another "illustrious victory" over the Americans.

Normally, the Beast gleefully made such announcements. This time, however, he had used the meeting time to search rooms and had found our hot plate. Apparently, when Hi returned to the room, Ishihara was waiting and knocked him unconscious with a heavy stick. For some reason, I was late in returning and when I arrived outside our room, I could hear Ishihara screaming: "You goddamn 'Molines' think you so smart. I show you I'm smarter." I could hear the thuds of the stick hitting Hi amid the Beast's screams.

It didn't take me long to realize that if I went into the room, it wouldn't help Hi and there would be two of us unconscious on the floor. So I ran down the hall making as much noise as I could, yelling, "Fire, fire!"

Out the back door I went and into the privy. I turned and looked out the privy door and saw a large number of Japanese and prisoners running toward our barracks. Ishihara's yelling stopped. I returned to our room and found Hi on the floor, but no Beast. Running outside again, I found Dr. Foley among those who had responded to my cries of fire and reported Hi's dilemma. By the time Foley and I returned to the room, Hi was trying to sit up, cursing the Beast.

Mr. Wu said we were both lucky to have escaped death, adding that the Japanese had tortured and killed many Chinese. He talked about how the Chinese Communists didn't torture or kill Japanese prisoners. Instead they tried to convert them to their way of thinking. (It is well known, however, that the Chinese Communists did torture and kill many of their own people as they fought the Kuomintang and did away with the landlords and officials of the Nationalist regime.) Mr. Wu ended the discussion with, "I hear some noise outside and I think it is the new interpreter."

We walked outside and met Lt. Liu Young, our new interpreter, and Captain Ling, the commander of the cavalry unit which was to escort us to the new Fourth Army headquarters. Lt. Liu, pronounced "Leo," was a young man of about 25, a stocky, clean-cut, good-looking young officer. He spoke excellent English.

My first question to him was: "Have you any word from Yenan about us and American airfields?" The answer was: "No, we haven't. You may have to stay here for a few days until we hear from our superiors."

This was not necessarily good news, but it would give us more time to learn something about the New Fourth and the Chinese Communist movement. I thought such information might be of value to our war planners when we finally returned to the States.

Johnny Mac asked if we could go straight west and switch over to the Nationalist Army once it was determined they had airfields used by American aircraft.

Liu said that was a possibility but told us of the many problems if we went that way. First, as we knew, they had been having trouble with the Nationalists, who might not want to talk with us. (The Chinese Communists under Mao and Chiang Kai-shek's Nationalist government had been fighting since about 1927.) Second was the problem of distance and the dangers from pockets of Nationalists and bandits. Liu said his instructions and those given Captain Ling were to escort us to their headquarters, where a decision would be made about what to do next. He finished with, "Sorry, but that is all I can tell you now."

To change the subject, Liu told us a little of his personal history. He had attended a university in Shanghai, but left the area in 1937 when the Japanese took over the city. (The International Settlement where the U.S. Fourth Marines and European troops were stationed was not taken over at that time.) He had gone north and crossed the Yangtze, along with the entire faculty and student body, to establish a university in Anwhei Province.

Unfortunately, the university had to be disbanded because of the insecurity of war and a blockade which prevented the importation of materials necessary for higher learning. The faculty and students joined the New Fourth to await a more propitious time for reestablishing the university.

Liu spoke good American English and was very intelligent. He was interested that we learn all about the Communist movement in China. He also wanted to hear of our experiences with the Japanese and to learn about American customs and philosophy. His humor was immediately evident when he was introduced to the Big Snooze. He wanted to know all the details of why we had nicknamed Hu Ping the "Big Snooze." When told, he laughed and said it was a good name.

The Big Snooze, getting into the act, asked Liu about the American woman who sang in the motion picture *The Wizard of Oz*. Surprisingly, he had seen the movie in Shanghai. He had questioned us about the movie before, but we had been away from "civilization" too long to know the answer. Liu immediately identified the woman as Judy Garland. The Big

Snooze said he really liked that singer. Later, when one of us would joke with the Big Snooze about his "girlfriend," Judy Garland, he would scowl and say, "I no like American girls."

Although the Big Snooze's English had improved greatly in the past few days, I still found it hard to understand him. We thought that we might lose both the Big Snooze and Mr. Wu when Liu joined us but were pleased with the outcome. We regretted losing Mr. Wu but were pleased to have Liu, an excellent interpreter, and retain our humorous relief actor, the Big Snooze.

Shortly after lunch, Liu announced that if we left quickly we could visit a school on the way to the headquarters. We said goodbye and thanked Mr. Wu and Captain Wong for their assistance and good service. Capt. Ling brought the horses; we mounted and trotted off.

Our reception at the school had been carefully planned. Still it was one to be long remembered. Handmade Chinese Communist and American flags at the gate snapped in the spring breeze. A large group of young students waved flags and sang songs. We stopped, dismounted, and entered. The building had been a sturdy stone residence of some wealthy person, but now it was in a state of disrepair similar to the school we visited near Ho Tan. A more cheerful atmosphere prevailed here, because there were better desks and chairs and, wonder of wonders, blackboards. The walls were almost covered with paper placards bearing phrases of welcome and praising the Chinese-American cooperation in the war against the Japanese.

We were welcomed by Mr. Chen, the headmaster, and two young women teachers. One of the women had attended school in Shanghai and spoke a little English. She was a good-looking gal in jodhpur pants, boots, and an English-cut coat. I don't know how she got away with wearing such an outfit in that tradition-bound area, but I suppose it was because she was a teacher and teachers were badly needed. We talked briefly about the old days in Shanghai—she remembered enjoying the Saturday parades of the Fourth Marines.

With the remark, "Let's go see our students," she led us back to the schoolyard. After the inevitable speeches and singing of national anthems, we mounted our ponies and continued toward the New Fourth headquarters.

Arriving there late in the afternoon, we caught the tail end of a pick-up basketball game among some troopers. Captain Ling, a rather tall Manchurian, persuaded us to try our hand at the game. I was dubious, but Liu and Hi said we should at least play a few minutes. Well, what was to be a few minutes seemed an eternity to me before we ex–POW collapsed and staggered off the field. When those Chinese fighters played basketball, they played as though life depended on it.

There appeared to be rules, as a referee was present with a whistle, but no one paid him any heed. He was used only to toss the ball at the beginning of the game and retrieve the ball if it went out of bounds. The running and jumping for any length of time was far beyond our physical endurance. Captain Ling and Liu graciously called a halt to our participation and led us to our quarters for the night.

After eating, Liu and Captain Ling came back to our hut for some light conversation, we thought. It turned out that they wanted information on our background and possibly information relative to our treatment in the prison camp. Liu did all the talking but was prompted by Captain Ling from time to time. I was questioned about my background first. When I stated that I had been stationed in Peking and was captured there, some of my earlier statements about being a pilot came back to haunt me.

Liu said it was their understanding that I was a pilot, and he was informed enough to say he didn't know that any marine pilots were stationed in Peking.

"I am not a pilot," I replied. "I was stationed in Peking with the American Embassy."

Well, that led to his asking why I told some of their fighters that I was a pilot.

"They were the only Chinese words I knew which I thought they would understand," I replied. "The first people I met couldn't read my pointee-talkee. I didn't know the word for infantry. They didn't understand the words for marine but they did understand *meigwo* and *feiji* (American airplane). It was only after Mr. Wu, our first interpreter, met with us that your fighters were really aware of what a marine was."

After some discussion with Captain Ling, Liu again asked, "Why did you say you were a pilot at first?"

"I have given you the reasons why I told them I was a pilot," I answered. "It was only to establish that I was an American."

After talking with Captain Ling, Liu turned to me and said: "We fully understand your reasoning and your position. But some of our people thought you might be a spy and that is why we questioned you. Everything is OK now!"

As the recital of our backgrounds and questioning continued, I was amazed at how much of the personal information my companions and I had given the Chinese in the very early days of our escape had been passed up to higher echelons. It seemed that every word had been recorded and sent by messenger ahead of us. In my opinion, the efficacy of their intelligence network was excellent.

Each of us, in turn, gave Liu and Ling a thumbnail sketch of his personal history. They were more interested in Bish's Flying Tiger background and experiences than in the rest of our biographies. They wanted to know why U.S. airplanes could not stop the rapid advance of the Japanese in southern China in 1944. Bish told them that there were not enough aircraft and that the base in Kunming was too far from the front. He also said that the Kuomintang forces did not hold and fight anywhere, but simply broke and ran. Kweilin fell in October 1944. The forward airfields for the U.S. Fourteenth Air Force in southern China were gone. Liu and Ling were satisfied with that answer.

I told Liu that I was impressed with the efficiency of their intelligence system, and I explained how Mr. Wu had described the way the system worked and how civilians were organized to provide information for the partisans. I said he had talked in terms of household groups, and we were wondering if he could give us a little more detail about the organization of both the civilian population and the army.

Liu began by explaining something that we already knew. Basic group loyalty in China is the family: family loyalty and worship of family dead (ancestral worship). Kinship is based upon family males, not females. The Communists wanted to change loyalty from family to work groups, communes, etc.

Liu went on to say that in the past his country had a collective security system based upon those family groups or households which provided both a police network and an intelligence network. Briefly, each household was responsible for the activities of its neighbors. Minor crimes or legal infractions would be handled by the family or clan organizations. Serious crimes would be handled by governmental authorities. Punishment for major crimes committed by an individual could be applied not only to his family, but also to his neighbors. The Communists had continued this system of collective punishment primarily to ensure that they received information on the movements of the Japanese and the Kuomintang.

Liu continued his explanation that since his people operated as partisans behind and adjacent to Japanese lines, they must always be aware of the positions and actions of their enemies. And, bragging a little, he said that North China had the best-developed lines of communication in China. The Japanese, having established control of the major lines of communication in North China in 1937, moved swiftly to the south from the Peking-Tientsin sector. In their tanks and trucks, they moved so fast that neither his people nor the Kuomintang could stop them. "Now, however," he said, "our local intelligence network keeps us well informed of Jap movements, and we react fairly quickly."

With such a close-knit network of people to furnish information, Kinney asked if there was any danger from spies or sabotage in this area.

"Sometimes," replied Liu, "the Japanese and the Kuomintang send spies into our areas. They also offer money for information. Occasionally, someone will try to kill our leaders or officers. I must caution you to be careful and always remain with your escort. Others may have told you, but I will repeat the warning: Some of our enemies may try to kill you and blame it on members of the Red Army. That would cause us to lose face with your government and make it difficult for us to negotiate."

I questioned Liu about letting us have weapons and told him we had heard that his forces did not have extra weapons to give us.

Liu said that was true, but also said that if we as foreigners had guns, some of his people might think we were part of the Japanese forces and shoot us. He admitted that didn't sound reasonable, but since many of his people had never seen a white foreigner before, the Communists thought it best to provide protection for us. Laughing, he added, "If we do get in a firefight and one of our fighters is killed, pick up his weapon and have a shot!"

Continuing, Liu pointed out that there were four possibilities of real and imminent danger for us. "First, there is the possibility of your being shot by a spy or a person ignorant of your being Americans. Second, if we move to the east and north we will have to take a junk across the Hungtze Hu (a lake in the northeast corner of Anwhei), which is heavily patrolled by Japanese in motor boats.

"Third, if you're to meet with the Kuomintang, we will have to cross the Pukow-Tientsin Railroad again. The Kuomintang forces are to the west of that rail line. Fourth, and probably the most dangerous, when you cross over to the Kuomintang troops, even with an escort, they may kill you and blame it on us."

"Well, that seems to take care of the possibilities," declared Kinney.

Johnny Mac spoke up. "Kinney, since you can't swim very well, crossing the lake will be more of a hazard to you than anything else. No need to worry about the rest of Liu's possibilities."

Bish asked Liu what would happen to spies and enemies if they were caught. Liu said that only the central government dealt with spies and landlords. Known spies were quickly "eliminated." If they were unable to reeducate landlords and capitalists, they too were eliminated.

Liu, continuing, told us that prisoners of war, Japanese or Nationalists, were reeducated and this had proven successful. Very few of them had to be eliminated. Liu mentioned that we would see some prisoners of war the next day and could determine for ourselves if the Communists' treatment of them was just. He explained that their goal was to convert all prisoners of war to their philosophy of government.

Liu, warming up to his subject, told us that in the long history of China, the greatest difficulties their people had experienced were with internal enemies—secret societies and peasant rebellions. External foes had captured or occupied part or all of China only when their people had been weakened by internal strife and difficulties.

Liu told how one peasant rebellion in the middle of the fourteenth century that was similar to Mao's revolution had been led by a peasant named Chu, a native of Anwhei. That rebellion overthrew the Mongol dynasty and established the Ming dynasty, which lasted until 1644 when the Manchus conquered Peking. Then the Ching dynasty took over and lasted until the Republican revolution of 1912 led by Sun Yat-sen, who was succeeded by Chiang Kaishek in 1925. Liu said China had had many internal difficulties during the last two or three centuries; he pointed out the Taiping Rebellion (1813–64) and the Boxer Rebellion (1900). He called attention to the fact that many of the rebellions were against the central government because of the mistreatment of peasants. Liu stated, "That is the base of Mao's Communist party and the core of our conflict today with the Kuomintang."

Our discussions with Liu continued long into the night. The talks were wide ranging, and some topics were of particular interest to us for possible use to our own forces. Our main focus centered around the organization, tactics, and strategy of both the Red Army units and the partisans or guerrillas. There were distinctions within these groups, however.

Organizationally, both the army units and the guerrillas, insofar as possible, were organized triangularly, three squads to a platoon and so on up through division level. Special task forces for specific missions were not necessarily triangular. For instance, the village guards had temporary organizations dependent upon equipment available and tactical value to overall strategy. Their primary mission was to protect the villages against bandits and to assist guerrillas and regular troops as directed.

The mission of the regular forces was to conduct operations against the Japanese in cooperation with Kuomintang armies when possible. The duty of the guerrillas was to occupy areas behind enemy lines and areas between and around enemy bases. (Although the Communists were allegedly cooperating with the Nationalists since 1936, there had been armed conflict between them and a growing threat of more severe conflict. There were armed clashes between the Communists and the Nationalists throughout World War II.)

The guerrillas' objectives were to maintain fluid defense of their areas, to deny the enemy use of supplies there, and to harass small enemy units while denying static combat with regular Japanese forces. By "controlling" their sectors, the guerrillas also provided intelligence networks and avenues for smuggling needed material to the regular forces. Being familiar with the terrain, guerrillas could avoid direct combat with regular Japanese forces and could assemble superior forces quickly to ambush small units or patrols. They also indoctrinated local populations in the policies of the Kungchantang.

The strategy of the Communists appeared to be "the death of a thousand cuts" (*lingchi*, fighting many small battles). There were few pitched battles between the Communists and the Japanese. Rather, the Communists were content to occupy existing gaps, consolidate their gains, and build up their regular forces and guerrilla ranks for future campaigns.

(The only large battle between the Japanese and the Communists, the Eighth Route Army, was fought in September 1937 at Pinghsingkuan, a narrow defile in the mountains of northern Hopei. Meanwhile, both the regulars and the guerrillas would ambush, harass, and retreat to safe areas when attacked by Japanese regulars.)

That evening and during the rest of our journey, Liu continually referred to the necessity for education in the Communist areas. Literacy for the civilians, guerrillas, and the regular troops was the main objective of the Communist party. Lessons in calligraphy and reading Chinese characters were a part of military training schedules. For civilians, sketches of an object and its Chinese ideograph were displayed in school rooms and on local bulletin boards.

Rote was the primary method of teaching, which I suppose is the only way to teach Chinese characters or ideograms. Character plays and Peking-type dramas carrying the messages of the Communist party policies were regularly shown in almost every village.

Liu referred frequently to the discipline of the Kungchantang. He spoke of it as the self-discipline which came from thorough political indoctrination. Each man believed in the Party doctrines espoused by Mao and wanted to do everything possible to reach stated goals.

Certainly such self-discipline was evident in the "Long March" by Mao's armies from Kiangsi Province in southeast China to Shansi Province in northwest China. It was a march of some 6,000 miles through 11 provinces, while under continuous attack by Nationalist forces, and lasted a year (from October 1934 to October 1935). Their force numbered 100,000 at the start of the march and was reduced to 10,000 when it ended. All Communists took great pride in and received inherent discipline from that achievement.

At the end of our long discussion, I could only say, from what I had seen so far, that the Kungchantang had done a great service to the people of the areas we had passed through. The discipline of both the guerrillas and the regulars had been evident to me from the first moment I was contacted.

I told Liu that we hoped we could see more of the New Fourth. He said we would see one of their arsenals the next day and perhaps visit one of their field hospitals the day after. He said he hoped by that time we would have word on where we were to go. He concluded, "It is now late. I think we should go to bed."

I couldn't have agreed more heartily.

CHAPTER TWELVE

Anwhei

L IU AND BIG SNOOZE awakened us early the next morning. Unfortunately, overnight an ugly infection had developed in my left
eye, which had swollen shut. A puslike substance was oozing from
the corners. I didn't feel like going to the arsenal, but it was a beautiful day
and I thought, "What the hell, I might as well go with the others. It won't
do any good to sit here on my ass." Besides, I had never seen a field arsenal.

I had studied naval ordnance and small arms manufacturing at the
Naval Academy and could not imagine readily how such work was done in
the many small, mud-brick huts. What was the source of power? What
types of lathes and boring machines were used? Where did the Communists get their steel, brass, and other necessary metals? It would be most
interesting to see such an arsenal in operation.

Further, it was our first chance to see New Fourth Army (NFA)
regular troops. I washed my eye and, at Liu's suggestion, applied hot tea
compresses. It seemed that there was nothing more I could do. Liu said
we would be near a hospital tomorrow or the next day. I figured I could
see well enough with one eye to look at their weapons, so off I went to join
the rest.

Liu told us that very few troops train this time of year, because it is
time for both harvesting and planting. All soldiers had to spend about the
same amount of time growing food as they did training. The one exception
was during combat operations. Each trooper received a daily ration. Any
excess food grown by soldiers was sold to the local populace. "Everyone
has to grow food," Liu said. "Even Mao cultivates a vegetable garden."

We were eager to see regular troops, since our experience had been
mainly with partisans or guerrillas. The one exception had been Captain
Ling and his small group of regulars at the crossing site. But we escapees,
as always, were interested in eating first. After a quick breakfast, we walked

132

about a mile to a huge training site about the size of ten football fields. A simulated battlefield had been constructed on one side. The principal feature was a reconstructed, Japanese-fortified blockhouse. Around it were the usual trenches, foxholes, and barbed wire entanglements. Blue-clad soldiers were practicing throwing dummy grenades over the blockhouse walls. Liu brought a dummy grenade to show us. It was a "potato masher" type, which we judged to weigh about two pounds. Each of us threw one. Hi was the winner at roughly 25 yards. The Communist soldiers were better. One threw a grenade almost 40 yards. We needed more strength and practice.

We asked Liu if the soldiers got to throw a live grenade before going into combat. He replied that it was customary for an officer to throw one live grenade to demonstrate its power. Live grenades were too scarce to use in training. The troops were instructed to remember the powerful explosion and to be careful with grenades.

Liu enthusiastically pointed to the various parts of the training area, particularly the obstacles, entanglements, and dummies around the blockhouse. He explained how the men would conduct an assault exercise on the blockhouse as part of their training. He told us to look to the north to see the rifle range butts. Each soldier and guerrilla got to fire his rifle several times. There was great competition among units to get the highest combined score. And, of course, Liu challenged us to fire a few shots.

Liu sent Big Snooze over to the officer in charge of the training to borrow a rifle. He brought one back and handed it to me. It was a Model 88, Hanyang arsenal type with a bore about the same size as a .30 caliber. I assumed it was a standard 7.9mm bore because it had the typical long barrel of Chinese-manufactured weapons. I appreciated its forward-locking lugs. I did not know how many times it had been fired, nor could I measure the head space. I didn't want any blowbacks in my face. In short, I was concerned for my safety in firing the weapon.

Liu asked me if all of us were familiar with that type of weapon. (We had found that the Chinese preferred to deal with one individual of a group, as opposed to dealing with the group as a whole. I, being the senior officer [if there was such a thing as seniority among us], was selected by the Chinese as the leader of the group. Normally, there was no need for me to repeat any instructions, as we all heard the same details.)

Knowing that we marines were familiar enough with the weapons, I turned to Bish and asked, "Did you fly boys get any instructions in this type of weapon?"

Bish replied, "Well, I had a little .03 rifle training (standard marine and army rifle in the 1930s). I think I can handle it. Let me have first crack."

I sighted down the barrel, which was clean and shiny. The lands were well worn, and I could barely make them out. I thought the weapon should have had more oil in the bore, as firing weapons was not on the program for the day. I took a ramrod and pushed a rag through the bore to be sure it was clean. I rattled the bolt a bit and worked it back and forth. It worked smoothly. Liu was watching. I thought, "What the hell? Go ahead and fire the weapon or you'll lose face."

Each of us was given a clip of five cartridges. (The weapon had an internal box for loading five rounds from a clip.) After trying several different positions, we all selected the prone firing position. It was best with such a long-barreled rifle. The targets were about 100 yards down range. Fortunately, my right eye was in good shape. If I had been left-handed, my swollen left eye would have given me trouble.

I handed the rifle to Bish and gave him a choice of firing at a target about 100 yards away or a magpie adjacent to the target. He chose the magpie, fired his first shot, and blew the magpie apart. He stood up, handed the rifle back to me, and would not shoot again. He said: "I now have a perfect score. Let's see who can beat it."

The rest of us fired all five shots at separate paper targets, but no one could beat Bish's perfect score. None of us pulled a "Maggie's drawers," however. (When you miss a target, the scorer in the butts waves a red flag — Maggie's drawers — to indicate a miss.) None of us had fired a weapon in over three years. Therefore, we marines felt good because no one had a score lower than 80 percent bull's-eyes. We had upheld the honor of the Marine Corps. But, of course, Bish kidded us for the rest of our time together that an ex–Navy lieutenant had a perfect score, whereas none of us had matched him. (Bish had resigned his commission in the U.S. Navy to fight with the Flying Tigers before the U.S. entered the war.)

We quickly learned one basic rule of the Red Army in battle. It was the same as on a Marine Corps rifle range. Liu said, "Our first order of battle is to pick up your brass before you move. Those brass casings are very scarce. The empty cartridges are reloaded time and time again."

We picked up our brass and handed it to the range officer, who grinned and thanked us. I knew those remarks of Liu's about reloading cartridges many, many times would stay with me. I would be reluctant to fire their rifles again unless we ran into a firefight. Weakened brass plus what I later observed to be excessive head space in some rifles did not create a great deal of confidence in their weapons. On the other hand, in an emergency, one does not worry about the condition of the weapon; one just fires it.

As we were walking toward another part of the arsenal, Liu pointed with pride to a large building and said it was their school where soldiers were taught to read and write. Lectures were also given on Kungchantang (Communist, Mao-type) policies, social behavior, and national and international affairs.

Liu was reluctant to confess that most Chinese could not read or write. He expressed hope that they were making progress in educating them. In camp many unit commanders posted characters together with sketches representing their meaning. During a long march, commanders pinned such sketches and characters on the backs of their soldiers in order that the man following would memorize the characters.

Liu said it was necessary that the soldiers learn to read and know some calligraphy since they were required to teach peasants. He said their men also made up stories to amuse the local people or composed plays and performed them for the villagers. Both the stories and the plays educated people on the thoughts and policies of Mao. He added that professional shows toured certain areas for the same purpose of promoting Mao's thoughts.

Liu wanted us to hurry over to other parts of the arsenal, but suggested we stop first to eat. We stopped in the village to buy *chou tsais* (small dumplings stuffed with meat or vegetables), baked sweet potatoes, and steamed bread. We sat on the ground near a small stream to eat. Food, native or otherwise, was always of interest to me. I asked Liu, "What do the NFA soldiers get for rations?"

He explained the ration system as follows: Each soldier received monthly about four or five catties of meat (one catty equals 1.1 pounds) and around 50 catties of cereals and vegetables. In addition, the soldier got enough salt, seasoning, oil, and fuel to cook his food. He asked us how that compared with the amount of food a marine received.

I asked Hi to reply because he had been the mess officer in Tientsin. I wasn't the one to ask, since my usual consumption of food, when available, was considered above the normal intake.

Hi answered that he couldn't say in terms of pounds or catties, but would guess a marine got about three quarters of a pound of meat or more every day, or about six times more than Liu's soldiers got. He guessed U.S. Marines ate about half again as much starch as Liu's soldiers ate and about the same amount of vegetables. Hi said: "Marines are primarily meat and potato eaters. If a marine ate only potatoes, he would be eating about 30 medium-sized potatoes each day. That's a lot of chow."

Liu continued to discuss their soldiers' rations and how they were issued to a group of men, perhaps a squad in his terms. The men took turns cooking. This saved both fuel and food. Individual cooking was not permitted. When engaged in fighting the enemy, cooked rice or other cooked grains were carried out to the location of the soldiers by local civilians. Liu laughed and said: "We welcome hot food. Cold food is not good."

"The canned food we marines eat during combat is not so good either," commented Johnny Mac. He explained how the Marine Corps had regular cooks for battalion-size units. He said he could see two big differences in the food fed their troops and ours. "First," he said, "marines eat a lot more meat. Second, your fighters have to grow a part of their own food. We marines don't. In fact, our men are discouraged from undertaking any work other than being a marine."

Liu thought the difference was because our country had a surplus of food, but China had been short of food for many years. Famines had been common. Only three years before, in 1942, there had been a devastating famine in the Honan Province to the northwest of Anwhei. Several million people died of starvation. Liu said that even though we ex–Japanese prisoners of war knew about hunger and starvation, we still hadn't walked where rotting corpses lay strewn along the roadside or smelled the stench of decaying bodies. He said that we had not watched a mother holding a dead baby for days on end because she did not have the strength to bury it. And he didn't think we had seen dogs digging up dead bodies to eat, nor the revolting practice of cannibalism which existed in Honan during the famine. He said, "People ate anything to stay alive."

Kinney asked if it was possible to get food in adjoining provinces. Liu explained there was food in Shensi and Anwhei, but that transportation was lacking to move supplies into the famine area. He personally believed that the central (Kuomintang) government did not act quickly enough to prevent a famine. He said that lack of transportation could be considered — after famine and the Yellow River — an additional curse to China.

Hi commented that perhaps the problem existed because there were too many people on the available arable land, and remarked that only about 15 to 20 percent of China was arable.

Liu nodded agreement and added that it was time to go back to the arsenal.

As we walked toward the main arsenal area, Liu told us not to expect any large buildings or factories. Most of the production was done in small huts which were widely scattered among many villages — not what one might call a factory. These people had had to build with little material because of the blockade by both the Kuomintang and Japanese. Some materials were smuggled through gaps in the blockade or bought in the black market from the Kuomintang and even the Japanese. He said, however, that their troops didn't require the large amounts of supplies American troops used. Living in an agricultural country with almost all of their people living on farms, they didn't need large amounts of fuel or parts for operating machines.

Machinery such as lathes and gasoline engines was rare here. The gasoline engines they did have were powered primarily by locally produced alcohol. Most of the machinery in this area was here before the Japanese invasion. Such machines were for making agricultural implements such as plows, harrows, and other farm equipment. "Fortunately," he said, "our people are very skillful and can repair captured Japanese machines."

Liu said that their most critical problem was still lack of fuel. Oil and gasoline were very scarce. There were no oil fields in Anwhei. Further, the Japanese controlled what big coal fields existed. The Communists' coal came from small mines operated by either Kungchantang troops or peasants. It had to be taken from the mine to factories on the backs of animals or in wheelbarrows.

The only reliable sources of power were men and animals. The Japanese were their primary source of material; the Kuomintang was another source. Of course, when the NFA troops moved north from the Shanghai area in 1941, they brought their weapons with them, but now there was not a sufficient supply for an expanded army. With no foundries in Anwhei, items of iron or steel had to be made from scrap iron. They utilized rails, locomotives, and other material captured from the Japanese. They also captured weapons from the Japanese and the Nationalists (Kuomintang) by ambushing patrols. They could also count on weapons being brought to them by Kuomintang or puppet troops deserting to their side.

As we approached one section of the arsenal, we could see a blind-folded donkey hitched to a huge, horizontal, wooden cogwheel. The donkey was walking around the wheel, closely followed by a small boy, stick in hand, who was prodding the poor animal. The large cogwheel was engaged to a smaller cogwheel at the end of a drive shaft extending into a long, low building. On entering the building, we saw numerous mechanical devices attached to the drive shaft by what looked to be leather belts. On closer examination, we could see that the drive belts were made of sisal or hemp treated with beeswax or resin.

Various mechanical tools were aligned in a row. Only one tool was utilized at a time because that was all the "one donkey-power" engine could pull. The biggest problem was that the revolutions per minute were not constant. It was all too obvious that there would be variations in the finished product.

The finished small cannon was a fairly decent-looking piece similar to a small mountain gun. It was mounted on two wooden wheels with a "V" trail attached to the axle. There was no recoil gear; it probably was not needed because of the very low velocity of the projectile. Black powder was the propellant. The best feature of the gun was its mobility. Still, I would not want to be the gunner because black powder is unpredictable. It does not burn like smokeless powder; it explodes.

I wondered aloud to Liu: "Is it worthwhile to spend so much time making this small cannon? Wouldn't it be more profitable to continue to obtain arms by blowing up trains or ambushing Japanese patrols?"

He replied, "Possibly true, but each time we blow up a train we can expect a large raid by the Japanese in the vicinity of the wreck and destruction of many homes. We have to be careful about the number of trains we attack and their proximity to a village."

Another item of interest was an attempt to make a mortar type weapon out of large pipe by winding it tightly with wire. From what I gathered from Liu, the partisans had better luck creating mines from pipes. Mines seemed to be a favorite weapon of the guerrillas because they could be laid under the noses of the Japanese. Although not considered an offensive weapon, mines greatly restricted Japanese movement and were effective against bandits or puppet troops attacking a village.

Hi asked how they could conduct offensive operations without weapons such as artillery and tanks.

Liu's answer to Hi was that small harassing attacks would wear down the enemy's will to continue to fight, but that they most urgently needed infantry weapons, rifles, machine guns, and some antitank guns.

Liu said they continued to defeat the enemy in small, well-planned operations, but for ultimate defeat of the enemy, large battles would be necessary. He said he thought that if they received some of the supplies our country was sending to the Nationalists, they could bring about defeat of the Japs more quickly. He said that the NFA had not received any supplies from Americans. It would be easy to provide them with such supplies since they practically controlled the coastline from the mouth of the Yangtze River north to Tsingtao.

They would continue to do what they could to build up their own forces, Liu said. At the same time, they would work to build support among the people for their system. In the end, he said, his country would be governed by a coalition of Communist and Nationalist forces, or the Communist party alone. He felt strongly that his country wouldn't remain divided between two parties.

While walking to another part of the arsenal, we saw peasants, primarily women, hard at work harvesting and threshing wheat and millet. The wheat was almost immediately being ground into flour. The flour mill was similar in operation to our old American water-powered grist mills, except for the power source. Two millstones about four feet in diameter and six inches thick were mounted on a wooden table horizontally, one on top of the other. Again, a donkey was the power source. Wheat being poured into a small hole near the center of the top stone was ground between the two stones. Around the edge between the stones, flour slowly emerged and drifted into a circular trough.

I thought it peculiar that the wheat was being milled before it was thoroughly dry, so I asked why they milled wheat immediately after threshing.

"Flour takes up less space than wheat and is easier to store," answered Liu. He explained that the farmer does not have the space to store wheat.

He can sell flour quickly and get a better price for it than for bulk wheat. He was reminding us that these people lived on a day-to-day basis.

Johnny Mac cautioned, "These people have been doing this for thousands of years, Mac. Don't try to teach 'em the Texas way of threshing and milling now."

The next arsenal unit was a black powder factory. The scene was very similar to that of the flour mill. A donkey was hitched to an axle extending through the center of a large, vertical, circular stone. The other end of the axle was fastened to a stable center post by bands of rope. As the donkey walked in his never ending circle, the stone rolled around and around in a horizontal, circular, wooden trough. Again, a small boy walked behind the donkey, prodding him to keep a steady pace. Behind the small boy walked a man with a wooden rake, which he used to stir the mixture. Another man occasionally sprinkled the mixture with water. Liu explained that wetting the powder reduces the chance of an explosion.

We watched the operation for a few minutes. The donkey was brought to a halt, and the man with the rake picked up a wooden shovel. He scooped the black material onto flat cotton sheeting. The sheeting and powder were carried to a nearby open field and left in the sunshine to dry. When dry, we were told, the powder was placed in silk bags (silk was produced in Anwhei) and stored under a waterproof cover in a distant hut. The man with the hoe and shovel returned with three bags on a wheelbarrow. He carefully took seven cans of white granular powder (saltpeter) and spread it in the circular trough. He then did the same with five cans of black dust (ground charcoal) and five cans of yellow powder (sulfur). Mixing the three elements with his rake, he spread the mixture evenly around the bottom of the trough. The donkey again began to walk his circle. The heavy stone ground the three ingredients into a fine powder and the man mixed it thoroughly with his wooden rake.

"There," said Liu, "you see a basic element of our combat operations — black powder." He further explained that black powder was a low-order propellant needing a large cartridge and bullet to be effective. "The bad part about it is we can't use it in our modern rifles," he said, "but it is good for mines and in older weapons."

I said that black powder could be used in shotguns by substituting a slug for shot and told how in southwest Texas, we used slugs in shotguns for deer hunting in the cedar thickets. "It's a damn good weapon at short range. You can blow a hole in a man you can walk through."

"Yes, that's true, Mac," said Johnny Mac, "but, Liu, what do you do for ammunition for your modern rifles and machine guns?"

Liu explained that first they capture as much ammunition as they can, but that their main supply comes from reloading old brass. They obtain the powder and caps for reloading from two sources: First, they use the powder from unexploded shells and bombs. Second, they buy smokeless powder, detonators, and regular ammunition on the black market.

"You mean you can buy those things from the Japanese?" exclaimed Kinney.

"Yes," Liu replied, explaining that they had things the local Japanese, Kuomintang, and puppet commanders needed. They more or less swapped or bartered, refusing to let war stop all commerce. Of course, in most cases, the people from whom they bought might not have known the ultimate use of the material. He said that in other cases, they did not care how the material was used. After a few more moments of explanation, he suggested that we move on to another part of the arsenal.

He led us to another hut inside high revetments, about a mile away. Upon our arrival, I could see in the revetments several stacks of unexploded shells and aerial bombs. The stacks were camouflaged by thick thatches of straw, which also helped maintain them at a low temperature. Inside were two men who had the job of defusing the explosive projectiles. The dismantling was done by other men in huts about a half-mile away.

Liu asked us if we would like to watch the men defuse one of the projectiles, but there were no volunteers. I certainly had no ambition to watch a bomb disposal unit at work on a rusty projectile, particularly at close range. Neither did any of the others. Liu told us that frequently members of the bomb defusing group had been killed, but there were always volunteers for the dangerous job. Apparently, the Japanese did not booby trap their bombs. Or, if they did, they didn't do a very good job.

We walked to the dismantling area to watch the operation. That was probably not too smart either. A spark here or there could have set off an earthquake from the several bombs scattered in the vicinity. Approaching one revetment, we heard the sound of hammering in a nearby hut. Liu stuck his head in the door of the hut and called for the person inside to come out. The hammering stopped, and a soldier appeared at the door and invited us inside.

Upon entering we saw an old, corroded, 500-pound bomb lying in the middle of the earthen floor. I glanced at the hammer the man had been using and was relieved to see a wooden mallet. Thank God. No sparks. With Liu as the interpreter, the soldier explained that he removed the powder from the casings, doing his best not to detonate it. After the powder was removed, he took a small portion over to another hut for it to be analyzed.

Liu asked the man if the work was dangerous. He replied that it was but *mei yo fa tzu* (there was no other way) and continued with his work. We made a rather hasty retreat.

In an adjacent area, there was a laboratory for testing the various explosives to determine their compositions. The technician in charge was a graduate chemist from a university in Shanghai and spoke excellent

English. It was strange to see familiar chemical apparatus—Bunsen burners, test tubes, etc.—in a mud hut in the hinterland of China. It was most interesting to me that the gas for the Bunsen burners was obtained from the familiar night soil jars. Human and animal excretions were mixed in a large earthen jar. The resulting gas was piped up to the laboratory. The technician said the only difficulty here was the lack of pressure normally found in the coal gas systems used in Shanghai.

Of course, that prompted the question to Liu about use of methane gas from night soil jars for cooking and heating. He said he supposed many farmers had not thought about it. The custom here was to allow the night soil to ferment, or to mature, before spreading it on fields.

The technician entered the conversation, explaining their difficulty in obtaining material for the manufacture of detonators or percussion caps. He said that they got most of their fulminate of mercury through the black market, but they were now attempting to manufacture some kind of acid from which they could make fulminate of mercury. He said, "We have not yet reached the stage of producing the necessary acids. When we do, we will be able to manufacture ammunition a lot easier and faster."

I remarked to Liu: "He seems to know what he is talking about, but isn't it about time to look at the rest of the arsenal?"

Liu readily agreed. We thanked the technician and moved on to another hut. There empty rifle and machine gun cartridges were forced into molds designed to ensure uniformity for each type of cartridge.

Watching some badly deformed cartridge cases being reshaped for reloading intensified my reluctance to fire any rounds. My fear of the brass being greatly weakened by many firings and by the constant reshaping was intensified. Reshaping and reloading were justified in this case, but all metal eventually becomes fatigued and has a breaking point. When questioned on that thought, Liu acknowledged that there had been several incidents where there had been injuries caused by exploding faulty ammunition. He also told us that the great variety of weapons used by the NFA caused difficulty in supplying ammunition to the troops and problems in the reloading process.

A separate hut was in use for placing new primers in ammunition. Brass and wooden tools were used to set new primers or detonators in cartridges. Such tools decreased the possibility of exploding the primers.

We walked another mile or so to a village where both black and smokeless powder were stored. The rifle and pistol cartridges were loaded with powder, and bullets were crimped in place. The finished products were carefully examined for deformed, long, or short rounds and fitted into clips of five. It was amazing how fast the workers could do the job and still find bad rounds to cast aside, particularly since the work was done by soldiers, many of whom were missing one or more limbs.

Johnny Mac commented, "With so much of this ammunition work done by hand, I don't see how you can supply enough ammo even to conduct ambushes."

Liu quoted another Red Army aphorism: "Each soldier has one bullet for the preparation, one for the attack, and one for the pursuit." He attributed this saying to Chu Teh, then the leader of the Eighteenth Army Group.

One could not help admiring the courage, tenacity, and ingenuity of the soldiers, as well as the workers in the arsenal. They were accomplishing their tasks despite almost overwhelming odds. The men were intelligent and eager to do their jobs well. Liu told us that the workers were treated the same as the men in the NFA or the partisans. They all received the same rations and pay as the soldiers.

"Pay?" said Kinney. "That's the first time I've heard the word. How do you pay soldiers and workers?"

Liu explained their pay system. Pay was in *renmenbi* (people's money), and the basic pay for an individual was one day's production. The usual rate was about 20 yuan a day, more if a man had a family. More was paid to highly skilled persons in short supply, such as a chemist. If a person did not receive food or clothing rations, then the pay was adjusted higher. Liu said he couldn't describe in detail the method of figuring how much pay a person received, but that it was approximately enough for a person to feed and clothe himself and his family, if any.

"When you mention that 'pay' is one day's production, that's sort of a vague statement," said Hi. "Do you mean the production of a farmer or a man making cloth? What's a day's production?"

"All I can tell you," answered Liu, "is that it equals what our leaders believe is the average production of all workers."

"Someone mentioned clothing," Bish said. "What is the clothing allowance for an active duty soldier?"

Liu told us he couldn't speak for the Eighth Route Army, but explained the allowance for fighters in the NFA as follows: First, the partisans and the regulars received slightly different allowances. All uniforms were of cotton cloth. Each soldier was issued for summer two pairs of trousers, two jackets, and one cap. For winter he received one heavy cotton uniform, one cotton padded overcoat, and a winter cap. As for footwear, he was issued two pairs of socks, one pair of cloth, rope-soled shoes for summer, and heavy cloth shoes for winter. Liu concluded by saying, "How does that compare with the clothing a marine receives?"

"Essentially that is about the same as far as I can remember," ventured Hi. "However, our marine also receives a set of dress blues over and above the winter and summer uniforms. In general terms, once a marine receives his initial outfit of clothing, he is credited with a clothing allowance of money from which he must buy his replacement clothing."

"Speaking of clothes," I said, "isn't it about time we washed ours? Mine are beginning to smell a bit."

Liu said: "That's a good idea. In fact, we want to get each of you a new set of uniforms today. We're to have dinner with the commander of the NFA tomorrow night. He's eager to talk with you about the possibility of Americans landing in or near our area."

"That would be great," responded Johnny Mac, "but that might be some time in the future. We'll take that proposal to our government. But if we have to go to Yenan, dodging Japs all the way, the war may be over before we get there."

Liu said that as of this morning, they had not had any word from Yenan about our next move, but he hoped that we would hear something the next day. Since it was rather late, he thought we should wait and have a look at more of the weapons tomorrow.

Liu suggested we take a look at some of their Japanese prisoners on the way back. They were in an area close to our path. He said he would be interested in contrasting how the NFA treated prisoners with the way the Japanese treated us. He added that Mr. Wu (our former interpreter) had given him brief notes on some of the ways the Japanese treated POWs, but he thought the general would like to know additional details. "We'll take a quick look at our prisoners as we pass," he added.

On our way to see the prisoners of war held by the NFA, Liu gave us general information on how their POWs were "normally" treated. Supposedly, the rules of the NFA were that no prisoner would be humiliated, coerced, tortured, or killed. Liu admitted that the rules were not always followed by troops in the field, but usually every effort was made to ensure the rules were followed. The purpose of such treatment was to convert the prisoners to the Communist doctrines.

A summation of Liu's remarks follows. Japanese prisoners were treated differently from captured Chinese puppet and Nationalist troops who were segregated by regions of origin and dialect. They were also separated from the regular NFA troops and partisans for several weeks. During this period the prisoners were questioned closely, and an attempt was made to determine if any were spies, "known criminals," former landlords, or high-ranking members of the Kuomintang. If a prisoner was classified as belonging to any of the foregoing, he was treated differently, sometimes severely. Once cleared of wrong doings or beliefs, prisoners were permitted to wander within prescribed areas. Their clothing was the same as the Red Army blue cloth uniforms but was identified by POW markings.

Once the Chinese prisoners were cleared and had completed their indoctrination satisfactorily, they were permitted to either return to their home area or join the NFA as regular soldiers. Generally the Chinese preferred to remain with the NFA, because they would risk brutal treatment or death upon return to their Kuomintang unit.

The Japanese prisoners seldom wished to return to their units, as the probability of harsh treatment, including death, clearly had been made evident in the past. Indoctrination was essential before the Japanese prisoners were allowed any freedom. The NFA supported some sort of an organization which might be called the "Japanese People's Liberation Movement" to which some Japanese prisoners migrated.

The purpose of the organization for the New Red Army was twofold: First, to utilize the ex-prisoners for propaganda purposes, i.e., possible use as a reverse "Tokyo Rose." The second was more meaningful: to smuggle them back to Japan to instigate resistance for the continuance of the war. Although Liu claimed the NFA had had some success, particularly in getting local Japanese troops to desert, I was doubtful of the efficiency of the exercise.

As we neared the POW area, however, we saw a Japanese dressed in the Red Army blue uniform with the telltale POW markings smoking one of those foul Chinese cigarettes. (From the smell I could understand why they called their cigarettes "rats," "tennis balls," etc.) He could speak a little English and informed us that he was being treated well. We saw no other Japanese POWs. There were many Chinese prisoners standing around, and they all seemed completely at ease and obviously much better off than we had been.

As we approached our quarters, I thought of my first shave and haircut from a Chinese POW at Magistrate Ting's village and how good it felt. I asked Liu, "How about a bath, a shave, and a haircut tomorrow morning?"

"OK, we'll do that first thing. We'll talk a little more about the Japanese treatment of prisoners of war tonight."

CHAPTER THIRTEEN

Water Cure

A S WE WALKED away from the prisoner of war area, we discussed the Japanese prisoner we had seen walking around without restriction. It made my blood boil. The thought that he was receiving the same rations, clothing, and shelter as the Red guerrillas and regulars made me even madder. Perhaps I shouldn't have reacted that way, but I believed my animosity was justified. The rest of our group agreed.

Hi asked Liu, "Why in the hell do you treat those bastards so well? Certainly you remember the 'Rape of Nanking' and all the other atrocities the Japanese have done to your people."

Liu explained that the Reds thought they received numerous benefits by such treatment. Prisoners had assisted many times in getting other Japanese to come over to the Red side without firing a shot. Others had been detained in reeducation camps until they understood and accepted the Reds' points of view. The others who had cooperated had been very useful for propaganda. Still others had helped take small outposts with little difficulty.

Johnny Mac said, "I just get mad as hell when I even think of those sonsabitches." We knew how he felt after the vicious treatment he had received on Wake Island and then in Kiangwan; it made Japs forever detestable to him. Kinney agreed that perhaps some of the rotten treatment on Wake was because the Americans had given the Japs plenty of hell when they attacked. Jap losses in men, planes, and ships had been much greater than they expected. The Japs thought they were going to have it easy and were pissed off at us for putting up a damn good fight.

Hi said heatedly that there was no reason for humans to be humiliated and beaten when they couldn't defend themselves. He said that both he and I had seen many Chinese beaten and bayoneted by the Japanese prior to the war. At no time had there been any apparent reason for such action.

He added that it appeared to him the Japs beat Chinese for pleasure or "just for the hell of it."

I said that at the railway station in Peking, it was common to see the Jap soldiers using bayonets to push Chinese civilians around. I told how often, when we walked along the Tartar Wall, which overlooked our marine compound and the railway station, we watched helplessly as the Japs beat Chinese civilians unmercifully. There was nothing we could do about it. Neither could the Chinese. The Nips had the guns. It was all too evident that, as Mao said, "Power grows out of the barrel of a gun."

Hi added that it was probably just as well we hadn't had weapons in the prison camp. Otherwise, he wouldn't be alive today. He said he would have butchered a few Nips after Ishihara and a guard had almost killed him.

I agreed that it had been one of our worst days and explained that I had just left the "tin shop" to bring Hi some metal containers for the "coal ball machine" he had been working on. I saw Ishihara and his bodyguard approaching but didn't have time to give warning. They slipped up behind Hi, and Ishihara hit him over the head with a big club. And I mean a big club — "two by four" size. That knocked Hi unconscious.

"The sonofabitch continued to beat you long after you fell, Hi. The guard put in extra blows with his rifle butt. Ishihara kept yelling his favorite curse as he hit you. 'You goddamn molines think you so smart. I boss now! Not you!'"

I told how they would have killed Hi if "Handle Bar Hank" hadn't been approaching the area at that moment. As Handle Bar Hank (the prisoners' name for Colonel Otera, the camp commandant) appeared around the corner, "Ishi" dropped his club, but strutted around, looking triumphantly left and right, as though he had won a great prize fight.

I said that even if Colonel Otera had been close enough to see Ishi hitting Hi, he probably would have turned his head the other way. He didn't discipline his troops at all. In fact, he didn't do much of anything. He was particularly oblivious to anything Ishihara and his guards did to prisoners. Captain Endo, his second in command, ran the camp, if it was run at all. Otera was almost never seen, and Endo was seldom around. Most of the time they sat on their butts in their offices and drank tea.

I believe if ole Handle Bar Hank had not appeared, Hi would have been a dead duck. As soon as I saw the club descend, I ran to our so-called sick bay for Dr. Foley. I hoped Dr. Shindo (the camp Jap doctor) would also be there. Neither was present. An American corpsman snatched a few supplies, and we ran back to where Hi lay. By that time, someone else had found Dr. Foley, who grabbed a bucket of cold water and poured it on Hi's head. When he didn't respond, Foley looked up and said: "Mac, he's in bad shape. Get a couple of men and take him to sick bay." He told the corpsman to go find Dr. Shindo.

"I hadn't realized how thin Hi was until another marine and I picked him up and dashed for sick bay. He was as light as a feather. Although we hurried, there wasn't a damn thing anyone could do for Hi in sick bay that we couldn't have done out by the coal dust pile. There was no special equipment in the sick bay to handle that or any other emergency. We laid Hi on a bench, and as his eyes opened, he began moaning and cursing, demanding to know what had happened. Dr. Shindo arrived. He and Foley took over and I left, relieved to know that Hi was alive."

"I didn't remember a damn thing about what happened," Hi said. "All I remembered was a sudden flash of light and then nothing until I saw Shindo and Foley bending over me."

Bish said he wondered why we bothered to call it a sick bay, since all that ever came out of it was sulphur, baking soda, and a few splints. And he asked why Hi and I always seemed to get beat up.

Hi and I had talked about that many times. His explanation was that we just seemed to be in the wrong place at the wrong time most of our prison days.

When Liu said it was strange that Hi and I were beaten so much, I tried to explain that for some unknown reason, Ishihara and many of the guards seemed to have had it in for us. Perhaps it was because we were much taller than they or they just didn't like our looks. The only time I thought there was a possible reason for being beaten severely was in October 1943.

A group of North China Marines and I were cleaning up the yard inside the compound. We were working alongside the western part of the tall cement block wall surrounding our camp. Weeds next to the wall had grown tall. We were ordered to cut them and clean up the area. Hoes and rakes were issued to do the job. As an officer, I was not required to work (Geneva Convention), so I had refused to use the hoe or the rake. Our guard did not seem to care about that. But he became nervous when he noticed me poking around the wall with a hoe handle.

When the Japanese built the wall, they had extended it down past the water level. When I kept poking around, the guard became very agitated. He probably guessed I was looking for a likely place to dig under the wall, which I was. As I made a deep thrust with the hoe handle, he charged me with his bayonet. I sidestepped, and his bayonet banged into the wall. Infuriated, he turned and hit me over the head with the butt of his rifle. That knocked me down, and he apparently was satisfied. After I got up and moved away from the wall, the guard followed close behind me.

Out of the blue, Ishihara and his bodyguard appeared. The guards who had been following me stepped back.

"What's the trouble?" asked Ishihara. "Why you no work?"

I replied: "Officers are not required to work according to the Geneva

Rules of War. I am supervising our marines cutting weeds." I should have known better. My remark threw gasoline on Ishi's fire.

"These men aren't your 'molines.' They my prisoners. So are you. Japanese no sign Geneva paper," shouted Ishi. "You no damn good."

As he continued his tirade against me and all "no damn good American molines," it dawned on me that all the SOB wanted to do was to degrade an officer of front of the marines. I couldn't stand the thought. I saluted and started to walk away. A blow to the back of my head knocked me on my ass. Apparently, Ishi had used the loaded end of his riding crop. I managed to stagger to my feet.

Ishi became hysterical, and his eyes bulged out. Spit spewed from his mouth as he continued to curse me and all "Amelicans." Blows rained on me from stem to stern. The two guards struck me with rifle butts. The last thing I remembered before I passed out was two other Japs joining in the fun. I learned later that one was a Sergeant Major Orai, called "One Round Hogan," because he usually knocked a prisoner down with one blow and then walked away.

Hi said that some marines carried me into our room and that my face and hands were covered with blood. I had kept my hands over my eyes, protecting them, I guess. The blood was coming from gashes on my head. Bill Foley examined me for broken bones but didn't find any. He said, "We all know Mac is hard headed, but to survive a beating like this is unusual. Let's call it a great accomplishment."

Liu said that Hi and I were lucky to have managed to stay alive. He continued to talk about atrocities in China, telling how many of his countrymen hadn't been so fortunate. He hoped at the end of the war they'd be able to capture the men responsible for the atrocities and punish them. He said it would be a hard job, however, because the bastards would be well hidden in the mass of civilians in Japan. "I personally don't believe we can ever deal out enough punishment for their savage acts in China."

As we neared our hut, a soldier met us and had a long conversation with Liu. The latter told us the gist of the message. The New Fourth Army (NFA) headquarters had radioed Yenan (headquarters of the Chinese Communist party and army) about what to do with us. NFA headquarters assumed, that since there were American military observers in Yenan, they would make a decision about what should be done with us. Several days had passed since the message was sent, but no reply had been received. That was not good news.

Liu explained the possibilities of getting to an airstrip. He said that Americans had not used any airstrips in the NFA area, so it was doubtful they would decide to fly here to pick us up. Further, he indicated his local group didn't like the idea of our crossing over to the Kuomintang area to reach an airstrip. He said that they had always believed it would be best to go northwest. That would give us the chance to go to Yenan and then cross over to the Nationalists. He added, "We have not been able to contact them, as Chairman Mao has not given us such permission."

I queried Liu about how far it was to the nearest Kuomintang area which might have a landing strip used by Americans. Liu indicated it depended upon the way we'd have to go. He guessed several hundred li, and we would have to avoid the many pockets of Japanese and puppet troops between us and the Kuomintang to the west. We would also have to cross the heavily guarded Pukow-Tientsin Railroad again.

Kinney asked if any Red forces in that area were in a position to negotiate with the Kuomintang.

"I don't know," Liu replied. "Perhaps when we have dinner with General Chang, the vice-commander of the NFA, we may find out. As I said before, I believe we would have to get permission from Yenan to contact the Kuomintang about any airfield used by your forces."

Throughout the day, my left eye continued to swell. I asked Liu if there was a doctor close by. He said there would be one in the hospital area we planned to visit tomorrow. He got me some hot water to bathe my eye.

That evening (27 May 1945), we had a very pleasant meal with General Chang, Colonel Lei (chief of staff), and Commissar Soong. General Chang was a short, stocky man, muscular but not heavy. His round face was wreathed in smiles except when he spoke of the Japanese or Kuomintang. His uniform was of the same cloth as the guerrillas but obviously cut to fit him. He bore no marks of rank, but his bearing and demeanor bespoke his position. He gave the impression that he could be kind and considerate of his fellow countrymen, but ruthless if crossed.

Colonel Lei, slight of build, was a little taller than the general, but not as gracious in manner. (To be nongracious seems to be characteristic of chiefs of staff.) His accent betrayed his southern Chinese (Cantonese) origin. Commissar Soong, who was very slender, mustached, and smooth of manner, was pleased when I told him that he bore a striking resemblance to Molotov.

All these men had spent most of their lives in either the Kuomintang or Kungchantang army. They were intelligent and lively, but only the commissar had been outside of China. He had spent two years in the Soviet Union. He spoke English and, of course, Russian.

I suppose circumstances had altered my thoughts about food. I had had plenty to eat for a couple of weeks, and food was not as important as it had been a few weeks ago. General Chang's dinner was delicious and well served but not as wonderful as that first bowl of millet gruel in the old farmer's house.

After eating, Professor Wei, who had been one of Liu's teachers back in Shanghai, joined us. Both he and the commissar spoke English fairly well. They added considerable breadth to the conversation as they discussed the plans of the NFA. No large-scale offensive actions were planned until more supplies were obtained. Meanwhile, their forces concentrated on guerrilla actions and training. Their first major offensive plan, once supplies arrived, was to cut the principal railroads at several points and decimate isolated Japanese troops.

The general told us, in essence, that the NFA could provide American forces with an unopposed landing anywhere between the mouth of the Yangtze and Tsingtao. It could also provide many landing strips for American aircraft to bomb Japan and support an invasion of that country if necessary. He claimed such action would not only shorten the war but would also prevent the Japanese army in China from holding out after the Japanese government surrendered. He thought the Japanese army in China would try to maintain its hold on China and continue fighting even if American forces invaded and conquered Japan. That was the message he wanted us to take back to our government.

I nodded agreement with the general's premises, as the Japanese had been in Manchuria since 1931 and had probably built a large industrial complex there. They could continue fighting for a long time. It appeared to me that a landing of U.S. forces in the Anwhei-Shantung area, as he proposed, would be good strategy.

The general also told us that so far, the NFA had not had any real contact with Americans or received any of the supplies our country had furnished the Kuomintang. He blamed the Kuomintang for not sharing supplies with the NFA. Regardless, he believed that they would drive the Japanese from their shores.

I assured the general that we would certainly tell the commanders of our forces what he had suggested. I anticipated that we would be sent to Washington when we got back to the States and that his ideas should be included in our reports.

Professor Wei talked about establishing secondary schools and colleges in the area. Again, it was a question of supply of materials as well as teachers, particularly in science and mathematics. Many teachers in Anwhei had been taught the old system of education of pure rote, but this was not the type of education the Communists wanted.

Finally, the conversation shifted to our group's possible courses of action. If the NFA received permission to negotiate with the Kuomintang in western Anwhei, there would be an opportunity for us to proceed to an American airstrip in southwest Anwhei. If this did not come about, we were to continue our journey to Yenan, where the Communist Eighth Route Army was in control. Of course, we hoped for a transfer to the Kuomintang, as that would cut several hundred miles or about one month off our journey to an airstrip used by Americans.

Sketch of author by a soldier of the New Fourth Army, Anwhei Province, China, 28 May 1945.

The decision was made to wait another day or two for an answer from Mao's headquarters. If an answer wasn't received soon, we would proceed toward the intersection of the Pukow-Tientsin Railroad and the Tung-hai–K'ai-feng Railroad south of Tung Shan. It would take several days to travel to that area. After we crossed the Pukow-Tientsin Railroad to the west, we would be in a position to either proceed to Yenan or negotiate with the Kuomintang troops about crossing into their territory.

"What do you think of the possibility of an American submarine picking us up off the coast of Kiangsu?" asked Hi.

The general replied, "That would be a possibility if we were in direct contact with American forces. Unfortunately, we are not."

Concluding that discussion, the general told us he had heard about the bad treatment American prisoners of war received from the Japanese. Knowing that Liu had given us a brief summary of the Red Army's treatment of POWs, he wanted to know what we thought of their methods.

"It is very lenient," responded Hi, "in view of the atrocities your people received from the Japanese. If you are satisfied with the results of your treatment of POWs, that is the only thing necessary."

Bish added: "You can't change the nature of the beast. Self-preservation is uppermost in your prisoners' minds."

Liu replied, "That may be true, but we have had fairly good results with our methods so far. If the desire to survive has brought about the behavior we want, then it is good. We still have to watch and control them. As long as they are in our area, we have the means of control."

Kinney said: "We certainly received very bad treatment from the Japs. Many of our men died as a result."

"General Chang would like to hear a personal story about your maltreatment," suggested Liu.

"Mac probably received some of the worst treatment by the Japs," replied Hi. "He'll tell you about his experience with the 'water cure.' You may be familiar with it. I am sure many Chinese have suffered the same treatment. How about it, Mac?"

I began by telling what brought about the brutal treatment I had received. The desire for more food than the meager rations the Japs furnished had prompted a few of us to try to buy extra food.

Some prisoners, myself included, had smuggled U.S. currency and yuan (nonoccupied-China currency) into the camps. If more food could be bought, that was what we wanted.

The Japanese observed that small part of the Geneva Convention that required paying officers a monthly pittance. The men, both enlisted and civilian, who labored on Nip projects were paid a small sum as well. The Japanese established a small canteen meagerly stocked with Chinese cigarettes, jam, and peanut butter. The prices were exorbitantly high.

Characteristically, the Japs deducted about 60 percent of the pay for starvation rations of prison camp food, as well as rent for shelter. In my case, a second lieutenant's monthly remainder amounted to about 50 Japanese yen or 250 yuan. Ten Chinese cigarettes cost 20 yuan and a small jar of peanut butter (about four ounces) cost about 300 yuan. So every month I could buy a small jar of peanut butter. I had some U.S. currency and desperately wanted more food.

We used three ways to change U.S. currency into the yuan of occupied China, the only currency accepted in the canteen.* Many enlisted men and civilians worked on a project called "Mount Fuji" some distance from the prison camp. Actually, the mound of earth they were building was butts for a rifle range. The Geneva Convention strictly prohibited such work and many of the other Japanese projects, such as polishing artillery shell casings and working on Japanese army vehicles.

The men working on the Mount Fuji project had contact with Chinese eager to make currency exchanges for the prisoners at a price. This was the most reliable and favorite method. Unfortunately, Ishihara and his cohorts were directors and supervisors of the construction of Mount Fuji.

Another method of changing currency, for me at least, was through a Taiwanese enlisted in the Japanese army, who served as a guard in the prison camp. He would exchange currency for me on rare occasions.

The third method was through contact with a Chinese peasant family across the barbed wire fences of our vegetable garden. (The officers were permitted to raise vegetables outside the two main electrified fences to supplement rations for both the prisoners and the Japanese.) For those who could speak a little Chinese, it was a convenient way of exchanging money, but it was not reliable. Your money might not be returned. You simply took a chance, tossed your currency over the fence to the peasant, and he would throw Chinese yuan back across the fence. Of course, this had to be done when the guards were not looking.

The Japanese became suspicious of how we obtained extra currency. First, more money was being paid into their canteen than the Japanese were paying prisoners in the camp. Second, some prisoners had constructed electric hot plates to warm extra food they had managed to obtain. This led to overloading electrical circuits, particularly in the evening. On several occasions, overloaded fuses melted and caused blackouts in the barracks. The guards went berserk during such episodes. In short, the Japanese became very suspicious and, in January 1944, decided to find out what was going on. Ishihara was placed in charge of the probe. We called his savage investigation the "Inquisition." It was his idea of how to extract confessions from prisoners.

The first few people Ishihara called to his office were simply questioned and returned to their barracks. Later, he summoned prisoners unexpectedly in the middle of the night. This continued for several days. During these questioning probes, civilians in the barracks near the guardhouse heard heavy blows and screams of pain. Those questioned during this

*There were two types of yuan: one from occupied China and another from Nationalist China.

period were then confined in the brig. Peculiarly, the usual slim rations of soup and rice were granted to those in the brig; these rations were delivered there by other prisoners, who were warned that no conversation in the brig was permitted.

The water cure began with Staff Sergeant Michael J. Shick of North China and a gunnery sergeant from Wake Island. Both men worked on the Mount Fuji project. Then Ishihara proceeded to expand the inquisition to include officers of the North China marines. Apparently, Ishihara had been told which prisoners were suspected of exchanging American currency for yuan. Some officers were questioned and returned to their barracks without maltreatment. Dr. Foley was not so fortunate. He was subjected to the water cure, badly beaten, and carried out of Ishihara's office on a stretcher to sick bay.

I was next. Two guards came for me about midnight. My feelings were not focused with the same calm deliberation I had the night I jumped off the train. Then it was my choice. Here I had some idea of what might happen to me. I had seen the results of the Jap torture on Chinese. The picture of Foley on the stretcher was vivid.

I was frightened by the unknown, perhaps more apprehensive than scared. As I walked ahead of the guards toward Ishihara's office, I knew struggle would be useless and probably fatal. Should I just tell what I knew so he'd let me go free?

Regardless of the consequences, the latter was impossible for me, a marine. To squeal on my comrades was unthinkable. I figured the least I could expect would be another beating. I had withstood a number of those. The next possibility would be a water cure similar to Foley's experience. And he was alive.

Then we were at the door of Ishihara's office. As I entered, Ishihara looked at me and said: "Here's guilty moline. He very bad." I didn't reply but looked at the paraphernalia scattered around the room. Four guards with bare bayonets on their rifles stood at the ready.

All too apparent was a sloping ladder with one end on the floor and the other end on a table. Several long wooden clubs lay in shallow water on the floor. The stench of blood and vomit engulfed me. Then the water cure began.

Ishi hit me on the head with his riding crop and yelled, "Lie down on ladder." I lay down on the ladder, my head on the high end. Ishi went into a frenzy. He struck me several times, yelling, "Turn around, you goddamn stupid moline!"

Before I could move, guards grabbed me by one arm and leg and tossed me in the opposite direction. They quickly tied me to the ladder and bound my head tightly to one of the rungs.

The guards with bayonets stood motionless close by. One guard stooped and held my nose. I opened my mouth to breathe! Another guard grabbed a large, metal funnel and forced it into my mouth. Ishi, waiting with a bucket of water, yelled: "Tell me where you get yuan. Tell the 'truf'." I didn't reply. He poured water in the funnel and I sputtered and tried to blow it out, finally gulped it in order to breathe. I could swallow only so much water before my stomach became full and distended.

As I gasped for breath, someone hit my stomach. Vomit spewed into the air and back in my face. I couldn't turn my head to avoid it. More water was forced into my mouth. I couldn't hold any more. My guts were churning. My head was exploding. Sweat mingled with blood from the head binding stung my eyes. A hard wallop on my belly forced vomit up again like a fountain.

Ishihara cursed louder, and I realized with a sweet tinge of revenge that he had been splattered. Hit by a surge of watery vomit, he exploded. He began to beat me incessantly.

I found it hard to keep my mind focused on anything but trying to breathe. I did my best not to panic. I didn't want to further antagonize the raving maniac who was alternately beating me and yelling, "Tell the truf, you goddamn moline!" The guard kept pouring water in my mouth. Between periods of vomiting and gulping water, I was questioned.

"You change money? Who change money for you? How much money you change? Why you break rules?" All the while, Ishihara was cursing, ranting, and beating me with a club. He said, "I know everything. You better tell the truf."

I could take the cure only for so long. I finally told him that a Japanese guard had exchanged money for me, but I had not seen him in several months. Ishihara screamed, "That's a goddamn lie." The treatment resumed.

Ishi was a madman. Blow after blow. To the side of my head, across my chest, against my knees. Again the taste of blood. Were my teeth knocked loose? More whacks on my stomach. More vomit. More questions. More blows. I stuck with my story. More water and blows. I passed out and awakened in the brig. I was sick as hell. My belly hurt like the devil, and my throat was on fire. Taking a breath was agony. Blood poured from cuts on my head, and blood covered my shirt. I could hardly move. My shoulders objected to any way I turned. Every nerve was raw, and body bruises gnawed my nerves. I ran my tongue over my teeth. Some were loose but thank goodness they were still with me.

My brig partner, Sergeant Mike Shick, said: "Shit, 'lootenant.' I didn't think you'd make it. You were out so goddamn long. What did you tell 'em?" I repeated my story about the guard changing money for me. Mike replied: "Good! That won't get anyone else in trouble."

I later learned that several other men were questioned and subjected to the same treatment after I was. I could only hope they had kept quiet.

Several nights later, Dr. Leo C. Thyson and Captain John A. White, both of North China, were thrown in the brig after questioning, but they had not received any harsh treatment. Apparently, between my treatment and the questioning of Captain Thyson and Captain White, someone had broken and told Ishihara the whole story of how the money exchange worked and who was involved. We learned later that Ishihara knew a great deal before he started questioning anyone. Colonel Ashurst, after learning that an informer had told Ishihara everything, had advised Dr. Thyson, Captain White, and others to tell the truth immediately when questioned.*

In a few days the accused were brought before Colonel Otera to be given punishment. Mike Shick and others were given 10 to 20 days in the brig. The usual slim rations were brought to them regularly. Fortunately, or unfortunately, in a few weeks they were back to the usual grind of hauling loads of earth up Mount Fuji.

I was given 20 days' confinement in my room in the barracks to repent and show remorse for my misconduct. No reading or conversation. A guard was stationed at my door. I lay on my bed, a plank platform, every muscle quivering in pain. Every breath rasped my throat. Blinding headaches tortured my head. An all-consuming rage engulfed me as though I was still tied to the ladder. I vowed, "I'll kill that sonofabitch once this war is over."**

I was allowed outside only to go to the toilet. That wasn't too bad because January 1944 in Shanghai was rainy and cold. My rage ate at my innards, tightened my stomach, and I had a hard time eating the slop brought to me.

There were many rumors as to who had chickened out and squealed. We had suspicions but could never confirm them. I believe the Japanese tortured the Chinese working at Mount Fuji with our marines, and the Chinese gave Ishihara at least some evidence. My friendly Japanese (Taiwanese, actually) guard was never accused, to my knowledge, nor was the family living just beyond our farm fence. They continued their miserable existence in relative peace.

Liu asked if I had been frightened when I was called to Ishihara's office.

"You're damn right I was!" I replied. There were rumors that the Japs were using the finger bending method. (Finger bending consisted of attaching two wires around the second joint of a finger, fastening the wires around the wrist and twisting the wires together closely, thus bending the finger back.) Bamboo slivers driven under the fingernails was another

---

*John A. White, North China Marines, pp. 97–114.
**Ishihara was tried by the War Crimes Commission in Shanghai in March 1946 and was sentenced to life imprisonment at hard labor. He died in 1956 while still serving his sentence.

diabolic torture used. "I'm not sure what I would've done had they used either of those methods on me."

General Chang replied in brief. "I know what you went through. I am a graduate of the Whampoa Military Academy and was in the Kuomintang Army at one time. As my thoughts toward Chiang Kaishek changed, I was subjected to similar brutal interrogations. I was fortunate in not being involved in anything specifically targeted against the Kuomintang at that time. Therefore, I was able to remain with the Fourth Army of the Nationalists, which as you know, became the Communist New Fourth Army."

It was time to leave, but as we were repeating our thanks for the evening and the assistance of the NFA, Liu said that the general had something for all of us for our journey.

Several soldiers filed into the room bearing gifts for us. We were given cloth saddlebags, a light cotton quilt for bedding, and 100,000 yuan (20,000 yuan each, Nationalist currency).

We thanked the general and did our best to refuse the money. Our pitch was that we had been furnished with food and shelter since meeting with the Communist guerrillas, and, so far as we could see, there was no use for us to have money. Our arguments were to no avail. Their claim was that we would not need money as long as we were with NFA soldiers or guerrillas, but we would need it if we entered Kuomintang areas. We pleaded with the general to take the money back, but he refused. After a short discussion among ourselves, we agreed he knew more about the situation than we, put the money in our saddle bags, thanked him again, and left.

As we walked back to our huts, we discussed the continuing expression voiced by the NFA officers about the close friendship between the Chinese and the United States. All of them, including the general, always referred to the friendship of the Chinese people, not China. This, perhaps, was indication of their intention to continue their struggle for the control of China.

We also talked with Liu about the money given to us. He repeated the general's words, "You will need it if you enter the Kuomintang area." He also said that if we went to Yenan to catch an American plane, we would be with his people most of the time and would not need it. Then, if we desired, we could give the money to the Eighth Route Army Commander.

I had noted in our travels that the guerrillas and the NFA soldiers always paid for food or any items taken from the peasants. Liu said that the Japanese, bandits, and some Nationalist troops took many things from the people without paying for them, but that by paying for everything his troops used or accepted from the people, they were able to maintain support.

After we reached our sleeping quarters, Liu brought me more hot

The author in Chinese Communist New Fourth Army uniform, Anwhei Province, China, May 1945.

water. I used my shirttail as a hot compress for my eye. Liu and I talked a little about religion and the changed demeanor of the people in the Communist area.

"As to religion," Liu commented, "our party believes in religious tolerance and encourages the foreign missionaries to remain with their missions. However, we do our best, through education, to discourage religious activities."

I questioned: "Aren't those two policies contradictory?"

He said that they might appear so to Americans but not to his people. What their party was trying to do was to change the people's loyalty from families and religion to the Kungchantang. He wondered if we had noticed that the common people were more direct and frank in both words and actions than under the old regime. This encouraged them to move away from the old customs of submissiveness. It also made them better soldiers.

I was too tired to pursue the discussion of the philosophy of the Chinese Communists. My left eye hurt like hell, and I could barely see out of it. The water for the eye compresses had become cold. It was time for bed. I said, "I sure hope I can see a doctor about my eye tomorrow." Liu agreed by saying, "I'll make sure you do."

I yawned and said, "Good, but right now I need some sleep." Liu nodded and left. I was asleep before he was out the door.

CHAPTER FOURTEEN

Guerrilla Hospital

L IU CAME TO our hut before daybreak. When I awakened, my left eye was stuck shut, and it felt as big as a baseball. Liu took one look and said: "Good thing we plan to go to the hospital today. You need a doctor."

"Well, let's eat first. I can do that with one eye."

"Mac's a tough old bastard," remarked Hi. "He'd rather die than skip breakfast. I think he'll hold out all right."

Liu told us that we could have a shave before we left. He had brought a barber with him. Again, I had the delightful experience of being shaved from my shoulders to the top of my head.

The barber wanted to put some of his medicine in my ailing eye. He claimed it was very good for sore eyes, but I refused. "Barber pole" treatment was not for me. I preferred hot water compresses until we arrived at the hospital. Liu took longer than usual getting the horses, so I had plenty of time for hot compresses and a shave.

Now I probably looked better to my buddies. I had acquired the look of a Manchurian. My natural tan complexion and dark, almost black eyes did not betray my European descent to many Chinese we met. My Communist uniform helped the disguise. As we passed through villages, peasants would say: "Look at those four foreign devils." They usually didn't detect the fifth foreign devil.

The morning was bright. A few small puffs of clouds floated lazily along. One could hear the metrical chant of the night soil men, "hu yuh, hu yuh," as they swung past us in columns to fertilize nearby vegetable fields. I missed the sounds of birds so common in the States on a warm spring day. I wondered what had happened to all the birds.

Before imprisonment, I saw hundreds of birds in rural parts of North China. There I hunted in sparsely populated areas, but here the dense population reduced the number of wild birds and animals. Although thick crowds of people milled in the villages, I hadn't seen anyone carrying a small bamboo cage with a bird in it. Such a sight was very common in Peking. There, in the city, wild birds were very scarce, but caged birds were always present.

If an elderly gentleman didn't have a bird cage in his hand, he probably would be carrying a cricket cage. Cricket fighting was conducted along the lines of our sport of cock fighting. Challenges were issued, and bets were placed. The noise level rose as each owner released his cricket for combat. As the crickets chewed on each other, the crowd grew noisier. More bets were placed. When one cricket fled or was rendered incapable of fighting, the winner triumphantly gathered his bets and his cricket and turned to seek another challenger.

Here, neither cricket nor bird cages were to be seen. Perhaps there was too much work to be done, or such activities were against the "new morality" of the Communist regime.

Liu and several militia arrived with Mongolian ponies. Liu explained that it was a long distance to the hospital, which was spread over a large area. He said that if we were to see most of it, we needed to ride there quickly. He reminded us that we must return early to see a local play being performed that night. He thought we would enjoy it, and he explained that traveling troupes regularly visited this village.

Mongolian ponies were good mounts but they could be mean. It was necessary to spin them to the "on side" (right side) in order to mount. Hi and I were used to mounting those tricky rascals and had little trouble, but our three prison mates had difficulty handling their animals. Bish received a sharp kick on the shin. It brought a gush of blood that soaked his new trousers. He complained loudly that he would get lockjaw and kick the bucket. Johnny Mac's comment that then we'd have peace and quiet didn't amuse Bish.

Liu told Bish that they hadn't had any tetanus cases in the area in a long time. He thought Bish would be safe enough. He said the doctor would wash the cut with alcohol when we reached the hospital.

Bish let us know he'd rather drink it. "That way, I'd feel better and alcohol might cure my other problems."

A sensible remark came from our pragmatist, Kinney. "Let's get going."

On our journey to the hospital, we were joined by two men and two women riding mules. Those animals placed their riders in the upper economic class. We learned they were going to the hospital to be vaccinated for smallpox. Knowing that such vaccine had to be refrigerated, Hi wanted to know how the vaccine was kept cold. Liu's answer was that it was smuggled in from Shanghai on ice. Of course, that meant it had to be given quickly, since ice became scarce as the weather got warmer, even though they had some stored underground from the past winter.

That reminded me of an incident about ice in Peking. There in the winter, ice was cut from the rivers and lakes, stored in pits, and covered with straw and earth. At a cocktail party in the home of a member of the Italian Embassy, the hostess was serving ice in drinks. One person asked, "Where did you get clean ice to serve in drinks?"

The hostess's reply was startling: "Oh, it's river ice, but it's all right in your drinks. I washed it off."

Most guests promptly emptied their drinks in the nearest flower pot and drank straight whiskey or gin from that moment on.

As we approached the area where the hospital was located, several bandaged men were walking alongside the path. Others hobbled along on crude crutches. Some were carried on stretchers. Fighting in and around this area had occurred recently.

From a distance, one village normally appeared the same as any other. But as we drew nearer our destination, I noticed hogs were missing from the hutungs and there were no wonks running loose. There were no uncovered night soil pits nearby, and the usual accumulations of filth and trash were missing. Many huts had clay-tile roofs instead of thatch. We had arrived at one of several villages constituting the hospital.

It was difficult for me to believe that a hospital existed within those huts of mud-brick walls. I could understand the probability of ancient Chinese medical treatment being used there, but could not conceive how even semimodern medicine could be practiced here. Had these local, rural Chinese cast aside the belief that diseases were caused by disharmonious relationships between the living and the dead, their ancestors?

In the back country where I had hunted, floods, crop failures, illnesses, and other such adverse events were said to be caused by the living incurring the wrath of ancestral spirits. This belief, in part, was the basis of ancestral worship. From time to time, offerings of food, fake paper money, and other gifts were presented to long departed ancestors to placate their spirits. Ancestral worship halls used for such activities were commonplace.

I knew that Christian missionaries were the first to introduce Western-style medicine into China. Conversations I had had with Mr. Trevor Bowen, the American administrator of Peking Union Medical College (PUMC) in 1940-41, had enlightened me about ancient Chinese medicine and the introduction of modern medicine. Early missionaries, repelled and appalled by the demonic medicine practiced in China in the early nineteenth century, used secular methods rather than religious ones to attract converts. They offered rice and modern medicine. With the introduction of anesthesia and antiseptics, the Chinese tendency was to combine the old with the new.

At first, Westerners had little use for Chinese medicine, but as their exposure to Chinese pharmacology, use of herbs, and acupuncture expanded, their respect for it increased. Gradually an amalgamation of the two methods developed in China, although in 1945 the practice of Chinese traditional medicine still prevailed in many rural areas.

As we approached one of the larger huts, several members of the medical community came out to greet us. To my surprise, several women were in the group. But my wonder at the unexpected appearance of women working in a hospital was cut short by the sight of the prettiest Chinese woman I had ever seen. She was standing in a doorway of a hospital hut. The shape of her small breasts was apparent through the light blue cotton gown she wore. Her dress was of a design used in Shanghai for women's clothing. The restraint of a small, high collar gave way to the boldness of slits up the sides of the skirt. She was a beautiful sight. I was surprised that she could wear such a dress in this area where the Communists frowned upon capitalistic clothes. She had very black short hair that accentuated her pale ivory skin. As we rode closer to the door where she was standing, she looked at us with interest. But it seemed she was looking straight at me, and she smiled. For the first time in a long time, I felt a stirring within that had been asleep for years.

After we dismounted, Liu introduced the assembled medical staff. At last, he turned to the young woman still standing in the doorway. He introduced her as Dr. Ssu, rattled off our names, and said we were marines. She bowed and said in excellent English: "How do you do?" That was another shock to me — as well as the rest of my buddies. We all stood staring at her. She was not disconcerted; instead she appeared rather amused.

Liu broke the spell. He told me Dr. Ssu would take a look at my sore eye while the rest would have some tea and look at the hospital. I was told to catch up with them later.

I couldn't have been more delighted. Dr. Ssu said, "Follow me," as though that was necessary. This was the first time I had seen a pretty woman wearing nice clean clothes in a long, long time. She appeared to be a lady, not the usual grimy, peasant-type female we had been seeing along the way. A hint of jasmine trailed behind her. I followed it like a bird dog stalking a pheasant. The rest of our gang disappeared into a hut across the hutung.

She led me into a room with smooth, whitewashed walls. The floor was covered with a closely woven reed rug. There was a modern bed covered with a clean white cloth. My soaring thoughts expanded. With no more time to dream, she told me in a businesslike manner to sit on a chair placed next to a table with an array of surgical instruments spread upon it. As she drew up a stool to sit beside me, I couldn't take my one good eye off her face. With one eye swollen shut and a big smile on my face, I must have been a sad sight. An attendant brought in an oil lantern and set it on the table. Her skin glowed in the light while her dark, almond-shaped eyes looked questioningly at me. I was mesmerized.

She wondered aloud, "Can't you talk?"

I stammered a heartfelt sentiment. "Yes, but seeing such a beautiful lady has made me speechless. I'm wondering how you happen to be here."

She laughed softly and said to me, "Thank you for the compliment. It's good to see an American. I'll tell you a little of why I am here. I was brought up and educated in Shanghai. In those years, I watched marines parade down Bubbling Well Road. I have always wanted to meet a marine. My parents wouldn't permit me to be near a marine or other foreigners. Then the war came along before I was old enough to consider defying my parents' wishes. I am pleased to see you."

Those last words awakened me. "Well, now you've met a marine. I'm very glad to meet you, too."

I thought it was great that she spoke English, so I asked if she would tell me more about herself. She said she would—"but first I will examine your eye."

She swabbed my eye, turned the lid up, and told me a pustule inside my upper lid was causing the irritation and infection. "I'll open the pustule and treat it with ointment."

She peeled back the lid again and deftly opened the pustule. Doctor's instructions followed. "Remain seated. I want to be sure the discharge has drained properly. Let your friends go on with their visit."

I was very happy to sit there, listen to her soft voice, and catch the scent of her perfume. She continued with her story.

She had been one of the few women to study medicine in Shanghai. It was over strong objections from her family and friends, who believed in the old Chinese ways. But she said she was determined to study medicine and bring modern medicine to the rural Chinese.

When I asked if she was married, she told me of her determination not to become a prearranged bride. (Often in old China, the bride and groom did not see each other until their wedding day. Their marriage was arranged by their families and a marriage broker.)

She had met an officer in the Kuomintang Fourth Army, and they were engaged to be married, but he was killed by Nationalist soldiers when the Kuomintang Fourth Army moved north of the Yangtze in 1941 to join the Communists. Because of her fiancé's death, she decided to go north when she finished her studies to join what had become the Communist New Fourth Army.

I listened, enthralled. God, it had been so long since I had been close to a pretty woman. Youthful hormones raced through my body. Weakened physically from those years of near starvation, one of the more prominent symptoms was missing. As I sat there and watched her, I wondered, had prison camp robbed me of my manhood?

She interrupted with a very different question, "Does your eye feel better?" I nodded yes and suggested that perhaps I needed additional treatment. She assured me my eye would improve now. But to my great pleasure, she asked if I would tell her how my friends and I happened to be there in Anwhei. I explained briefly about our long trek with NFA guerrillas and said that we were on our way to an area near Tung Shan. I added that there had been many difficulties en route, but that meeting her was the highlight of the trip.

"Speaking of my trouble getting here," I said, "it must have been difficult to establish a hospital in this area."

"It has been," she said, and she went on to explain that the blockade of this area by the Kuomintang and Japanese had prevented the Communists from getting many of the things they needed. Without autoclaves, they boiled their instruments to sterilize them. They used locally produced silk thread to suture wounds. Many of their surgical instruments had been made in a nearby arsenal. She said the hospital was in constant danger of being destroyed by the Japanese during their routine raids. They had prepared waterproof cases for burying instruments when the Japanese raided the area. She added, "We must be ready to leave the village within an hour of being warned."

An attendant brought us cups and a pot of tea. Dr. Ssu made the suggestion that since my friends had probably had their tea by now, we could just sit and chat a little longer. "I haven't spoken English in a long time. It is a pleasure to do so." I could vouch for that.

The beautiful doctor continued her story, telling how their primary duty was the prevention of widespread and recurrent diseases. They conducted mass campaigns against epidemic diseases such as cholera, malaria, and typhoid fever. Improved hygiene resulted.

They had trained their barefoot doctors to perform low-level medical services and to educate peasants in public and personal hygiene. But it was difficult to improve hygiene when soap was hard to get and very expensive. Dr. Ssu mentioned that soap could be made with vegetable oil and wood ashes, but the peasants needed the oil for food. The choice between oil for food and oil for washing was an obvious one. I said I had heard some peasants used the inner bark of a tree they call a "soap tree." Its inner bark (and some say its beans) made suds similar to soap. I wasn't surprised to learn that more than half of the babies born died before reaching one year of age. Such a death rate was the result of poor personal hygiene.

She said that many local citizens believed in ancient methods of treatment, such as wearing amulets and casting spells to cure diseases. It had been hard to get them to accept new methods. This hospital group found it best to use some of the old methods, such as acupuncture, along with modern medicine to gradually win the local Chinese over to the new way. Acupuncture had been used as an anesthesia, both local and general. She said old herbal remedies were used because of scarcity of modern medicines. She also said the ointment she had put in my eye was an herbal remedy with a slight narcotic effect. Whatever it was, I was transformed. It gave me courage to say, "I wish it were possible to see you again."

With a smile she said, "I would like that, but you are leaving the area." She asked which direction we were going. When I told her we were on our way to Tung Shan, she was quiet a moment. Then she said, "Perhaps I could arrange to visit the small regional hospital near Tung Shan when you are there. I will see if it can be done." Then she added, "It would be wise for me to examine your eye again."

My spirits soared. Gratefully, I accepted a pair of sunglasses she said she had brought with her from Shanghai. She said, "Please wear these glasses. They will help your eye to heal, and perhaps you will think of our meeting." I assured her that I would wear them and hoped for the chance to see her again and return them. She gave me some ointment to use three times a day. "And now you must join your friends," she said, walking with me along the passageway. Before the others came into sight, she brushed the side of my face with her lips. I couldn't believe the wonder of it.

As we joined the others, they were watching a Chinese dentist using an ancient, foot-powered dental drilling machine on some poor soldier. What a rude awakening for him—and for me. It reminded me of our days in Woosung prison camp and the dental chair Hi rigged for our dental officer. Hi was a genius at making many things. He spent hours making a chair which had a foot-powered drill similar to the one we were now watching. He and I looked at each other, remembering the difficult time we had using a speedometer cable as the transmission element to make the foot-powered drill. Hi said, "Mac, if we'd had some of the equipment we saw in the arsenal, we could've made a better chair."

Johnny Mac said that most of us had been lucky to have fairly good teeth not requiring much dental work. Our dentist was able to take care of some of the severe cases. Quite often, when someone bit down hard on a rock in the rice, his expertise was put to a test.

Bish said it would have been a lot better if novocaine had been available. "I pitied those poor birds who had to have dental work in camp. But the fate of those older civilians from Wake Island who had lost their false teeth was even worse." He went on to explain to Liu how those POWs tried to eat boiled field corn. "It took them hours to gum the stuff enough to swallow. Even after a lot of chewing, the hard corn jammed their guts tight." (He stopped short of explaining that relief came only when one of the corpsmen would dig out the log-jam with his fingers.)

As I watched the soldier occupying the chair in front of us, I could feel his pain. He sat there with no novocaine and several acupuncture needles inserted in his body. One needle had a blob of something burning on the end sticking out. I asked: "What's that burning?" Dr. Ssu didn't know the English word for it. Liu thought it was called *wormwood*, but wasn't sure. He said that wormwood was supposed to keep infection from spreading.

Hi wanted to know why opium was not used to ease pain. One of the male doctors informed us that opium was taboo in many places in the Kung-chantang area. Anyone caught with it or using it risked immediate death. I wondered how the guerrillas escaped that dictum. When we first met with the guerrillas, we had been given opium and something similar to paregoric to control diarrhea. Distance from a central government dilutes control.

Liu glanced at his watch and reminded us it was time to go back to the NFA headquarters. Hoping for more time in the village, I reminded Liu that I hadn't seen all the facilities. "You all could have some more tea and perhaps Dr. Ssu could show me the rest of the hospital."

"It would be nice to stay longer," Liu remarked, "but tonight, we are to see a local play with the general. He expects us soon. I believe you will enjoy the play."

I thought, Christ, I've seen enough Chinese plays to last me a lifetime, but I guess I'll have to go along. We waved to the medical staff who had gathered to say goodbye, but the only one I could see was Dr. Ssu.

Hi asked, "Mac, what took you so long for a simple eye exam? All I can see the doctor did for you was to stick some ointment in your eye and give you a pair of glasses."

"Did you take a look at Dr. Ssu?" asked Johnny Mac. "Boy, I know why Mac was there so long. If Dr. Ssu would look after me, I'd get sick quick."

Liu was prompt in saying, "Dr. Ssu is a good-looking lady. I understand she is one of the best doctors at the hospital. I would like to become better acquainted with her myself."

Kinney added, "From the way Mac looked as we left, I think he would, too."

While riding back to our huts, I took out the picture of my fiancée back in Maryland, looked at it longingly, and wondered what five years of separation had brought about. The few letters I had received were most reassuring that she would still be there for me when I returned, but it was still a big if as far as I could determine.

Wasn't it too much to ask or expect of a young lady to wait so long? Many of my fellow prison inmates had received "Dear John" letters. One of my close friends had received a letter from his wife stating: "I want you to know before you return that I am in love with another man and will marry him as soon as I can divorce you." He was not the only one to receive such devastating news.

I pondered my fascination with Dr. Ssu. She was beautiful, seemed to like me, and was (almost) available. Was now the time to test my manhood? Had it been derailed by three-and-a-half years as a poorly fed prisoner of war? I'd like to find out. Would I have the opportunity to at Tung Shan? As I thought of the possibilities that could occur in the next few weeks, I mentioned to Liu that Dr. Ssu had said something about the authorities frowning on close relationships between unmarried males and females.

Liu talked a bit about the Communist's views toward relationships between the sexes and other moral questions. He said Communists took a dim view of close relationships between unmarried couples. It was still a problem because most of the soldiers weren't married, and the authorities did not permit camp followers or prostitutes. If a soldier got a woman pregnant, he was forced to marry her.

Women were equal under Communist rules and could select their own marriage partners. Prearranged marriages and concubinage were forbidden. The policy was to teach men to treat women respectfully, as equals. These rules had made the Red party very popular among peasant women.

Shortly after we arrived at our huts, a soldier came and talked with Liu. His message, unfortunately, was that no word had been received from the headquarters in Yenan about plans for our escapee group.

Liu told us we would go to a guerrilla area south of Tung Shan, where he hoped we would receive information about further travel and our destination. He said we could reach the guerrilla base faster by going across the Hungtze Hu, a very large lake located in eastern Anwhei near the junction of the Grand Canal and the Tung-hai Canal. He added, "At the northern end of the lake at Chung-hsing-chen, there is a large concentration of Japanese soldiers."

Liu told us that the Japanese patrolled the lake in motor boats. They randomly inspected many boats and often selected several to search thoroughly. He said that the Japs were looking for smuggling going on around the lake and the Grand Canal. Since many junks, sampans, and houseboats swarmed the lake, they would offer cover for us. Sometimes advance warning of Japanese boats was passed along by signals from one boat to another. If they came near us, we could hide below deck in the cargo. If we were close to shore, we would "bank in" the junk and we could hide in the reeds. Liu warned that there was a good chance we could be found. Also, the possibility of betrayal by puppets was always present. He said, quite seriously, "We will burn a little offering to the lake gods for good luck before we leave."

Bish asked how long it would take us to get to Kunming if we couldn't cross over to the Kuomintang. Liu said it would probably take a couple of months with many detours around enemy troops. Further, he said we would have to walk the greater part of the distance to Yenan because horses were not readily available in that area.

It would be best to sail across the Hungtze Hu because there were large numbers of Japanese and puppet troops northwest as well as east of our present location. Describing the approach to the Pukow-Tientsin Railroad, he mentioned numerous fortifications and blockhouses. It did seem we could move faster by going across the lake. "Now," he said, "it is time to eat and go to the play."

After eating, we walked to the "theater area," which consisted of a bare platform with a roof of reed and bamboo matting. A few benches were placed near the stage, but most of the spectators sat on the sloping ground in front. We sat in the front row with the general and other NFA officers and were introduced to the audience. The response was much cheering and clapping for America. At the end of the play, the cast and audience sang the "Internationale" and we were asked to sing our national anthem. Again, we responded with "The Marines' Hymn."

Liu told us that the play was typical of those presented to the peasants. It opened with a scene in a farmyard with a farmer pouring night soil into an open pit. A passing NFA soldier told the farmer that he must place a cover over the pit to prevent flies from breeding—an illustration of the attentiveness and kindness of the NFA soldiers.

Although the scenes and players' actions were obvious, Liu's interpretation of the dialogue helped. As the play proceeded, a farmer's child became ill because he had drunk unboiled water. A practitioner of the ancient, demonic medicine appeared and cast spells to drive the demons out of the boy. A barefoot doctor entered and told the family they must always drink boiled water or they would die. He also said the family must take the boy to the hospital for treatment. The practitioner of ancient medicine was rejected, and he slunk off the stage. The scene changed to the hospital. The boy was treated with "modern" medicine and recovered.

Lessons learned: Keep night soil pits covered, always drink boiled water, avoid ancient demonic medicine, seek modern medical treatment, and the barefoot doctors are good at what they do.

There were other scenes which promoted hygiene and health and the goodness of NFA soldiers. For instance, an NFA soldier received food from a farmer, but the soldier surprised him by paying for the food. (Apparently, the Japanese, puppet, and Nationalist soldiers didn't pay for the things they took.) All scenes were designed to teach lessons and show that the Communist party and army were friends and protectors of the people.

According to Mao, as the author of this book interprets him, literature and the theater exist not for the expression of private opinions but for the indoctrination of the masses with the Party's thoughts and policies. Liu indicated that it was the only way to teach the people quickly. He said that the Peking operas I had seen in North China portrayed ancient culture — of little or no use in the world today. Such operas had been changed to emphasize the sacrifices and actions necessary to obtain the goals of the Party.

The play was conducted with a scarcity of props. The music performed by a small group with stringed instruments tried to represent the moods of the play, and sometimes it succeeded. The play was entirely different from the usual Peking dramas where stylized roles were performed by an all-male cast. Here women played the roles of women. The lively country production provided amusement, hygienic and moral lessons, and political support for the Party. The audience laughed, clapped, gestured, and quoted some of the better-known lines in concert with members of the cast. Meanwhile, they ate dried, salted pumpkin and melon seeds, and peanuts, and drank white tea. They were having a marvelous evening. The Party's system of using traveling troupes to "educate" and entertain the peasants was apparently successful.

As the play ended, a soldier walked up to Liu and handed him a message. I hoped it was a message for us to report to an airstrip for transportation to Kunming. It wasn't, but it was a delightful surprise.

Smiling broadly, Liu handed me the paper. I glanced at it and my blood pressure went sky high. In small, feminine handwriting in English, the note said: "I have arranged to visit the area you will visit near Tung Shan. I hope to see you there. Ssu." The play had ended on a high note. It couldn't have been better unless I had been handed a ticket home.

Hi said, "Mac, I haven't seen you this happy since the day your team beat us in polo in Tientsin."

All I could say was, "It's better than polo."

Bish said, "Come on, tell us what it says."

I replied, "The note says, 'The hospital people wish all of you a fast and happy trip home.'"

We were surprised the next morning when Liu brought Mongolian ponies for us to ride. We had expected a long, fast walk. A group of NFA officers, including Colonel Lei, came to wish us a successful trip. We rode quickly to the northeast toward the Hungtze Hu and the Hwai River.

In 1938 Chiang Kaishek, in an attempt to slow the southern advance of the Japanese, had deliberately destroyed the dikes of the Yellow River (Huang Ho) below Sanmen. The river flooded much of Anwhei and Hopei provinces, drowning over a million peasants. The Yellow River was diverted from its old bed south, with floodwaters flowing into the Hwai River. The latter then became a very large and volatile stream that periodically broke through its dikes, flooding the land and drowning more people.

The Hwai River drains into the Hungtze Hu, and the overflow finds its way into the Yellow Sea and, at time of floods, into the Yangtze. The area around the Hungtze Hu is an alluvial, loess plain studded with ancient, eroded hills and marked by many swamps, lakes, and a very dense population. From village to village, as the crow flies, it would have been only about a 15-minute walk, but detours around swamps added to the walking distance.

The area is still subject to devastating floods. Once the river breaks its dikes in areas where the river bed is higher than the surrounding plain, it's very difficult to return it to its old bed. In short, the Hwai, with or without the addition of Yellow River floodwater overflow, is a blessing and a curse. It brings water for irrigation, but frequent floods are often bitter disasters.

As the sun moved overhead, the weather became very hot for late May. Liu told us that this was only the "little heat" on the Chinese calendar. During the "big heat," no one moved unless absolutely necessary. Sweat poured from us and our ponies. We stopped at several shacks along the way for white tea. Once we were fortunate and were served delicious honeysuckle tea made from dried blossoms.

At another stop, a thin, very old man with a scraggly white beard served the "tea." He carelessly dipped a dirty, cracked bowl into the jar of tea as he ladled out our portions. He also seasoned or sweetened each bowl with his long, dirty fingernails. He took the money for each bowl and secreted it in his vermin laden clothes. It was not appetizing, but we had long since become accustomed to such surroundings.

We left and followed a deeply rutted, single-lane dirt road. A zigzag trench wound from side to side, cutting across the road every half mile or so. These obstacles were to prevent the Japanese from utilizing motor vehicles. Liu told us that many of the roads in Anwhei had such ditches.

Several times during the day, we passed small groups of guerrillas walking in the opposite direction. We learned they were heading for the NFA area for training. I thought that rather strange in view of the season. It was both harvest time for millet and planting time for summer vegetables. Late in the evening, we crossed a magnificently carved, camel-back bridge over a wide stream and entered a large town, Kuo-chuang (32°54′N, 118°18′E).

We spent the night in an imposing wooden house which reflected better days. The family made us comfortable despite the large number of ducks and chickens brought into the house for safe keeping during the hours of darkness. I was thankful for hot water to bathe my eye and the ointment Dr. Ssu had given me. The swelling had decreased to where I could open my eye and see out of it. Awakened early by a braying donkey, we ate and saddled up for another day's ride.

We crossed the Yellow River twice to reach our destination of Chang-pa (33°08′N, 118°41′E) the next afternoon. Our first crossing was close to

Wang-chia-ying (32°56'N, 118°17'E). Liu had difficulty finding boats to accommodate both us and the horses. The river meandered among torturously many islands in the swampy area. The water was shallow, and the current wasn't a problem. Liu finally located "ferries," and after much pushing and shoving to get the horses aboard, we made it across the river.

Once on land, we entered a swampy area covered with tall reeds. There were many areas that appeared shorn, giving evidence that local people had cut reeds for fuel and for building houses. It was the first time I had seen swamps of such massive size in China. The air was thick with mosquitoes that stuck to us and our horses. Our thin cotton uniforms offered no protection.

Cantering through swarms of mosquitoes was similar to riding into the face of a sand storm. I was lucky, however; Dr. Ssu's sunglasses protected my eyes. The ponies energetically switched their tails, shuddered their shoulders, and flung their heads to and fro to be rid of the pesky bugs. We vigorously puffed on Chinese cigarettes, but the smoke had little effect on the mosquitoes. We asked in one small village if they had punk to burn to drive off the pesky rascals, but there was none.

"Do these damn bugs carry malaria?" I asked Liu.

"Some do and some don't," was his unsatisfactory reply.

"That's real comforting to know," Johnny Mac said sarcastically.

"I've had malaria before, and it ain't too bad if you have quinine," remarked Bish. "The Japs had plenty of quinine in Indo-China, but, of course, they wouldn't give us prisoners any. Then it was hell. High fever and terrible pain."

About noon we came to our second crossing of the Yellow River. It was almost a half-mile wide and fairly deep. Several small ferries were plying back and forth across the thick, yellow, muddy water. Oarsmen used *yulohs* to drive the ferries across the river. (A yuloh is a curved oar working on one fixed point and fastened to a rope attached to the gunwale. When one pushes and pulls on the rope, the yuloh makes a motion similar to a propeller.) The river appeared to be one broad band of yellow sand with scarcely a ripple. Only the high pointing of the ferries gave evidence of a current, roughly two to three knots.

We led the horses down a stone ramp to the ferries. They were agitated and frightened by the water. After considerable difficulty, the first ferry was loaded and sent on its way. With a load of only three horses, a sparse freeboard of a mere six inches remained. I was afraid the horses would move and capsize the boat, but with great skill and patience, the oarsman made it to the opposite bank. He made a repeat performance with the second ferry.

Loading the third ferry was not so easy. We used whips and blindfolds to get two animals aboard, but the third horse refused to get any closer to the ferry. We finally had to leave him with a soldier to be returned to the NFA headquarters.

As the ferry left the shore, one horse jumped off, dragging a soldier with him. We watched anxiously as both made it ashore to the bank we had left. As we neared the opposite bank, the last horse tore loose from a soldier, jumped about, and capsized the ferry, throwing all on board into the water. Thank God it was shallow and near the shore or we might have lost one of us and all our gear. We were wet and dirty but safe. Most of our gear was recovered, including the five 20,000 yuan money bags. We helped the ferryman push his boat to the shore, climbed up the bank, and went on our way.

Three hours of walking brought us to the San Ho, a small stream just outside Chang-pa (33°07′N, 118°45′E). The latter was a large, prosperous town of stone houses and cobbled streets. Many small wayside shops lured our appetites, particularly those with fresh fruit, including apricots. We were welcomed at a magnificent old home by its mistress. She immediately sent her children and husband on various errands to make us comfortable. Her husband returned with the town's magistrate to welcome us, and the children brought merchants bearing bowls of food. We sat and ate and ate. For the first time, we enjoyed fresh fish, river shrimp, mounds of white rice, and fresh apricots.

The immediate business at hand was to hire a junk to sail to P'ei-chia-su (33°32′N, 118°28′E), a small village at the northern end of the lake, a two-day journey. Liu went scouting for the junk. The rest of us relaxed and prepared for the night. I treated my eye with hot water compresses and Ssu's ointment.

Hi suggested that my thoughts of the person who gave me the ointment did as much good as the salve itself.

"Perhaps," I acknowledged, "but whatever it is, it has been good for my eye."

Kinney, changing the subject, let us know that he was just "damn glad" to see the thick reed-and-grass sleeping pads that were offered instead of wooden doors. "I look forward to a night of sound sleep. But I'm worried about tomorrow. I'm not looking forward to you two 'canoe school' boys navigating us across deep water for two days. I don't believe your alma mater gave you lessons in sailing junks."

"Don't worry," laughed Johnny Mac. "That water is so muddy you can walk on it."

"You guys can jabber all night if you want to," Bish said, "but I'm going to sleep."

Except for the murmur of the children in the next room, the house was silent. Sleep comes easily on a soft reed-and-grass pad.

CHAPTER FIFTEEN

The Hungtze Hu

A COCK CROWED next door. A hen proudly announced she had laid an egg. Somewhere nearby a donkey brayed loudly. Street noises echoed through the room. I heard the family scurrying about in the kitchen amid the prattle of children. Some of these sounds reminded me of a small town in Texas. The smell of stirfry cooking wafted my way, but the appealing aroma of percolating coffee was missing. Still, I looked forward to a good breakfast. I was up and about before my friends awakened. Hot tea is almost as good as coffee. Liu came into the room and loudly announced that he had hired a good junk for the next two days. Awakened, the rest of our group began questioning him about the junk and the weather. Liu reassured them of the seaworthiness of the boat and capabilities of the crew. As to the weather, he informed us that there was a good breeze and added that if it kept up, we should make good time. Hi said he was looking forward to the trip, but my other three companions were not happy with the prospect.

I admitted I hadn't had a great deal of experience with junks, but I had sailed one time on a junk at Chingwantao on the Po Hai (Gulf of Chili, a bay off the Yellow Sea). A friend's number one boy named "Goo" had a cousin operating a junk out of the old Kailan Mining Administration port. Unfortunately, in the fall of 1940, a severe storm blew the junk ashore, breaking it apart. This ended my junk sailing career.

I went on to explain that Goo had told me later about the storm that wrecked the junk so that I now knew what not to do. Don't anchor near the beach with a strong onshore wind blowing.

Liu explained that the junk we would be on would be fairly easy to sail. He said it was not large and warned us that good sleeping spaces didn't exist. We were to sleep on deck during good weather, in bad weather in the holds. He emphasized again that if Jap boats came near during the day, we were to hide in the hold amid the cargo.

The crew consisted of a young man (the owner), his wife, his father, and two small children.

I had slept well the night before on soft reed pads, a real treat. And my eye wasn't painful that morning—a good beginning.

Looking at my reflection in a pail of water, I could see the swelling had lessened and I looked almost normal. Ssu's ointment had worked wonders. Always cautious about my eye regardless of what seemed like improvement, I bathed the sore eye with hot water and applied a little ointment.

I was looking forward to the trip on the lake. I had sailed Starboats and many other small craft. Sailing had always been exhilarating to me, so I was eager to learn more about junks and how to sail them. An added advantage was that sailing would save our butts.

Before breakfast, we checked our quilts and extra clothing to see if they had dried during the night. Our clothing was dry, but our quilts were still wet. To hell with the sodden quilts, we had to get moving. We rolled them into tight bundles, counting on drying them aboard the junk. Surely there was enough rigging to hang out quilts. Our personal gear plus the food Liu had bought for the journey made a heavy load. We divided it as best we could for each of us to carry to the dock.

Thanking our host and hostess, we started for our junk's anchorage and arrived within 30 minutes. Already the sun was high in the sky, close to the yardarm. We were late in starting our voyage.

The so-called dock was an old stone sea wall that was probably built by Kublai Khan. I couldn't see the need for it because the water's edge was a good distance from the wall. Liu told us the depth of the lake changed rapidly from dry to rainy seasons, however. After the diversion of the Yellow River into the Hwai, the change in the lake's water level was radical. At the height of the rainy season, the water came over the top of the wall. The full flood waters of the Yellow River hadn't yet reached the lake.

Along the lake front, I saw houseboats of all types, shapes, and sizes. They were moored to poles or logs anchored in the bottom of the lake. Each appeared to be a floating junkyard. Several different types of material had been nailed or tied together to create a floating raft of jetsam. Rusty kerosene tins, reed matting, frayed cloth, and varied sizes and kinds of wooden planks formed jerrybuilt but apparently livable houseboats. It looked as though the poorest of poor villages had been suddenly transferred to the surface of the lake.

In addition to the houseboats, a hundred or more junks swayed at anchor. Their main decks were more orderly. Sails were stowed neatly, rigging was taut, and cargo stored properly. Each junk had a lake or river god painted on its bow. Also, displays hung on each mainmast showing the type of cargo carried or advertising what was aboard for sale. Large, medium, and small size junks intermingled, but the small, single-mast junks out-numbered the larger junks with two and three masts. Liu told me the single mast variety were the most numerous on the lake because of their shallow draft and simplicity of sails and rigging.

Liu estimated a floating population of about 200,000 or more on the Hungtze Hu, a lake measuring about 50 miles long. It narrowed from a cir-cular southern end (25 miles in diameter) to a 10-mile-wide, 30-mile-long neck in the north. From Liu's figures, there were roughly 250 persons per square mile of water. These people were born and raised on their boats an-chored near the coastline. All their work and play was directly connected with the lake. Several rivers flowed into the lake and the nearby Grand Canal. Many of the lake dwellers were fishermen, others freight haulers, and still others merchants who served the water-borne city. Merchants rowed sampans about, trading in all types of merchandise.

As we walked toward the shoreline we could see the activities aboard the houseboats and junks. There were chickens, dogs, cats, ducks, and even hogs living with families on the houseboats. Chickens were tied closely to the "gunnels" or kept in boxes dangling over the crafts' sterns. Ducks had more freedom and swam about while tethered to their mother boat. Liu told us it was difficult to keep pigs aboard because they had to be taken ashore frequently to feed. Ducks were easier to keep since they could find much of their food in the lake. Chickens were fed the few scraps remaining after a meal, or perhaps their owners could afford to purchase some grain from the floating merchants.

Serving as a conveyance to our junk was a small sampan about twelve feet long with squared bow and stern, a beam of four feet, and a depth of about 24 inches. Its weathered and beaten appearance did not breed con-fidence. It had no rubbing board or fenders, and its sides were heavily scarred and splintered. This sampan had seen heavy usage. The oarsman was a young man of about 25, slight in stature, but lean, tough muscles bulged out on his arms. He welcomed us as we approached his boat, but he appeared worried by the size of our heavy loads. Perhaps it would be too much for his sampan. I was worried also because its bottom sagged when Hi stepped aboard.

The oarsman shot volleys of words at Liu, and the latter replied with equal fervor. This exchange resulted in two of us being rowed to our junk first, leaving the rest of us on the dock. Even with only two persons and the oarsman aboard, the gunnels were practically awash. Fortunately, the lake was calm, but the sight of water lapping near the gunnels made us all fear the sampan wouldn't make it to the junk. Our luck held, however, and we made the trips safely.

I looked at the houseboats and junks as we were rowed past them. Small children wandered about their decks seamanly surefooted. No one

Sketch of a junk similar to the one in which the author and his four companion escapees crossed the Hungtze Hu in northeast Anwhei Province, June 1945.

seemed worried about their falling overboard. A small dog barked fiercely when we came close to his berth. Women on each vessel were busy preparing vegetables, washing clothes, nursing a baby, or pushing trash off the side. Junkmen were working on sails or rigging. Houseboat men were covering holes in their houses with odd pieces of boards or tin. Some were rigging mattings of reeds for shelter from the summer sun. Others squatted in the sun talking with nearby fellow boatmen.

Each vessel had a small sampan similar to the one we were riding in moored alongside or close astern. Cormorants lined the gunnels of one long fishing sampan. Liu, on the last sampan trip with me, pointed to floating restaurants and what he thought was a bathhouse. We were surrounded with the amenities of a city. In this myriad of floating dwellings, we must be safe from any pursuers, I thought. Certainly the Japanese could not find us here.

Hi waved to us as we approached our junk. He, an old sailor, was already poking around to see how the junk functioned. We threw our gear over the junk's gunnel and climbed aboard. Liu introduced us to the crew. Mr. Ching was the master and owner of the junk. His complexion was darker than that of many Chinese. Short, stocky, and muscular, with rough calloused hands, he appeared capable of handling the laborious duties of a junkman. His old father, a frail, shrunken individual with a thin, wispy, white chin beard and watery slits for eyes, was living evidence of many arduous years on the water.

The master's wife and two small children stood in the background, awaiting their turn to bow to the foreign devils. The wife was referred to as "the children's mother"; later we called her "Nian." The two children were both boys, a three-year-old and a baby of six months. Instead of given names they were called according to their sequence of birth, Yi (number one), and Erh (number two). It seemed remarkable to me that the children called their father "Da-da," but the mother was "Nian." The old grandfather was called "Yieh-Yieh."

Our junk was about 45 to 50 feet long, with an eight-foot beam amidships; it curved to about five feet at the bow and stern. It had a flat bottom and had a depth of about four feet with a draft of about 18 inches when loaded. A small shed forward of the transom served as quarters for the family. The junk had two bamboo masts — a short foremast and a mainmast. Each mast was strengthened with wrappings of rope. The sails were heavily patched cotton cloth with closely spaced bamboo battens. Each batten was fixed to its own bamboo-rope parrel (a ring made of rope, iron, bamboo, etc., encircling the mast). That arrangement kept the sails relatively flat and permitted sailing fairly close to the wind even though the junk did not have a ballast keel or sailing boards to provide transverse stability. The sails were hoisted from a point about one-third along the yard; consequently about a third of the sail was forward of each mast. Fortunately, the masts were not high (about 12 feet), and the sails were small. It would have been impossible for one man to hoist a large mainsail because of the weight of the sail with battens. According to Liu, this was a typical lake trading junk.

We helped Mr. Ching as much as we could, but we probably got in the way more than we helped. By the time information was passed to us through Liu, it was almost too late to help, but we did tie down a cargo of reed mats. The mother, Nian, was a better deck hand than any of us. She kept the youngest, Erh, slung on her back most of the time and was still able to help Ching hoist the sails and do her housework. When ready to get underway, Hi and I hoisted a four-fluted anchor and "whistled" for better wind. The breeze was about four knots, but to my surprise, we were able to move out on the foresail from the mooring and into the lake. When we hoisted the main sail, the junk surged forward on a northerly course. We at last believed we were on the way home.

Nian managed the tiller as she nursed the baby. Ching kept a weather eye on the sails as he placed a small brazier on a tripod near the family shelter and started a charcoal fire. He cooked rice in a wok and placed it in a large covered dish. Then he took over the tiller. Nian, having finished nursing Erh, laid him on a cotton quilt and turned to prepare the rest of the meal. She and Yi chopped cabbage, turnips, and a small piece of what looked like meat into little chunks. Nian poured peanut oil in the hot wok, added the vegetables and meat, and in a few minutes we were eating. I was glad we had our own small bowls and chopsticks. Was I becoming fastidious? Each had his bowl of rice, but we ate communally with chopsticks from the stirfry wok. It was good.

After a late start, we were eager to keep moving. As soon as we cleared the arm of the lake where Chang Pa was located, Ching changed course to due west. Hi questioned Liu about why he directed our course west. Liu told us he wanted to make any spies or puppets in the floating city believe we were going to land just north of the Hwai River. He said that after dark our course would be changed to due north, but we would stay close to the western bank of the lake. This course would permit us to land quickly if Jap patrols came close to us. We could hide in the thick reed beds ashore if necessary. Liu's explanation suited us, and we lay on deck and discussed the rigging and sailing of a junk.

Bamboo battens were common to junk and sampan sails for many reasons, the most important being that bamboo was strong, cheap, and plentiful. Sail cloth was very costly, and the battens protected the sail from damage. Bamboo battens would maintain sail area even if there were many holes in the sails. Some junks had sails so full of holes you would think the boats wouldn't move, but somehow they did. Some small sampan owners used reed sails, which rotted rapidly, lasting a year or less. Tradesmen selling bundles of reeds seemed to be about the only ones using reed sails. Cotton sails, even when treated with solutions to prevent rot, lasted only a few years and required frequent and extensive patching.

Another advantage of bamboo battens was that each was tied to its own parrel, enabling one to reef sails quickly. Further, with the weight of bamboo, one could douse sails in a moment. One disadvantage was that the sails had to be tied securely the length of each batten. That was a lot of work and made sails expensive. Cutting the cloth to a certain shape for sails also added to the cost.

As darkness approached, we prepared for the night. The junk's hold was divided into five cargo spaces, three ten-foot-long holds and one five-foot hold at both the bow and stern. Most of the junk's cargo had been shifted to the bow and stern holds and one ten-foot hold. The other two spaces, our places of refuge in bad weather or for concealment, were partially filled with reed mats and ropes of various materials. The reed mats were being taken to the north end of the lake to be sold. They made good sleeping pads. But more important, we could hide under them if we were stopped by Jap patrol boats.

The bottoms of the holds were flat on either side of the keel plank to the point where the side of the junk sloped slightly upward. The tops of the transverse ribs and the keel plank rose slightly above the bottom. The reed mats and ropes filled the gaps between the ribs for better sleeping. After placing our pads for as much comfort as possible, we gathered on deck for an evening meal of bread and pears Liu had purchased in town. The night was calm and peaceful. A few clouds hovered on the horizon, and the reflection of the moon on the water was very relaxing.

We talked about the fortunes or misfortunes of our former fellow prisoners. I expressed concern that there may have been mass punishment after we left.

Hi was wondering about the prisoners in the same car with us when we escaped. If there had been any retribution, they were the ones who would get the worst beatings.

Johnny Mac said he thought we were all fortunate that Ishihara had been transferred in February. If he had been around, he doubted we'd have gotten our tools on board the boxcar.

"Hope the sonofabitch's ship was torpedoed," growled Bish.

Kinney said, "I'm sure those on the train who tried to hold us back will regret the day they didn't leave with us." He added, "It's hard to imagine the food in Japan being worse than the food we had. Anyhow, I'm damn glad to be here. Still, I hope no one was punished because of our escape."

We came to the general belief that the prisoners left on the train probably did not suffer severe punishment.

Since we had been sailing close to the lake's western shore and in shallow water, Ching decided to anchor until first light. After anchoring and finding the water to be only about four feet deep, Ching took off his pants and jumped overboard. We stripped and joined him. Using sand for soap, we took off the grime of the last few days. The water was cold but felt good.

Hi, Bish and I were to sleep, head to toe, in one large hold and Liu, Johnny Mac, and Kinney in the other. The only way we three could fit in the hold was to lie athwartship on our backs. I fell asleep immediately despite the uncomfortable position, but I awakened shortly because the air in the hold was stifling and my back felt as if it would be bent forever. I went topside for fresh air and found Ching was up and had decided to get underway. Nian took the tiller, and Ching stood in the bow with a sounding pole to prevent us from running aground.

Soon all the others appeared on deck as the noise of the creaking masts and lapping water awakened them. We spread out on deck, glad to be in the fresh air, and tried to get a little more sleep. Toward morning a thunderstorm overtook us, and we were driven below deck again. Ching doused sail and anchored to ride out the blow. Our junk rolled violently, but we were fortunate that the wind was from the southwest. Had it been from the east, we could have been driven hard aground. I prayed the anchor would hold. It crossed my mind that my hold mates might become seasick. Unfortunately, Bish did.

He tried to stand to make it topside, but no such luck. Hi and I escaped the vomit plumes by squeezing against the transverse bulkheads. The smell of vomit was bad enough, but with hatch covers on tight, the holds recaptured the aroma of long dead fish and other previous unsavory cargoes. I tried to raise the hatch cover, but Ching had fastened it tight to prevent its loss and to keep water from flooding the holds. We sweated as we thought of possible entrapment if the junk capsized. To ease the tension, we cursed poor Bish for his contribution to our misery. We banged on the cover for Ching, but there was no response.

Finally, the storm blew over, and a wet, smiling Ching removed the hatch cover. We were damn glad to see him. He apologized for not removing the hatch cover sooner. He told Liu he was too busy trying to prevent severe damage to the junk. He said he was never fearful the junk would capsize or sink or he would have removed the covers. We thought it was a weak excuse, but Ching was the captain. Bish took on the task of cleaning up our hold, while the rest of us sat on the deck and laughed at him. He cursed us roundly and asked for some help, but his request was refused.

Ching, to distract us, asked for help in getting underway. The breeze was fair, about six knots. We hoisted anchor. The sails filled and carried the junk away from the shore. It was good to hear the swish of the bow through the water. Breakfast was the eternal boiled millet, along with some hard boiled eggs Liu had bought.

Nian was a remarkable woman. She sat cross-legged for hours on end with one hand on the tiller and the other taking care of Erh. The tiller, a five-foot pole attached to a large balanced rudder, enabled Nian to steer a course with a light touch. The slightest luffing of the sails brought her automatic correction. Ching walked to and fro, adjusting the rigging, checking on Yi, and talking with Liu.

It was a pleasant, sunny day. We sprawled out on the deck and caught up on the sleep we had missed while in pretzel positions in the holds. About two hours before noon, we joined a group of junks sailing north, believing there was safety in numbers. I leaned against the mainmast in company with Yieh-Yieh as we watched Nian and her children. The sun's reflection off the water was painful to Yieh-Yieh's eyes, and he constantly shifted position to avoid it. Since my eye was better, I gave some of Ssu's ointment to Ching for his father's eyes. Neither wished to take the ointment, but I insisted, and, with much bowing, they accepted it. I also decided at that point I would give Yieh-Yieh my sunglasses upon completion of our voyage.

Watching Yi was like observing a typical three-year-old. I thought he might slip and fall overboard, but not once did he appear to be in any danger. In fact, displaying good sea legs, he played a favorite game of Chinese children. The game consisted of tossing a small bean bag in the air with his feet and trying to keep it in the air by using only his feet. The rule was no hands. I had often seen other children play the game ashore, but playing it afloat on a rolling deck was most surprising. Yi could keep the bag in the air for only three or four kicks but doggedly kept trying to do better.

Hi said he had tried that game once in a village, but all he could raise was laughter from the villagers. He said it was a difficult game.

I agreed, having seen very few youngsters keep a bag in the air more than a few minutes. I also remembered several young boys who could kick the bag over their shoulder, catch it on their heel, and toss it back to their toes.

Ching was proudly watching his son but not so intently as to miss a signal that a Jap motorboat was approaching our fleet of junks. We quickly moved into the holds and covered ourselves with reed mats. Although Bish had worked diligently to clean our hold, the stench was still strong. The junk was too far from shore to bank in, so all we could do was wait, hope, and pray. We could hear the motorboat approaching, stop for an eternity, then start again. Finally the sound faded in the distance. Time hung in balance until Ching rapped on the hatch cover as an "all clear" signal. Liu cautiously poked his head up and asked if it would be all right for us to appear. The answer was yes.

We breathed collective sighs of relief and climbed back on deck. According to Ching, the Jap motorboat had stopped close aboard. Its crew looked at Ching's proof of ownership, glanced at the cargo on deck, and left. The Japs did not attempt to board our junk. Two other nearby junks, according to Ching, were boarded but neither was taken in tow. The Japs then went to the east side of the junk fleet and disappeared to the south. There was a strong possibility we could be stopped again and checked by the Japs on their way back north. Their main base was at Chung-hsing-chen, a village on the Grand Canal at a junction of several main roads. Their motorboat flotilla base was at Wu-chang-tsui at the north end of Hungtze Hu, some ten miles south of the main base. The Japs would return to their base as soon as the sun was low. Liu said, "The sons of turtles do not like darkness in our part of China."

As the devil would have it, the little bastards came roaring back as we approached the opening to the lake's long neck. We dove back into our holds. Again we held our breath and prayed. Our junk was close to the western edge of the junk fleet. Fortunately for us, the Japs steered a due north course and stopped a couple of junks on the eastern edge. They took one junk in tow and buzzed off to the north. Again, Ching tapped an "all clear" and we emerged, sweating but relieved.

I am sure Ching sweated as much or more than we. If the Japs had found us aboard his craft, it would have meant death for him and his family, as well as Liu. There was reason for both Liu and Ching to worry since the Japs offered substantial rewards (reputedly $5,000 in U.S. currency) for any American turned over to them. Neither Ching nor Liu could be sure whether or not some person in our fleet had seen us get aboard the junk and would turn us in for the rewards. Ching had taken a great risk in helping us escape.

The next day after we left Ching's junk, I asked Liu why Ching was willing to take such a chance when he knew he and all of his family would be killed if the Japs found us aboard his vessel.

Liu's explanation: "He's a member of the Party. We pay Ching for the voyage but he charges us no more than he would for his countrymen. Many of our Party members take such risks constantly, just as the first few families you met did after you escaped from the train. We think such actions help us to rid China of the Japs more quickly."

Our course changed to the northwest as we swung into the narrow neck (called the Ch'eng-tzu Hu) of the big lake. Ching wanted to stay close along the western shore for safety. The rest of the junks sailed a similar course. For us, it was chow time again. Nian and Yi chopped more vegetables as Ching prepared the fire. Liu brought out some sweet rolls he had bought, and we had a real feast.

After eating, our talk turned to a favorite subject of all sailors, sea stories and superstitions. Liu reluctantly agreed to query Ching about local beliefs, and his answers were very interesting.

Geomancy (foretelling the future by occult or mysterious means) dictates when and where the junk should be built. The geomancer also specifies the heading of the junk. It's similar to the *fengshui* (wind and water) belief that tombs must be placed at certain spots and that a corpse must be properly aligned.

I thought there was similarity between smashing a bottle of champagne on the bow of a U.S. ship when it is launched and the Chinese custom of killing a chicken and sprinkling its blood on the bow of a junk. Ching showed us a clay model of the lake god which he kept mounted on a shelf in his shelter. His lake god helped ward off the multitudes of evil spirits which constantly attack junks and their occupants. Among all the lake gods of which Liu spoke, my favorite was the "Concubine of Heaven," who blesses the junkmen with children. This was my favorite because, while the word "concubine" to Westerners implies immoral customs, here the "Concubine of Heaven" depicted not only pleasure on earth, but the desire of the Chinese to have many children—their heaven.

Hi described the antics and ceremonies our country used to initiate landlubbers when crossing the equator or the international date line. Liu was hard pressed to repeat our descriptions to Ching while laughing at our silly ceremonies to initiate "polliwogs" into the realm of King Neptune. He was hilarious when Hi described that a blindfolded polliwog had to "kiss the navel on the belly of some fat seaman" as a part of the initiation. We told him it was all in fun and no one believed in such creatures as King Neptune. We didn't want him to think we Americans were superstitious.

As darkness came, we were at ease and sprawled on the deck for the night. The shore was close by on the port side, where Ching could quickly ground the vessel in the event of trouble. I used one reed mat for a sleeping pad and a second one between me and my damp quilt for warmth. It was slightly chilly but comfortable enough in the open. I much preferred it to our stinking hold. To end our long conversation on superstitions, Hi then asked Ching for a knife and stuck it in the mainmast to ensure good wind.

The knife brought us luck. The next morning, a southeast wind, about six knots, was blowing in our favor for our journey. We had to sail up a narrow waterway leading northwest to our destination, a village called Pei Chia Su. Junks going in the opposite direction had to be towed. A long, plaited bamboo rope was fastened halfway up the mast of southeast bound vessels. The other end was fastened to the harness of a pair of donkeys or mules. Liu told us that men pulled the junks if the owner could not pay for animals — men were cheaper.

Tall reeds rose on either side of the waterway. Gradually reeds gave way to solid land. At the village of Pei Chia Su, our landing area was about a foot and a half higher than the water level. Instead of reeds there were rice paddies and fields of vegetables. Water buffalo pulled harrows through the muck of the paddies, leveling them in preparation for planting rice. Men and women were busy planting rice in leveled fields. Ching had a difficult time threading through sampans and water buffalo near our landing.

A soldier standing beside a huge stack of reeds signaled to Ching, who dowsed sails and coasted alongside the bank. He stuck a pole in the mud to hold the junk and threw a line to the soldier. The latter pulled us close to the shore. Liu jumped onto the bank and began talking with the soldier while we gathered our gear and said goodbye to the Ching family. It was difficult since they had become, in those two days, a part of our lives. We each bowed to Nian, hugged the two kids, and shook hands with Ching. When I came to the old man, I looked at his watery eyes and the white puslike material that had gathered in their corners. To me he appeared almost blind. There was little we could do for him, but I gave him the sunglasses Ssu had given me. They would help a bit, and I felt sure Dr. Ssu would approve.

Once ashore, Kinney and Bish immediately discussed with Liu the possibility of landing a plane for us on the level fields nearby. Liu told us they had tried a couple of times to level an emergency strip, but each time the Japs sent in a large force to destroy it. They had abandoned the thought of an airfield here until the military situation became suitable.

We walked through the village to a point where the narrow canal intersected a road. Liu told us to wait while he and the soldier found horses for us. They disappeared up the road, and we squatted by the side to watch the hordes of humanity passing. The peasants parading past paid us little attention because we were looking more and more like Chinese. No longer can I squat for hours as I did then.

The village was obscured from our view by huge stacks of reeds. Many small sampans and water buffalo choked the waterway. Boatmen had difficulty sculling around the numerous buffalo. One scene caught my eye: two peasants, each carrying a bundle of straw on their heads, appeared simply to glide across the canal. At the same time they talked and waved their hands with complete abandon. Each was standing on the back of a water buffalo. Such was the ferry system.

Liu and the soldier returned with several horses. Lengthy discussion ensued about who would ride which horse. I finally quieted the talk by choosing the one large Jap horse, and the others seemed satisfied with the smaller Mongolian mounts. My mount walked faster than the other horses, forcing me to go ahead, then wait. I tried letting others go ahead a mile or more, then I would try a gallop to catch them. Neither idea worked well, as "Clop-Clop" (my name for the gelding) did not know one pace from another. He simply leapt from one spot to the next. Each jolt drove my spine further into my head. By noon my butt was raw and my brain scrambled. And we still had to ride for three or four hours longer.

We were headed for the headquarters of the Fourth Division of the NFA. As was the case with our search for the NFA headquarters, no one was sure where it was located. By luck, we rode into a village enfolding the arsenal of the Fourth Division. The arsenal was similar to the old NFA arsenal except for their power plant. The manager was very proud to have a captured Jap motor, a power boat engine that he had installed at his central power plant. A series of overhead drive shafts, belts, and pulleys delivered power to the machinery.

I questioned the manager about fuel. Grinning broadly, he said: "We use grain alcohol. Gasoline is too difficult to get." As though to prove his fuel was alcohol, he took a small cup, opened a petcock at the bottom of the fuel tank, and filled his cup. To show us the fuel was nonlethal, he tossed the fluid down his throat without a grimace and raised his cup in salute. He then filled a cup for each of us and raised his second cup in recognition of the friendship of the Chinese and American people.

I gulped the flaming liquid down my throat and felt the fires of hell arise in my belly. I did manage to croak, *gam bei* (bottoms up) and turned my cup upside down. I looked at my comrades; they appeared as stunned as I was.

Hi, with difficulty, squeaked: "Thank you. Better than mao-tai" (a powerful national drink).

The manager was very pleased and poured us another round. It was our turn to make a toast to our friendship. With difficulty I raised my cup, we clicked cups, and it was another "gam bei." I could barely see straight, much less walk straight.

The manager insisted we make a tour of his facility. Being marines, we had our pride. Straightening up, we pasted smiles on our faces and followed our jovial host. Somehow we managed to show interest in everything. We passed machines making bayonets, knives, traditional Chinese broad swords, etc. But the only thing I could see clearly and remember well was an old familiar friend, a single naked, electric light bulb hanging over a work bench.

We returned to the entrance, and there, much to our surprise and delight, was a table spread with rice, hard boiled eggs, fish in garlic sauce, and tea. Unfortunately, small toasting cups lined the table. We ate our fill and, to our dismay, again came the courtesy toasts with cups filled with motor fuel. Toasts flowed like water: to Truman, Mao, Stalin, and, at last, to the friendship of the United States and China.

Not being used to drinking such potent liquid, we all needed guidance to our horses. The outside world was blurred, and the path wobbled. Although my mind flickered out now and then, I managed to climb aboard Clop-Clop. Once aboard, I said a prayer that I could stay on his back as he thundered onto a path. I hoped it led to the Fourth Division headquarters.

CHAPTER SIXTEEN

Nationalist Army

WE WERE GREETED at the Fourth Guerrilla Division Headquarters by our old friend and interpreter, Hu Ping. He had remained behind at the New Fourth Army hospital for treatment of a stomach ailment. Hu had both good news and bad news. The good news was that there was a strong possibility of establishing negotiations with the Nationalists in the southwest part of Anwhei. There was an airstrip used by Americans in the Nationalist sector. Once we were with the Nationalist Army, it appeared it would take only about two weeks to reach it.

These excellent prospects overwhelmed my disappointment to learn that Dr. Ssu had remained at the NFA hospital. Hu Ping handed me a note from her explaining her decision not to come to the hospital near Tung Shan. Apparently she had been thinking along the same lines as I had. It wouldn't be good for either of us, in view of the Communists' unfavorable view of such liaisons. She expressed regrets and wished me well in the future.

I felt both keen disappointment and immediate relief that she had not come to see me. A romantic encounter with Dr. Ssu might have caused bad relations with our hosts. Frankly, I was pleased she had made the decision not to come. All these thoughts reminded me of some sage advice I received from an old bos'n mate during my first cruise as a midshipman in the summer of 1936.

I was aboard the USS *Arkansas* in the harbor of Cherbourg, France. I had looked forward eagerly to going ashore in France, but I was assigned duty during the first few days of our visit there.

As I stood near the gangplank checking out other midshipmen going on shore leave, I watched some of them and the sailors being warmly greeted by good-looking French girls on the pier. A pall of disappointment settled over my face.

A grizzled old bos'n mate with many "hashmarks" on his sleeve who was checking out sailors on shore leave noticed my dejection and offered some words of advice. He said, "Son, there is nothing so overrated in this world as a 'piece of ass' and nothing so underrated as a good shit. You can do without the first but you damn sure can't do without the second." This bit of droll advice was accurate and gave me some cheer. I'd had more than enough of the second part of his advice during my POW years when there was no chance of making a comparison with the first part. Neither was there much chance for comparison here. The Communists, with a strict puritanical code about the relations between men and women, had made a decision for me.

The Fourth Division commander had decided that we would stick around in his area for a while to see what negotiations developed with the Nationalists. For several days we rode around the countryside with a small troop of cavalry as we looked at schools and small arsenals built by the Communists. They were very proud of their achievements in this region that had been devastated by the Japanese.

It was a beautiful sight, our column of Mongolian ponies silhouetted against the sky on top of the dikes surrounding the fields. These ponies had long tails but little mane. Their tails streamed out behind them as they trotted. Such scenes reminded me of Chinese paintings of Kublai Khan's troops.

Mongolian ponies, once in column, obeyed bugle calls, even to the extent of lying on their sides to provide protection against enemy fire. Such actions brought to mind the paintings by Russell and Remington depicting battles of the U.S. Cavalry with the Plains Indians. The commander of the troops gave us a demonstration of our mounts obeying bugle calls.

Although our ponies were well trained for battle, early morning scenes of troopers saddling and mounting were entirely different. As the bugle sounded for saddling and mounting, a maelstrom of activity and noise ensued. The ponies resented troopers mounting. To prevent being bitten or kicked while mounting, the troopers had to spin their ponies. The sound of snorting ponies and cursing troopers filled the air. After they had mounted and the bugle had sounded "move out," the troopers quickly formed a column in good order and we moved swiftly. The areas through which we passed gave evidence of having been thoroughly ravaged and pillaged. What had once been prosperous villages were now gruesome skeletons. Most bridges had been destroyed, and ashes marked the locations where villages had once stood. Very few farm animals remained.

Looking back on this tour through the Communist controlled territory, I view it as a maneuver to keep us there several extra days to absorb fully the utter destruction of the area by the Japs. In addition, they also wanted us to see what the Communists had done toward reconstruction and revitalization.

New Fourth Army cavalry unit with which escapees traveled a few days in central Anwhei Province, China, May 1945.

One indication of the devastation that had been perpetrated on the area and the people was that we had difficulty finding huts for billets. We traveled extensively at night because the troop commander believed this would prevent any spies in the area from reporting our presence.

At one village, I was assigned sleeping quarters in a hut occupied by an elderly gentleman and his grandson. Their evening meal was a vivid lesson in poverty and frugality. To prepare the meal, the old man lit one end of a bundle of three or four kaoliang stalks. By careful and patient adjustment of the flame, he kept it directly under a small bowl of water. When the water began to boil, the old man dropped a scant handful of millet and a pinch of salt into the bowl. He let the water and millet boil for a few minutes and then carefully extinguished the flame. The remainder of the kaoliang stalks was set aside for future use. A small bowl of boiled millet and a tiny dollop of preserved cabbage constituted the meal for both the old man and his grandson. The emaciated bodies of the old man and the boy were grim evidence of the area's poverty. We had existed on that same amount of food while in prison camp.

In another demolished village, we were assigned delapidated huts to shield us from the hot noon sun. Unfortunately, the fleas there proved to be more vicious than any we had previously encountered. They must have been waiting a long time for a meal. We gathered in a small open shed, rested in its shade, and talked about what might occur next. As we sat there picking and squashing fleas, we tried to decide what we should try to do next if the Nationalists and Communists did not come to an agreement.

Again I argued that going over to the Nationalists would place us in an unknown situation and that we should go on to Yenan, but I was voted down, three to two. Later that afternoon I noticed a change in direction of movement from the northeast to the southwest. I wondered why, if we were going to negotiate with the Nationalists in the southwest part of An-whei, we had not gone in that direction in the first place. I supposed the Communists did not know if the Nationalists would agree to accept us.

Explaining why we had moved to the northeast, Liu told us that two downed American aviators had waited a couple of months for the Nationalists to accept them. They finally had undertaken the month-long trip to Yenan for a flight back to Kunming.

It seemed to me that we were moving back toward the area where we had jumped off the train. I really could not understand all the circular movements unless the Communists were dodging enemy troops.

The morning of 10 June we were awakened by the troop commander with excellent news. He had received word that the Nationalists had finally agreed to negotiate for our transfer to their side at a village called Lo Shan (33°20′N, 117°40′E).* Further, there was an emergency airfield in southwest Anwhei in an area controlled by the Nationalists. The troop commander verified the fact that once we were with the Nationalist troops, we could reach the airstrip in about 15 days.

We rode to the headquarters of the Third Guerrilla Brigade and arrived there in the late afternoon. Again, we were greeted with good news and bad news. Negotiations with the Nationalists were continuing, but had not been completed. We were to remain at the Third Brigade headquarters until the next morning, 11 June. Again, we were cautioned to stay close to the Communist troops. Liu warned us that the Nationalists might kill us and blame it on the Communists in an effort to create bad relations between the Communists and the United States. This caution from both sides was an old one and was repeated many times by both the Communists and the Nationalists. Although we did not believe such would occur, we exercised due precaution by staying close to the troops of our current host.

Lo Shan, the village where we were to be transferred to the Nationalists, was located among small, rocky hills rising abruptly above a flat plain. Contrary to the usual mud-brick huts, many of the buildings in this area were quite substantial and of permanent stone construction.

---

*Richard Vernon Hill, Major, USA (Ret.), My War with Imperial Japan: Escape and Erasion (New York: Vantage, 1989), p. 322.

We walked up one of the hills facing west toward what we were told was the Nationalist occupied area. Here we found that the Communists had set up defensive positions along both the military and geographical crests. In the distance we could see the Nationalists' defensive positions, which were similar to those of the Communists. We could well imagine that this area had been the scene of recent conflict between the two forces. All that separated the Nationalist and Communist areas was a small stream. The geographical distance between the two forces was minimal, but the political distance was infinite.

Liu pointed to a nearby village and said, "That is Lo Shan." He added that about 40 or 50 miles to the west there was a good sized city called Ko Yang (33°31'N, 116°12'E).

We returned to brigade headquarters in a jubilant mood. Our festive spirit continued into the evening as we celebrated with a toast of mao tai to Chinese-American friendship.

The next morning (12 June) two Nationalist majors, carrying a flag of truce, walked over to the Communist position. As they approached, I could see the expression on their faces change from one of intense apprehension to one of great relief when they saw us. They appeared delighted to see us and shook our hands vigorously. Liu told us later that the Nationalists had suspected a trap by the Communists. One of the majors returned to the Nationalist lines to inform their commander that there were five Americans with the Communists as reported. Just before midday, he returned from the Nationalist line and informed Commissar Soong that all was set for the Nationalists to receive the five Americans. The commissar lined us up for pictures with our interpreters and the two majors.

Commissar Soong told us a battalion of Communist troops was deployed for our protection during the transfer. Looking toward the Nationalist lines, I could see a similar number of troops deployed in defensive positions.

It was difficult to say goodbye to Liu and Hu Ping, who had been with us for over a month of difficult times. When we were getting ready to leave, Soong presented us with pictures taken that morning. The prospect of getting to an American airfield overrode deep regrets of leaving our friends, whom we knew we would never see again.

Shortly after noon on 12 June, Commissar Soong of the Third Brigade joined Liu, Hu Ping, the two Nationalist majors, and the five of us for the walk to the middle of the plain between the Nationalists and the Communists, where the transfer was to take place.

As we walked across the plain toward the small stream, sights of battlefield wreckage confirmed our suspicion that this was an area where fighting between the two forces had recently occurred. That was not encouraging, but having two Nationalist majors walking with us toward their

Lo Shan, China, 12 June 1945. Left to right: Liu Young, Communist (Kungchan-tang) New Fourth Army (NFA); 2nd Lt. John F. Kinney, USMC; 2nd Lt. John A. McAlister, USMC; James D. McBrayer, Jr., USMC; Lewis Bishop, AVG pilot; 2nd Lt. Richard M. Huizenga, USMC; Commissar Soong, NFA; a soldier, NFA; a major, Chinese Nationalist Army (Kuomintang or KMT); Hu Ping, interpreter, NFA; a soldier, NFA.

own troops was some assurance that the Nationalists would not fire. Commissar Soong, Liu, Hu Ping, and we five Americans stopped about 200 yards short of the Nationalist forces. The two Nationalist majors continued on to their positions.

With some apprehension, we five escapees walked the last 200 yards to the Nationalists, where we were received with great ceremony by Colonel Tien, commander of the Second Regiment of the Nationalist Army, north of the Hwai River. Greeting us also was a Dr. Chang, who was to be our interpreter while in this region. He told us that a big reception had been planned. I thought he meant another feast and had no conception of the warm welcome that awaited us. It was almost dark when we reached the outskirts of the village of Lo Shan, but we could see in the fading light long lines of soldiers on both sides of the road leading into the village.

It was a Roman welcome. Children and older people stood nearby, waving small paper American and Chinese Nationalist flags. The biggest surprise of all was the sight and sound of strings of firecrackers hanging from the buildings, exploding as we passed. Firecrackers were thrown in front of us, too, as we marched down the street. This was certainly more than we had expected. Unfortunately, rain began to fall, but that did not dampen our spirits as we walked toward our billets for the night.

A hot bath, a banquet, and clean, dry Nationalist uniforms rounded out our reception. Colonel Tien told us if we would stay another day at Lo Shan, he would have uniforms tailor made for each of us. We declined with thanks because we were eager to continue our journey to an American airstrip, whose exact location was still undetermined.

Dr. Chang, our new interpreter, displayed a map, outlined an area in southwest Anwhei about the size of a Texas county, and said, "The airstrip is in that area." Looming large on the map well to the west of us was the Yellow River, the old nemesis of China.

We left Lo Shan early the next morning, 13 June, for a long day's ride to Ko Yang (33°31′N, 116°12′E). We were surprised when we were informed we would cross the Pukow-Tientsin (P-T) Railroad in daylight. We had been told that the railroad was heavily patrolled by both Jap and puppet troops.

When questioned about the risks, we were informed that the Nationalist troops in this area had good working relations with both the Japanese and puppets, i.e., there were very few or no hostile actions. The puppet troops apparently kept the Nationalist forces informed about the location of Japanese patrols and armored troop trains. This was a very convenient arrangement for all concerned.

Despite the good working relationship with the puppets and Japs, we had a large cavalry escort across the P-T Railroad. We crossed the railroad from east to west at a point north of Ku Chen (33°19′N, 117°18′E) with no trouble.* Light rain was perhaps more of a blessing than a hindrance because it provided additional cover for the crossing.

During the long, hard ride to Ko Yang, we saw standing houses in fair condition that confirmed the lack of Shermanesque activity and proved that relations were good among the local forces. The lack of destruction contrasted vividly with the utter devastation in some areas controlled by the Communists. It made one wonder if there was an agreement among the forces that the Japs would concentrate their combat efforts in Communist-controlled areas.

We noticed another contrast on the long ride to Ko Yang, one that we much appreciated. Not once did we visit a school, a cottage industry, or an arsenal. Our hosts seemed to understand our desire for speed in reaching the still mythical airstrip.

Our royal reception at Lo Shan was but a small rehearsal for the receptions at Ko Yang and succeeding cities in our journey. Disregarding our late arrival and weariness from the ride from Lo Shan, another 4th of July salute of exploding fireworks greeted us at Ko Yang. We were entertained far into the night with an elaborate banquet and a Peking drama.

*See map on page 2 of this book.

Ko Yang, China, 14 June 1945. Standing, left to right: First three men are Kuomintang (KMT), soldiers; Col. H.M. Liu, 1st Brigade, KMT; Major Gen. Li Hwa, 1st Brigade, KMT; next three are staff officers, 1st Brigade.

Sitting, left to right: John Wu, KMT interpreter; Magistrate of Ko Yang; 2nd Lt. John A. McAlister, USMC; 2nd Lt. John F. Kinney, USMC; 2nd Lt. James D. McBrayer, Jr., USMC; 2nd Lt. Richard M. Huizenga, USMC; Lewis Bishop, AVG pilot; KMT staff officer.

The drama was about a monkey who ruled the jungle but also wanted to rule the seas. After a long, drawn-out battle between the king of the seas and the king of the jungle, the latter was killed and the king of the seas ruled supreme. The drama was a poorly masked version of the then current worldwide conflict. The Chinese were delighted with the show and roared with laughter.

We acquired another interpreter, John Wu, who spoke English better than Dr. Chang. Wu, a former resident of Shanghai, came to us after the drama and offered to take us to a "sing-song" house where we could have women. We refused and then joked among ourselves, "Are we really marines, refusing women?" One of our group asked, "Do you want something with a stamp of approval by the U.S. Department of Agriculture on it? You don't find that even in the States."

Our reception at Tai-ho (33°08′N, 115°38′E), a large city on the

歡迎美國盟友脫險攝影紀念

Tai Ho, China, 16 June 1945. Standing, left to right: W.C. Wang, Blockade station master; Protestant missionary; next five are KMT staff officers. Sitting: Major Gen. Tang, Vice–cin C, Kuomintang (KMT) armies north of the Hwai River; Gen. Lu, cin C, KMT armies north of the Kwai River; 2nd Lt. John A. McAlister, USMC; 2nd Lt. John F. Kinney, USMC; 2nd Lt. James D. McBrayer, Jr., USMC; 2nd Lt. Richard M. Huizenga, USMC; Lewis Bishop, AVG pilot; the Reverend F. Paul Greck, Catholic missionary from Malta; Shu Han Sung, magistrate of Tai Ho.

Yellow River, was the most elaborate of our journey. Dignitaries greeting us included General Lu, commander of the First Provisional Brigade; the Reverend Chen, a Protestant missionary; and Father Greck, a Catholic missionary from Malta.

We attended a banquet at 5 P.M. given in the local Protestant church. It was unusual in that it was presided over by the Reverend Chen and Father Greck; it was followed by a Peking drama, but at least it was one that was amusing. It was about one of the emperor's concubines who smuggled a man into her royal apartment for an obvious purpose. After a long skirmish conducted toward getting what she wanted, she discovered the man was a eunuch and erupted in outrageous anger from frustration.

Protestant Reverend Chen, who interpreted the drama at the request of General Lu, was obviously embarrassed, as was Father Greck, but the rest of us enjoyed it and laughed with the locals attending.

General Lu had graciously provided billets for us in his private home, a Western-style house with bathtubs and flush toilets. An amusing small detail came to our attention: coolies were required to fill the bathtubs and provide water to flush the toilets. The toilets were flushed into a holding vat that also required honey-bucket coolies.

Dr. Chang came to our billets after the drama was over and asked me for some money for his return to Ko Yang. He had noticed the large number of bills in my saddlebags when I was packing before dinner. I took out a wad of bills and gave some to him. Wu saw the transaction and threatened Dr. Chang with his pistol. I restrained Wu, who was ready to kill Dr. Chang. The latter ran from our room. Wu yelled after him, "That son of bitch shouldn't do that. I'll kill that son of bitch!"

The next morning, 16 June, we attended another banquet in the early morning that was sponsored by the local Kuomintang party. General Lu presented each of us Americans with a large red banner emblazoned with big, white Chinese characters meaning "Ride the wind and cleave the waves." He told us it was a commendation for bravery from the Nationalist party and the First Provisional Brigade.

Soon after the banquet we left for Fow Yang (32°53′N, 115°48′E). Neither Wu nor Dr. Chang was present for our departure. About 20 miles down the trail, Wu galloped up to us. I asked, "Where is Dr. Chang?"

Wu slapped his pistol and shouted, "I fixed that son of bitch."

I asked Wu where the money I had given Dr. Chang was. He smiled smugly and patted his saddle bag, but he did not offer to return the money. Justice is swift in China. Executions are usually at the scene of the crime. Apparently, Wu was the accuser, jury, judge, and executioner in the case of Dr. Chang's crime.

At Fow Yang we were greeted by Nationalist troops stationed there as a part of the area's American Air Ground Support Team (AAGST). The AAGST had the mission of assisting downed pilots and air crews to reach the air evacuation field, i.e., Valley Field (Wu Kia Tien) (31°25′N, 115°35′E).* At last we had definite information about an American airstrip.

We were treated to another banquet by the Nationalist troops. We spent the night and departed early the next morning (17 June) for what we were told was an American outpost called Roger Two Sugar (R2S, 33°02′N, 115°21′E).** We hoped we were finally on the home stretch.

The AAGST at Fow Yang furnished us fresh horses, a small escort, and a guide to R2S, an OSS (Office of Strategic Service) station.

Rain continued to hamper our progress. At a swollen river, the ferry was too small to take our horses across. We left the horses, crossed the

*_Hill_, My War with Imperial Japan, _p. 323_.
**Ibid.

Banner presented to author at Tai Ho, China, 16 June 1945, by Gen. Lu, C in C, KMT armies north of Hwai River as a memento of his escape from danger.

Translation: Presented by the people of all circles of Tai Ho, Anwhei Province, Republic of China. "Ride the wind and cleave the waves." [Surmount all Difficulties.]

river, and proceeded on foot through the muddy fields. To our dismay, it appeared our guide was unsure of the station's location because we were walking in an increasing spiral. Tired and annoyed with him, we finally contacted a Nationalist patrol whose officer, after much discussion with the guide, pointed out what we hoped was the correct direction. Daylight was fading fast, so we knew we had to move quickly.

Later, as we stumbled along in the darkness, a beam of light caught me full in the face and a strong American voice rang through the night, "Halt, who goes there!"

CHAPTER SEVENTEEN

Meigwo, at Last

I yelled, somewhat in disbelief, "Is this Roger Two Sugar?"
"Hell, yes! What 'ya expect, the White House?"
Overcome with relief, I shouted triumphantly, "We've found Roger
Two Sugar!" My companions chimed in, "Thank God, we've made it."
The White House it was not. Some 300 miles inside Jap lines, Roger
Two Sugar appeared to be another small Chinese village. It was the
challenging shout through the night that made me feel I was on my way
stateside. A lone American voice had relieved the five of us of our worries.
We were jubilant. The long-sought American contact was Roger Two
Sugar, the beginning of the road home. We congratulated each other with
thumps on the back and broad grins.

I quoted the name "Roger Two Sugar" (R2S) almost reverently. A
damn good name for the place of encounter with American forces. From
now on, it all had to be downhill.

The challenge had come from a U.S. Army captain. He was immediately surrounded by the five of us. Where is the airstrip? How long
will it take to get there? When can we expect a flight to Kunming? Our
rapid-fire questions smothered his attempts to reply.

The captain, amid the noise, told us to calm down. He said there was
an airstrip called Valley Field that had the mission of evacuating personnel.* It was located six or seven days of hard riding from R2S. He added
that a C-47 usually made a flight from Kunming about every two weeks to
bring supplies to the strip. According to his latest information, a supply
plane was due to land there in about ten days, plus or minus a day or two.
He told us the landing times were staggered for obvious reasons.

The captain said that R2S was the radio call sign of their intelligence

*Hill, My War with Imperial Japan, p. 323.

station, a part of the Office of Strategic Services (OSS). We learned that
Captain John M. Birch, the officer in charge of R2S, was on a trip to a
nearby airstrip called "Pasture Field" that was located a few miles from
R2S.

Pasture Field (radio call sign "Sleepy") was used only to furnish sup-
plies for R2S, but, since it was often under water, it was nicknamed "Bog
Field." Captain Birch was scheduled to return to R2S the next day, 18 June.
We were told he would arrange an escort and guides for us to Valley Field.
Meanwhile, R2S would be in radio contact with Valley Field to find out
when the next supply plane was due from Kunming.

On the evening of 17 June, we enjoyed the fringes of Western civilization—steaks (of water buffalo), fried potatoes, and onions topped off with
a generous belt of good Kentucky bourbon and a fine cigar. We listened
to music from station KGEI in San Francisco and began to feel that all was
well with the world.

The next day Captain Birch returned, and I became acquainted with
a legendary individual of great courage and dedication. Captain Birch, who
had been a missionary in China prior to World War II, had been stationed
in Shanghai before the war started. Foreseeing the Japanese onslaught, he
had left Shanghai the night before the outbreak of hostilities, carrying with
him a radio receiver, transmitter, and spare parts. He served deep inside
China as an intelligence agent, first for the American Volunteer Group
(AVG) and then in succession for the 14th Air Force and the OSS. He was
killed by Chinese Communist soldiers at Huang Ko, a small village 35
miles west of Tung Shan, on 25 August 1945.*

Birch's name was used (some say smirched) years later in 1959 by
Robert Welch when he established the John Birch Society, an anti–Com-
munist organization. Welch proclaimed John Birch the first casualty of
World War III.**

At R2S we spent two days relaxing and walking around the countryside. It was a relief to stretch our legs after those long days in wet, wooden
saddles. Some of us had developed sores on our butts and genital regions
from being continually wet and bouncing in uncomfortable wooden
saddles.

A Chinese captain was in charge of the defense of R2S. Belonging to
the old Chinese school of defense, he had directed that a deep moat and
earthen wall be constructed around the station. There I had my first glimpse
of a bazooka, a weapon developed after I had left the States. That weapon
was the captain's first line of defense. It was also his weapon of choice when
on raiding parties along the Hankow-Peking Railroad west of R2S.

---

*Hill, My War with Imperial Japan, p. 349–351.
**Robert Welch, The Blue Book of the John Birch Society (Boston: Western Islands, 1959).

The day after we arrived, a bazooka shell was the cause of a local tragedy. Some peasants nearby had found an unexploded shell and had tried to use it to drive wooden pegs into the ground. The shell exploded at the first blow and blew the farmer and several others out of existence.

While we were with the troops manning R2S, we were of course encouraged to tell our escape stories. Captain Birch seemed surprised that we had survived the jump from the train and our journey around the area. He said that just staying healthy in China was not easy and that we were unusually fortunate, or, as we argued, we had acquired subclinical immunity in the prison camp.

A P-51 pilot joined us as a traveling companion on 19 June. He had been on a mission strafing trains on the Pukow-Tientsin Railroad near Suchow and had been hit by small arms fire. He said he had been picked up by puppet troops and held prisoner for several days. Using the gold sovereigns in his escape kit, he bought his way to Nationalist troops. The latter guided him to R2S.

The pilot had injured his left leg when he hit the ground after parachuting from his plane. He required a sedan chair and bearers to make the trip with us. We went with Captain Birch to the nearby village to hire a sedan chair and bearers.

We questioned the pilot to learn if his squadron had been briefed on the location of our Kiangwan prisoner of war camp or the fact that POWs were being transported along the Pukow-Tientsin rail line. His answer was a resounding no. That squelched a long-held belief by many POWs that American forces, aware of the location of POW camps and POW movements, avoided bombing or strafing those areas.

Our group for the trip to Valley Field was now composed of us five escapees, one P-51 pilot, three enlisted men stationed at R2S who were due for rotation, and Captain Birch. We had an escort of about 20 Nationalist soldiers. On 20 June we left R2S for Valley Field.

Captain Birch told us that the armed escort was necessary because we would travel through very rugged parts of the Ta Pien mountains in southwest Anwhei. That area was notorious as a hideout for large numbers of bandits and troops belonging to nonaffiliated fiefdoms.

Our progress over the steep, narrow, mountainous trails was very slow. Much of the time we had to dismount and lead our horses. At night we had to move very slowly and carefully because of precipitous cliffs on one side of the path. Many times a rock dislodged from our path would bounce once or twice and land with a sickening thud far below. A continuous drizzle made the trails even more hazardous.

One of the enlisted men, a sergeant, fell, injured his leg, and could not walk. We draped him over his horse and tied him to the saddle until we could reach a village. There we hired another sedan chair. Two sedan chairs further slowed our progress. We had to watch the sedan chair bearers' every move because they attempted to flee at any opportunity.

There were four episodes which differentiated this dreary, tortuous journey from the rest of our trip. First, the constant requirement to draft sedan bearers; some coolies escaped despite the guards' vigilance. Whenever a bearer escaped, our escort would go to the nearest village and return with another bearer, a reasonable carbon copy of the original, gathered under threat of death.

Second, our cloth shoes were soon cut to ribbons on the slick, rocky paths. We tried to buy shoes at several small villages but could not find any that fit. We finally resorted to draconian measures — using pistols as the purchasing agent. Our guard simply stopped every peasant we passed. Each of us then tried on the peasant's shoes. When at last one of us found a decent fit, the lucky one put on the peasant's shoes and left the poor man wondering what cruel stroke of fate caused him to be shoeless.

A third bizarre event will always be imprinted on my mind. The rocky, steep paths took their toll on both horses and men. My mount lost a shoe and became lame. The others, leaving me and one guard behind, continued to the next village in search of fresh mounts. My companion and I limped behind, with the guard carrying an old Thompson .45 caliber submachine gun and leading my horse. We were walking up a rocky stream bed when suddenly a wild stud horse charged us and tried to mount my saddle horse, a mare.

The guard dropped the reins and tried to beat off the stud using the Thompson as a club. The stud turned his attention from the mare to the guard and savagely bit the guard's right arm. In agony, the guard dropped his Thompson. I picked up the gun but had difficulty getting it to fire because of dirt in the firing mechanism. The stud turned his attention from the guard to me. Fortunately, the mare whinnied and caught the stud's interest again. I finally got the Thompson to work, and we left a dead stud in the creek.

The guard's arm was bleeding badly, and I could see the bone in his forearm. I tore some strips of cloth off my shirt and bound the wound as best I could, hoping we would soon reach Valley Field and get better treatment for him.

At the next village, a very small one, we found that Hi and most of our group had left and gone ahead again since fresh mounts were not available. I followed with the sedan chairs, their occupants, the wounded guard, and part of the escort.

We finally straggled into a large village and found Hi, Captain Birch, and the others waiting for us. They had fresh mounts and bearers ready for us. A local barefoot doctor treated the guard's wounded arm. After a brief rest and hot gruel, we pushed on through the night for Valley Field. Fortunately, the terrain became much less rugged, and we could proceed more easily.

At dawn we left our escort and sedan chairs and forced our mounts to a gallop to cover the last few miles quickly. Our desire for speed probably caused the fourth unusual episode. My pony slipped and fell with me in the saddle. I hit the ground hard, my back was twisted, and the pony and saddle were on top of my legs. I tried to move but couldn't; there was no feeling in my legs.

For Christ's sake, I thought, here I am a few miles from getting out of this Godforsaken land, and I, a Texan, have broken my back because my horse fell.

Hi and the others came back to help me. I asked them not to move me because I thought my back was broken. The others went on to the airstrip, hoping to hold a plane, if present, until I could reach the airstrip.

Hi and a guard remained with me. I lay in the muddy path for what seemed like ages before feeling gradually returned to my legs. Finally, I could move them. Hi helped me back on my pony, and we proceeded slowly toward the strip. Hi kidded me about being hurt by a falling pony. I claimed that the mud on my new shoes caused my feet to stick in the stirrups, preventing me from jumping clear. Take it or leave it, I had to save face.

It seemed as though we were moving at a snail's pace; besides, we were worried now that if a plane landed, it wouldn't wait for us. A plane on the Valley Field airstrip was in a very vulnerable position to any Jap fighter plane in the area.

Riding over a small knoll, we saw what we wanted to see: a twin-engined transport sitting on the end of the airstrip. I wanted to run and jump for joy, but not wanting to trust my legs, I settled for a few whoops.

We were welcomed by First Lieutenant Vernon Hill, the officer in charge of the Air Ground Aid Section in that sector, and the crew of the C-47.* Disregarding the danger of remaining on the airstrip for a long period, the pilot, a major, USAAC, had waited for us overnight. Meeting the crew, I discovered that the navigator was the brother of a classmate and friend of mine from the class of 1939, U.S. Naval Academy.

Before we left Valley Field, I realized that we were back under the jurisdiction of Uncle Sam and had been since we arrived at Roger Two Sugar. This revelation dawned on me when Captain Birch presented me with a bill for 62,400 dollars in Chinese Nationalist currency (CNC). (See Appendix 4.) This total consisted of 22,400 CNC for board and lodging for seven days for the escapees and 40,000 CNC for travel expenses. I thought

*Hill, My War with Imperial Japan, p. 323.

it ironic that the money with which I paid the bill was the money the Chinese Communists had given us.

We were naturally excited and very happy as we boarded the aircraft for takeoff to Kunming. Always hungry, we asked for food and were given K-rations, which we devoured quickly. The GI crew members were amazed that we liked K-rations.

As the plane reached cruising altitude, our exuberance knew no bounds. Flying over the Jap lines, each of us walked back to the plane's latrine and did something we had wanted to do for a long time: shit on the Japs.

Upon landing at Kunming we were taken immediately to the commanding general's office to establish our identities. With no identification cards to present, we marines established our identities with the commanding general and the paymaster by naming their officers who were commissioned at the same time we were. To add to our identity, Hi and I sang the last two verses of "Navy Blue and Gold" while our comrades booed.

Once we had been identified, but still had no cards, the Navy paymaster allowed us to draw some of our back pay to buy necessities while we were at the 14th Air Force base in Kunming. With money in hand, we went to the exchange store to buy suitable clothing, only to discover that we couldn't buy anything without a regulation identification card. We returned to the adjutant general's office for the required card, but instead of receiving the card, I was given top secret orders for the escapee group to proceed to the Marine Corps Headquarters in Washington, D.C. We were ordered not to discuss our escape with anyone until we had been debriefed in Washington.

The top secret orders did not solve our problem of identification cards for everyday items. After some persuasion, the adjutant took us to the Red Cross office, where we were given Red Cross khaki clothing, a musette bag with toilet articles, and a Red Cross ID card and collar insignia, which entitled us to treatment as officers.

We were then ordered to the local dispensary for a physical examination and necessary inoculations to leave the CBI (China-Burma-India) theater of war and enter the United States. There we encountered the first of several obstacles barring our return to Meigwo. The doctors at first claimed we would have to remain in Kunming for several weeks for two reasons.

First, they declared we would have to take every inoculation in the book. Some would require several injections at one per week. We objected strenuously, claiming acquired subclinical immunity. We finally won our case with the aid of the commanding general. One obstacle removed.

Second, one doctor asserted that we would have to remain there for a week or more. He claimed the sores in the genital and butt regions could be symptoms of syphilis or some strange Oriental social disease. We claimed they were simply saddle sores from riding horses in the rain and chafing from wooden saddles. The doctor wouldn't believe us and thought he had found a humorous and bizarre occurrence of intercourse while on horseback. This would have given him bragging rights throughout the armed services for treating a social disease resulting from the most peculiar of circumstances. However, we again won our case, and it was concluded that our problem was simply saddle sores. A second obstacle removed.

Physically, I was in fair shape, weighing in around 145 pounds because I had regained some 30-odd pounds while with the guerrillas. I believed that our ability to ride and walk about 800 miles over a period of some 48 days provided evidence that we had received good treatment from both the Communists and Nationalists.

Our top secret orders imposed other obstacles at every stop on our flight from Kunming to Washington, D.C. At each landing— Karachi, New Delhi, Cairo, Casablanca, etc.—we had to find an officer with top secret clearance in order to get a flight to the next airfield.

The most exasperating obstacle that barred our entry into the States was posed by the U.S. Customs and Immigrations officials at Gravelly Point Air Field at Washington, D.C. We had no identification, other than the top secret orders and the Red Cross card. None of the customs and immigration officials had top secret clearance, and therefore they could not review our orders. Further, since they would not recognize our Red Cross cards as proof of U.S. citizenship, we were refused permission to enter the U.S. until we could be positively identified as citizens. We finally received permission to call Marine Corps headquarters. We asked to have a marine officer come to the airport and identify us.

I immediately thought of Colonel Leo Sullivan, who had been our quartermaster in Peking in 1940. He might be at headquarters, and, if so, could certainly identify Hi and me. We asked for him and other officers to come and identify all of us.

Colonel Sullivan and several officers came as requested. A customs official accompanied them into the room where we were waiting. The colonel looked at us with a stern, penetrating stare, turned to the customs official, and said in a loud voice, "I never saw any of these sons of bitches before in my life." Then he roared with laughter. We all joined him, much relieved. At last we were permitted to enter Meigwo.

With little ceremony, we were taken to headquarters the afternoon of 9 July 1945 and assigned to a debriefing officer, who took his time extracting the information he wanted. At last we were taken to a hotel, where each of us rushed to telephone our families, girlfriends, and the families and girlfriends of those POWs we had left behind. It was sad to find that many of us were calling girlfriends who should have written "Dear John" letters.

Without hesitation, I called my fiancée, Skip, and asked, "Are you still interested in marrying me?" A swift and positive yes was the answer. No obstacle there! Skip and her youngest sister came over from Baltimore that same night.

The next morning, 10 July, I had to ask the commandant of the Marine Corps for a couple of days off to get married. General A. A. Vandegrift's reply, vivid in my memory, was, "I don't give a shit what you do after five o'clock."

As a result, my fiancée had two very busy days on 10 and 11 July, arranging for our long-delayed wedding. The marriage license bureau in Westminster, Maryland, normally closed at five o'clock, but the bureau agreed by telephone to remain open on 11 July until we arrived. A jewelry store clerk in Washington, with raised eyebrow, sold a rather embarrassed lady a $5 wedding ring. With much pleading, a Methodist church pastor in Frederick, Maryland, agreed to perform a wedding ceremony "after hours." Friends worked a miracle in wartime D.C. They were able to reserve a room for us in a fashionable hotel.

On the afternoon of 11 July, Skip and her sister arrived at the parking lot of Marine Corps headquarters and confidently parked near the main entrance. A sentry came up to her car and told her she couldn't park there. After he listened to her story, her pretty impassioned face prevailed. The sentry not only permitted her to remain but, unknown to her, arranged for help from the District of Columbia police.

At five o'clock, I rushed past the crowd leaving headquarters and joined Skip in her car. To our surprise, the sentry brought over a D.C. motorcycle policeman, who turned on his siren and blazed a trail for us out of the Washington area at peak traffic time.

At the license bureau in Westminster, the clerk had all documents prepared for us to sign. With marriage license in hand, we dashed to a phone to alert Skip's family, who were waiting to know where to join us. Then, with little sister in the back seat, we took off for Frederick and the church some 30 miles away.

From there on it was easy. Skip's family and a few friends arrived at the Calvary Methodist Church. The minister, unfamiliar with the church's lighting system, had difficulty finding the main light switches. But at 10 o'clock in a dark church with only one small light over the organist's console, we were married.

One might say it was a tough, six-year fight from promise to consummation, but well worth the struggle.

*   *   *

I returned to China in 1987 with Skip. Peking was a far cry from my earlier China days. The creation of Tiananmen Square had destroyed the marine barracks, and the Tartar Wall was gone. Camels and rickshaws had disappeared from the scene. My old house was still there, but was now occupied by several Chinese families instead of two bachelors. Still, the Forbidden City and the winding hutungs had the same intrigue of an ancient city and its culture.

The mystique of China is inescapable. I am glad I was caught up in its mantle of what could be called the "good old days." I am glad also, and most grateful, for that small window in a boxcar and the friendliness and help of the Chinese people.

If we left a legacy in Anwhei Province, it is the belief that "The Marines' Hymn" is the American national anthem. Semper Fi.

Epilogue

A fter being debriefed in Washington, D.C., in July 1945, the paths of the five escapees diverged widely and rapidly as each of us sought to make up for lost time.

We four marines remained in the corps. Huizenga entered and completed flight training at Pensacola, Florida. Kinney and McAlister were stationed on the West Coast of the United States. I was assigned duty in the Panama Canal Zone, and Bishop resumed his career as a pilot in the U. S. Naval Reserve.

Soon after our arrival in the States, Bishop, Huizenga, Kinney, and McAlister were awarded the Bronze Star for their escape. I was awarded the Legion of Merit with Combat "V."*

Within a few months, Bishop divorced his wife, as five years of separation resulted in marital difficulties. About the same time, he was released from active duty to serve as a pilot in the Chinese National Airlines (CNAC). It was during Bishop's tour with the CNAC that I lost touch with him.

All four marines got married soon after our return. Again, our duty assignments were diverse and kept us widely separated. Huizenga and Kinney each commanded several different fighter squadrons, including one during the Korean conflict. McAlister and I remained in the marine ground organization. Both of us served in the 1st Marine Division in Korea. Most of my duty in Korea was with the United Nations Armistice Commission, where I negotiated with Chinese and North Korean Communist officers. Some of those Communist officers probably were from the New Fourth Army, and, I am sure, had assisted us in our escape from the Japanese.

*Colonel Ashurst, USMC, the senior officer in our POW camp, recommended the author for the Legion of Merit because he considered him the leader of the escape group.

Once during a negotiating session, I noticed that a Communist soldier was busy making a sketch of me. I interrupted the proceedings by remarking: "If you want a picture of me, get one from the New Fourth Army, as I was with the NFA for almost two months in Anwhei Province in May and June 1945." That remark broke up the negotiating session for that day.

In 1947, during my tour of duty in the Panama Canal Zone, our first son, James David III, was born. Our second son, John Alexander, was born in 1949 in Washington, D.C. when I was on the staff of the inspector general.

I attended the Marine Corps Senior Course in Quantico, Virginia, 1949-50 and was later assigned duty with the 2nd Marine Division. There I served as the commanding officer, 3rd Battalion, 8th Marines, and later as executive officer, 8th Marines, before being transferred to the 1st Marine Division in 1953.

After my tour in Korea, I served as an operations officer on the staff of the commanding general, Fleet Marine Force Atlantic, Norfolk, Virginia. I was promoted to colonel in 1956 and assigned duty as an operations officer on the staff of the commander in chief, Specified Command, Middle East (CINCSPECOME), in London. My family and I arrived in London just in time for the Suez Canal conflict in 1956. I dropped my family off at a flat in London and departed immediately for the Sixth Fleet in the Mediterranean. After two great years in London and many trips to the Middle Eastern countries, we returned to the States, where I attended the Naval War College in Newport, Rhode Island. I was first a student there and then an instructor and executive officer of the Senior Course. During my tour at the Naval War College, I attended evening classes conducted by Boston University and earned a masters degree in international relations.

Our next move was to Atlanta, Georgia, where I served as the director of the Sixth Marine Corps Reserve and Recruiting District. It was there that my experiences as a prisoner of war caught up with me, and I was retired in 1965 because of physical disabilities.

Pursuing a second career in the educational field, I taught at Georgia Tech, 1965–72, while attending graduate school at Emory University, where I earned a Ph.D. in political science in 1972. I transferred from Georgia Tech to a teaching position at Georgia State University in 1973. I later retired as a professor emeritus from Georgia State University in 1983.

Retirement meant a slower lifestyle, so in September 1983 Skip and I moved from Atlanta to the Isle of Palms, South Carolina, and in 1994 to Birmingham, Alabama. Our eldest son, Jim, lives in Steamboat Springs, Colorado, and works for the Bureau of Land Management. John A., an attorney, married Susan Woodruff in 1979. They now live in Pelham, Alabama, with their two sons, Daniel, age 9, and Timothy, age 6.

Huizenga and his wife Lucy adopted two children—a boy, Richard Reid, and a girl, Geri Lou. After retiring in 1960 as a colonel, Huizenga taught at Hargrove Military Academy in Chatham, Virginia, until his death in 1970.

John Kinney retired as a brigadier general in 1959. He worked for Lockheed Aircraft Corporation in Sunnyvale, California, for several years. He and his wife June now reside in Portola Valley, California.

John A. McAlister retired on 1 July 1965, after having served on the staff of the commander, Naval Forces, Philippines, 1962–64. He died in 1974. His widow, the former Mary Elizabeth Turner, lives in San Diego, California.

Looking back on our days in the Japanese prisoner of war camp and the subsequent events in the lives of the marines involved, it is very gratifying and noteworthy that each marine simply took his POW experiences in stride. The four marine escapees pursued their careers to successful and distinguished conclusions.

While in the POW camps, all marines conducted themselves in an exemplary manner. Of those who remained in the Marine Corps, as well as those who entered into civilian life after World War II, all had successful careers. In each case their success can be attributed in a very large part to their marine training. The Japanese tried very hard to break the spiritual ties and solidarity of the marines, but were unsuccessful.

The U.S. Marine motto, Semper Fidelis, proved to be much more than just words or an empty slogan. I am very proud to be a MARINE.

Appendix: Documents

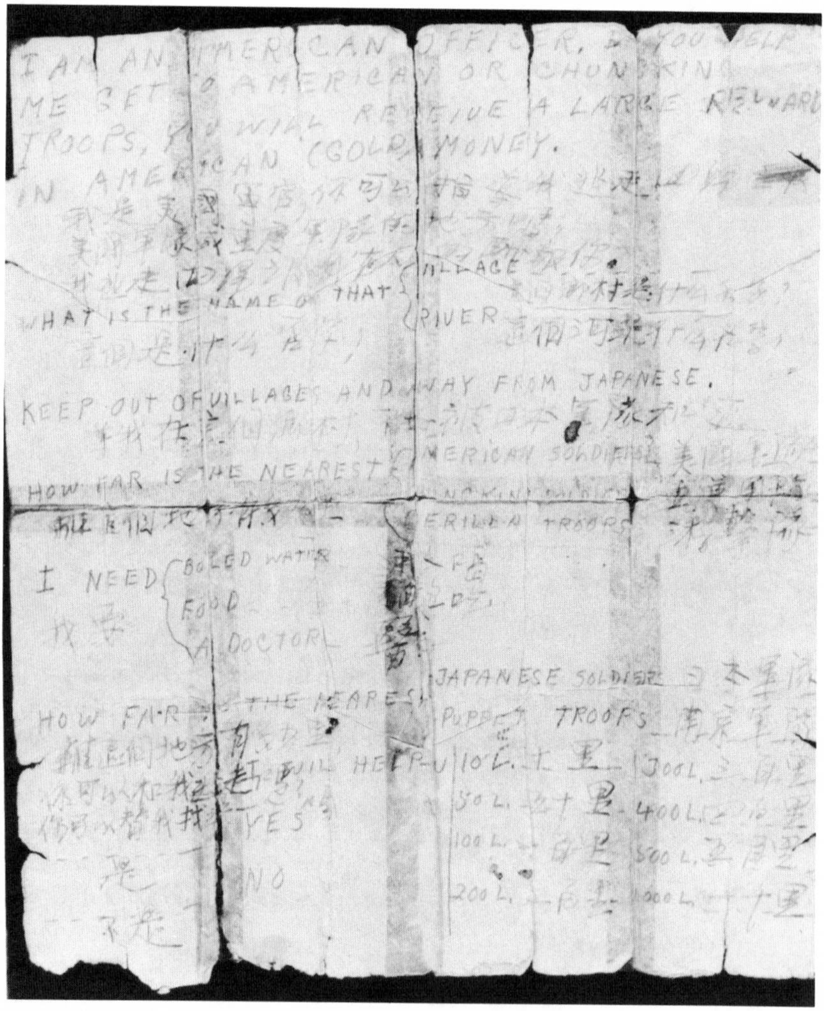
I AM AN AMERICAN OFFICER, IF YOU HELP
ME GET TO AMERICAN OR CHUNGKING
TROOPS, YOU WILL RECEIVE A LARGE REWARD
IN AMERICAN (GOLD) MONEY.
WHAT IS THE NAME OF THAT VILLAGE
RIVER
KEEP OUT OF VILLAGES AND AWAY FROM JAPANESE.
HOW FAR IS THE NEAREST AMERICAN SOLDIERS
GERILLA TROOPS
I NEED BOILED WATER
FOOD
A DOCTOR
JAPANESE SOLDIERS
HOW FAR IS THE NEAREST PUPPET TROOPS
WILL HELP U
10 L.
50 L.
100 L.
200 L.
300 L.
400 L.
500 L.
1000 L.
YES
是
NO
不是

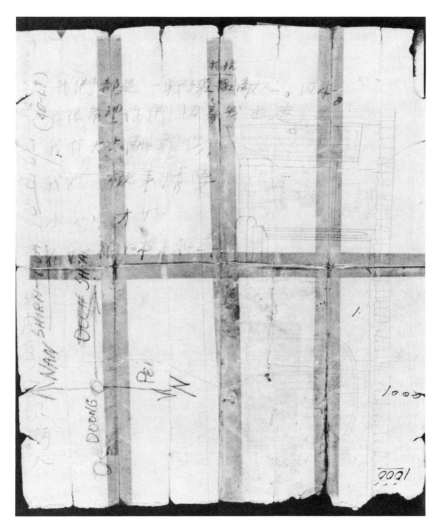

AFFIDAVIT

Colonel James D. McBrayer, Jr., then a 2nd Lt., while interned as a Prisoner of War of the Japanese at a Prisoner of War camp near Shanghai, China, suffered from various diseases at various times during the period 7 December 1941 to May 1945 when he escaped from a prison train. These diseases were as follows:

a. Sever Dysentry on many occasions, both bacillary and parasitic, as these were prevalent in the prison camp and in China.

b. Infestation with worms and parasites of various sorts particularly of the intestinal tracts. Such afflictions were common in the prison camp.

c. Pellagra and beriberi manifesting the vitamin deficiencies.

d. Severe pains in the legs and arms, particularly the legs, apparently arthritis, inflamation of the joints and tendons.

e. Severe headaches from sinus trouble.

f. Pains in the lower bowels or colon at times separate to attacks of dysentry and the like.

g. Severe loss of weight.

h. Various other afflictions suffered by Prisoners of War of the Japanese, particularly those of the stomach and the flu and repsiratory type.

I served closely with Col. McBrayer, then 2nd Lt., in North China prior to our capture on 7 December 1941 (8 December, U. S. time) and knew him to be then a vigorous, healthy, and active young officer who participated in all sports and Marine training and exercises. He, Col. (2nd Lt.) McBrayer, served in North China from the period of about June 1940 to 7 December 1941 and did not suffer from the afflictions which later beset him in the prison camp.

Luther A. Brown

September 9, 1966

TO WHOM IT MAY CONCERN

The undersigned participated with Colonel (then Second Lieutenant) James D. McBrayer, Jr. in a successful escape from the enemy on or about May 10, 1945; and also travelled with Colonel McBrayer on the trip by horseback from the escape site inland into China to the point we were recovered by U. S. forces -- and thereafter on the return flight to this country.

The actual escape was from a rapidly moving train of freight cars in which we were being transported, in company with our fellow prisoners of war, from the Shanghai area northward in China enroute to an eventual relocation in Japan.

Although we did not jump from the train together, I am well acquainted, from personal experience, with exactly what happened to Colonel McBrayer on that occasion. In my case it was a matter of pure chance that I did not sustain a back injury of major proportions. The circumstances of my "crash landing" on the railroad bed were such that my injuries (in addition to cuts and bruises) were confined to the rib cage. The pain and discomfort I suffered during subsequent travel across China was later diagnosed to have resulted from a number of cracked ribs. In Colonel McBrayer's case, I distinctly recall that his back bothered him considerably during our long horseback ride with the guerrilla forces with whom we travelled.

There was a later incident that most certainly added complications to Colonel McBrayer's back condition. For that matter it could very well have been the cause of spinal damage, whether or not there had been previous injury. In this instance I was a direct witness. The accident occurred while we were riding at night in an all-out effort to meet the aircraft being sent in behind enemy lines to pick us up. Needless to say we were not inclined to accept any delay in this final phase of our efforts to rejoin friendly forces. Our "China Pony" mounts were far from predictable under the best of circumstances. Travelling rapidly at night only added to the hazard. It was under those circumstances that Colonel McBrayer took a bad spill. The incident comes vividly to mind for a number of reasons. First of all, he was riding directly ahead of me. I was forced to rein in to avoid trampling him. In the process I almost become unseated myself. Then too, it turned out that he was disabled to the extent we were delayed in effecting our rendezvous with the recovery aircraft. Finally, after it became apparent Colonel McBrayer could manage to continue with us, there was a certain amount of good natured ribbing. This stemmed from the fact he is a Texan, and had been practically raised on horseback. It is not too often one has an opportunity to needle someone in this category about his ability to remain in the saddle. However, to be fair about it, I'll have to admit the horse stumbled badly and that we were all sleepy and the worse for wear at the time the Texan came a cropper.

Events similar to the above don't normally become a matter of official record. In a tight situation, and under war conditions, military personnel are not inclined to evaluate future implications of emergency action they are required to take. Several accounts of our escape may appear in official files; yet it is highly doubtful these documents contain specific information on personal injuries or other such matters we considered to be somewhat incidental at the time. Incidental, that is, in comparison to the single objective of any major importance to us, namely to escape and to rejoin our own forces.

It is my understanding Colonel McBrayer has been experiencing considerable difficulty with his back, both prior to and since his retirement from active duty. This is to certify that in my opinion this could very logically have resulted from the incidents described herein. Both were exceedingly traumatic, and either could have caused internal injuries of the type that develop into a painful back condition at a later date.

R. M. Huizenga
Colonel, U. S. Marine Corps (Ret'd)
05950

State of Michigan
County of Allegan

Sworn and subscribed before me this 9th day of
September 1966.

HOWARD BRYANT
Notary Public, Allegan County, Mich.
My Commission Expires Nov. 20, 1966

As the escapees prepared to board the plane at Wu Kia Tien to fly to Kunming, Captain John Birch walked up to me and said that he didn't want to put a wet blanket on such a joyous occasion but that I owed him some money. Astounded, I asked how much and what for? Captain Birch said that I owed him 62,400 yuan for food, lodging and travel expenses. I said, "John, you must be joking. We traveled with both the Chinese Communist and Nationalist troops for almost two months and didn't have to pay for anything." Captain Birch explained that because we had been with American forces for seven days, he must account for the extra expenditures.

At that point, with the plane poised on the end of the runway and ready for takeoff, I handed Captain Birch a big stack of Chinese currency which had been given to me by the Chinese Communist New Fourth Army. Captain Birch gave me receipts for the money, copies of which are shown below.

22 June 1945

RECEIVED, of 2nd Lieutenant James D. McBrayer, USMC, for board and lodging for four men for fxxxxxx seven days: the sum of Chinese National Currency TWENTY TWO THOUSAND FOUR HUNDRED DOLLARS (NC$22,400.00)

John M. Birch
JOHN M. BIRCH,
Captain, A.C.

22 June 1945

RECEIVED, OF 2nd LIEUT. JAMES D. MCBRAYER, USMC, for travel expenses incurred by personnel in the U.S. armed forces (four Marines, two pilots, and one army radio operator) between 18 June and 26 June, 1945: the sum of Chinese National Currency FORTY THOUSAND DOLLARS (NC $ 40,000.00)

John M. Birch
JOHN M. BIRCH,
Captain, A.C.

IN REPLYING ADDRESS
COMMANDANT OF THE MARINE CORPS
WASHINGTON 25, D. C.
AND REFER TO
SERIAL 05927
DGP-298-bw

HEADQUARTERS U. S. MARINE CORPS
WASHINGTON

FEB 28 1947

MC- 876763

From: Commandant of the Marine Corps.
To: Lieutenant Colonel James D. McBrayer, Jr., USMC.,
            Marine Barracks, 15th Naval District, Balboa,
            Canal Zone.
Via: (1) The Commandant, 15th Naval District, Balboa.
            (2) The Commanding Officer, Marine Barracks, Balboa.

Subject: Award of Legion of Merit with citation.

1.   I wish to express my gratification upon the recognition of your exceptionally meritorious conduct in the performance of outstanding services to the Government of the United
States while a Prisoner of War of the Japanese, in China, from
December 1942 to May 1945, as evidenced by the award to you of
the Legion of Merit with citation by the President of the United
States.

2.   Be assured of my deep appreciation of your devotion
to duty and exemplary service which were in keeping with the highest traditions of the United States Marine Corps.

A. A. VANDEGRIFT

- -

Index

Military History of Author

J AMES D. MCBRAYER, JR., was born and raised in Lorena, Texas. He graduated from the U.S. Naval Academy on 1 June 1939 and was commissioned a 2nd Lieutenant, U.S. Marine Corps. After graduating in May 1940 from the Marine Corps Basic School, Philadelphia, Pennsylvania, he was ordered to the Marine Embassy Guard in Peking, China. A year and a half later he was captured on 8 December 1941 by the Japanese.

McBrayer was imprisoned in two different Japanese POW camps in China: Woosung and Kiangwan, both near Shanghai. When the POWs were being moved in May 1945 from Kiangwan to Japan, he and four fellow POWs escaped from the boxcar in which they were being transported. With the assistance of Red guerrillas, they made their way across China to an emergency U.S. airfield inside Japanese lines and were flown to Kunming and thence to Washington, D.C., where they arrived 9 July 1945.

McBrayer was immediately ordered to the Marine Air-Infantry School, Quantico, Virginia, having been promoted to captain and then major subsequently. Upon graduation in 1946, he was assigned duty as the executive officer of the marine barracks in the Panama Canal Zone. He was then promoted to lieutenant colonel and from 1948 to 1950, he served as a member of the Marine Corps inspector general's staff and traveled in the United States and worldwide, inspecting marine posts and installations. In 1950–51, he attended the Senior Course, Marine Corps Schools, Quantico, Virginia. After graduating, he was transferred to the 2nd Marine Division, Camp Lejeune, North Carolina, where he served first as the commanding officer, 3rd Battalion, 8th Marines, and later as the executive officer, 8th Marines.

Ordered to the 1st Marine Division, Korea, in 1953, McBrayer was assigned duty as a member of the United Nations Military Armistice Commission for negotiations with the North Koreans and Chinese. Following this assignment, he became executive officer, 1st Marines, 1st Marine Division, also in Korea.

July 1954–July 1956, McBrayer served as a deputy operations officer on the staff of the commanding general, Fleet Marine Force Atlantic, stationed in Norfolk, Virginia.

July 1956–July 1958, he had duty as an operations officer on the staff of the commander in chief, Specified Command Middle East headquarters in London, and he traveled extensively throughout the Middle East.

July 1958–July 1961, he was first a student and then the deputy director of the Senior Course, U.S. Naval War College, Newport, Rhode Island.

July 1961–July 1965, he was the director of the 6th Marine Corps Reserve and Recruiting District with headquarters in Atlanta, Georgia.

1 July 1965, he was retired because of physical disabilities.

1 July 1965–1 July 1972, he taught international politics and political science at Georgia Tech, Atlanta, Georgia.

In July 1972, he was awarded an earned Ph.D. in political science by Emory University, Atlanta, Georgia.

1 July 1972–1 September 1983, he taught political science at Georgia State University, Atlanta, Georgia.

31 August 1983, he retired as a professor emeritus from the university system of Georgia.

Decorations: Two Legions of Merit, one with combat V; one U.S. Army Commendation Ribbon with pendant; one U.S. Navy Commendation Ribbon with pendant; two Purple Hearts; Korean Presidential Unit Citation; American Defense Service Medal; Asiatic Pacific Medal with Bronze Star; National Defense Service Medal; Korean Service Medal; United Nations Service Medal.